W9-AVJ-920

Handbook to American Democracy

Volume III

The Executive Branch

Handbook to American Democracy

Volume III

The Executive Branch

Lori Cox Han
and
Tomislav Han

An Infobase Learning Company

Handbook to American Democracy: The Executive Branch
Copyright © 2012 by Lori Cox Han and Tomislav Han

All rights reserved. No part of this book may be reproduced or utilized in any form or by any means, electronic or mechanical, including photocopying, recording, or by any information storage or retrieval systems, without permission in writing from the publisher. For information contact:

Facts On File, Inc.
An Imprint of Infobase Learning
132 West 31st Street
New York NY 10001

Library of Congress Cataloging-in-Publication Data
Han, Lori Cox.
  Handbook to American democracy / Lori Cox Han and Tomislav Han.
    4 v.. cm.
  Includes bibliographical references and index.
  Contents: vol. 1. Foundations of American democracy — vol. 2. The legislative branch — vol. 3 The executive branch — v. 4. The judiciary.
  ISBN 978-0-8160-7854-7 (alk. paper)
  1. United States—Politics and government—Handbooks, manuals, etc. I. Han, Tomislav. II. Facts on File, Inc. III. Title.
  JK31.H36 2011
  320.473—dc22   2011005185

Facts On File books are available at special discounts when purchased in bulk quantities for businesses, associations, institutions, or sales promotions. Please call our Special Sales Department at (212) 967-8800 or (800) 322-8755.

You can find Facts On File on the World Wide Web at http://www.infobaselearning.com

Excerpts included herewith have been reprinted by permission of the copyright holders; the author has made every effort to contact copyright holders. The publishers will be glad to rectify, in future editions, any errors or omissions brought to their notice.

Text design by Julie Adams
Composition by Hermitage Publishing Services
Cover printed by Yurchak Printing, Inc., Landisville, Pa.
Book printed and bound by Yurchak Printing, Inc., Landisville, Pa.
Date Printed: December 2011
Printed in the United States of America

10 9 8 7 6 5 4 3 2 1

This book is printed on acid-free paper.

KENNEDY

3 9222 03059 394 6

CONTENTS

Volume III

The Executive Branch

DuBOIS

INTRODUCTION

The study of American government and politics is both fascinating and complex. An enduring symbol of democracy around the globe, the government of the United States has evolved greatly and expanded since its inception in 1789, yet it remains true to the basic principles laid out by the framers of the U.S. Constitution. While many aspects of the day-to-day governing are based on seemingly basic principles such as representative democracy and majority rule, other aspects of government, such as the committee system in Congress or the Supreme Court's power of judicial review, are more obscure and require a more in-depth understanding of the American constitutional system. *Handbook to American Democracy* provides readers with the essential tools for understanding the governing and political processes of American government. In this four-volume set, the constitutional foundations of government, as well as the three branches—the legislative, executive, and judicial—are clearly explained for students who are seeking a better understanding of American government, whether from a historical or from a contemporary perspective.

While the study of American government and politics is a standard course for high school and college students alike, the importance of political knowledge goes far beyond the classroom. As citizens within a representative democracy, all Americans have a civic duty to stay informed about their government and its policies. The strength of a democracy can be measured by both the rate of political participation and the depth of political knowledge of its citizens. Not only did the framers provide a unique system of government to its citizens, but the democratic elements found within the Constitution require that citizens be informed to fully participate in this representative and deliberative democracy. Aside from the evident benefits, familiarity with the American political system has a broader contemporary significance. During the past few decades, the pace of global change has triggered political and economic reforms that has made other governing systems more like the one in the United States. The American political system is being used as a model by activists and politicians in various countries to reap the rewards of global change through closer cooperation with the United States on political and economic issues. The traditional differences between the United States and much of the rest of the world are gradually decreasing while the similarities are growing. From today's perspective, the American system may eventually become the global system, and that provides an additional important reason to become better acquainted with it.

CHAPTER 1

The Historical Foundations of the Presidency

The American presidency is one of history's most fascinating institutions. Dynamic, powerful, and unusually intricate, it seems to defy comparison to anything before or since. Enhanced by a unique international stature, the executive branch of the American government has become a yardstick by which its counterparts around the globe are measured. Individual presidents have come and gone, serving their country with varying degrees of success and gradually receding into the backdrop of history, but the presidency has stood front and center since 1789. Buffeted by recessions, embargoes, and disasters, it has survived assassinations, scandals, and wars. The office of president has been occupied by great men whose political contributions are unforgettable and fallible men whose accomplishments are quite forgettable. Still, the presidency has endured. Built lean and lithe for the 18th century, it has become muscular and mighty for the 21st, but the essential characteristics of the American presidency are as recognizable today as they were more than 200 years ago.

Of all the political structures created by humans, the American presidency has been one of the most resilient. Its resilience is the proud legacy of the Founding Fathers, as is the capacity to inspire and promote America's political ideals. Those ideals rest on constitutional principles that define and animate the American political system and support the evolution of institutions such as the presidency. Like the rest of the American political system, the institution of the presidency emerged from an 18th-century political culture that encouraged intellectual innovation and the perfection of human potential. The American Founding Fathers believed that such perfection was possible through the application of the right ideas to matching circumstances. Convinced that the key to society's problems lay in the inseparable link between politics and ideas, they dedicated themselves to an understanding of the ideas that would serve as the foundation for an American presidency.

THE RISE OF POPULAR SOVEREIGNTY IN AMERICA

Perhaps no other concept is more critical for an appreciation of the development of the American presidency than *sovereignty*. For centuries, executive power was merely an extension of the natural sovereignty of kings, and the equation of sovereignty with monarchy seemed indisputable. Philosophers, kings, and clergymen all agreed that the inherent right to govern belonged to the executive and that the sovereignty of the executive could not be divided, delegated, or diluted. Even after the intellectual innovations of the Enlightenment revealed the possibility that the sovereignty of the executive was not absolute, the relationship between *executive power* and sovereignty was never questioned. And, to this day, long after ideas of indivisible sovereignty have been rejected, the link between sovereignty and the executive remains inviolable.

The Centrality of Representative Government in the West

In many ways, the history of executive power in the West is also the history of sovereignty. Since the dawn of civilization, generations upon generations of political leaders, commentators, and philosophers have worked diligently to discover the true meaning of political rule. They have carefully examined their traditions, the historical evolution of political communities, and even reality itself in order to create proper governing structures. With the aim of promoting political stability and longevity, these men embraced various systems of rule whose common denominator was the necessity to control people and institutions. Convinced that effective control was a function of the appropriate distribution of power in a political community, the men who established or maintained history's most famous regimes promoted the concentration of power within the executive. Consequently, justifications of executive power became justifications of sovereignty, and the two concepts have not been separated since.

Sovereignty as a function of absolute rule by the executive has been the norm rather than the exception throughout the past 6,000 years. Until very recently, the historical evolution of executive power has coincided with the development of absolute authority by sovereigns. Whether as kings, emperors, dictators, tyrants, or any one of a number of other types of nondemocratic heads of state, sovereigns have possessed the inherent power and authority that has qualified them for rule. Of course, as Americans and many others in the West are aware, alternatives to absolute rule eventually arose. English deviations from absolute monarchy during the late medieval and early modern eras paved the way for a unique system of constitutional government that would, in time, exert a profound influence over political practices in British North America. The British system, and especially the political culture it spawned in the American colonies, embraced the idea of representative government, and it legitimized rule by consent while it simultaneously undermined rule by decree (or fiat). Over the almost two centuries between the English settlement of Virginia and the creation of an American republic in 1787, the concept of representative government, which was linked to broader theories of popular sovereignty, became one of the cornerstones of American democratic politics.

The history of representative government is one of the keys to a proper understanding of the development of executive authority in America, and, as a result, it has attracted more than a little attention from writers of all sorts. Its importance, and especially that of the notion of popular sovereignty, should be obvious to anyone even vaguely familiar with the American system of politics. The idea of popular sovereignty has animated liberal-democratic political thought for quite some time, and its gradual implementation during the last 60 years has been crucial for the maintenance of peace and stability in the Western world. Despite some recent changes to the contrary in Latin America, Africa, and Asia, democratic political ideals have not lost any of their appeal as symbols of legitimacy and progress. The concept of rule by the citizenry is a powerful incentive for governmental reform throughout the globe, and it continues to inspire regimes both old and new.

What Is Sovereignty?
At the risk of oversimplifying a complex political dynamic, sovereignty is about power and authority. Concepts such as power and authority are central to an understanding of sovereignty itself. Unfortunately, these are not easy terms to define, and they have been habitually misused over the years. In most cases, power simply refers to the ability to influence or determine the actions of others through the possession of physical force or the potential to use or acquire physical force. However, power does not necessarily entail the presence or use of physical force. At a more abstract level, power involves the ability to compel, direct, or subdue the behavior of individuals or groups through some type of leverage. Such leverage may be actual or apparent, but it depends on a fundamental disparity between those who can (or may) successfully employ such leverage and those who cannot (or may not). Authority, on the other hand, refers to a kind of power, one that is inherently more valid than others. Power without authority is unlawful, and its ability to control

behavior is almost exclusively based on physical force, whereas power backed by authority is more legitimate because it is based on law. Unlike any other sort, power backed by authority invokes the right of designated individuals to rule and protects their ability to access, delegate, or use force or influence.

As the real source of political authority, sovereignty justifies the right to make decisions about the basic principles of government and its fundamental laws. Sovereignty asks questions about the distribution of power in a political community and those authorized to use it. These questions revolve around theories of rule and focus on the right to govern, so they seek to identify the individuals who possess the legitimate authority to exercise power as a ruler, or sovereign. A sovereign is the ultimate ruler in a political society but is not necessarily the person or institution that serves as chief executive, although that has usually been the case during the last 6,000 years. In this context, ultimate refers to final or original, so the ultimate ruler, or sovereign, in a political community is the person or institution that authorizes the use or possession of political power. The sovereign is the true source of all political authority and is responsible for the allocation of political power in a society. All political institutions, representatives, and officers are accountable to the sovereign and must promote the interests, principles, and priorities established by the sovereign.

Despite the Western world's reliance on relevant theories of sovereignty, sovereignty has been a historically recent concern. The concept first attracted the attention of philosophers attempting to comprehend the political transition from feudalism to early modern forms of rule during the 15th and 16th centuries. Prior to that time, most political writers assumed that rule follows power, because the possession of power apparently implied both the authority to use it and the right to rule others. However, during the early modern era, as concerns about political authority surfaced and people started to question prevailing explanations of the relationship between power and the right to govern, the topic of sovereignty could be ignored no longer. Almost overnight, the need to understand the true nature of that relationship and the actual sources of political authority became much more important than ever before. Political commentators of all sorts realized that addressing questions of authority and the legitimate use of power was impossible without considering related questions of sovereignty.

The earliest theories of sovereignty may seem unsophisticated, since they rested on the assumption, which no longer holds, that sovereignty is indivisible. Until well into the 17th century, if not the 18th, most definitions of sovereignty stressed the fact that it cannot be divided among people or institutions and that it has a single, unified source. This underscored the conclusion that monarchy is the only type of legitimate regime, whose power and authority are secured through hereditary rule. This is one of the main reasons why

16th- and 17th-century English monarchs were unwilling to share sovereignty with Parliament. To them, Parliament was little more than a manifestation of the royal prerogative to grant privileges, but it could never be accepted as a valid source of political authority itself. Accordingly, sovereignty could not be delegated, separated, or allocated in any fashion, since, by definition, sovereignty was incapable of division.

The concept of the indivisibility of rule is known as unitary sovereignty, and it provided a compelling defense of theories upholding the divine right of kings during the early modern period. During this time, theories of sovereignty were used to substantiate claims that the only legitimate rulers were kings, whose authority was confirmed by their status as God's direct representatives on earth. Supposedly, kingly rule was a divine right that conferred com-

Frontispiece of Thomas Hobbes's *Leviathan*. In his book, Hobbes addresses questions of authority, power, and sovereignty. *(Wikipedia)*

plete and unified authority on hereditary monarchs, who were part of a long lineage that led back to Adam himself. Not much imagination is required to see that notions of unitary sovereignty fit hand in glove with theories about the absolute and final authority of kings. In the end, the existence of a direct connection between sovereignty and the divine right of kings would depend on the likelihood that sovereignty is indeed unitary. By the time the American Founding Fathers began their experiments in representative government, the likelihood had become rather low.

Although the concept of unitary sovereignty enjoyed widespread popularity among rulers and writers for much of the early modern period, its appeal began to wane after only a few centuries. The lack of appeal was most apparent among an emerging class of politicians and philosophers whose application of Enlightenment ideas about the perfectibility of man to republican theories of government offered alternatives to unitary sovereignty that seemed more appropriate for the times. In Great Britain and America, this trend was so pervasive that, by the 18th century, conceptions of unitary sovereignty had been almost totally discredited and competing ideas about the divisibility of sovereignty had gained the upper hand. Eventually, long-held beliefs about absolute monarchy and concentrated political power succumbed to the awakening of a more democratic spirit across the rest of Western Europe, and ancient notions of the indivisibility of sovereignty seemed vulnerable throughout the West. None of this is meant to imply that support for monarchical, or even absolute, government had disappeared as a result of these developments, for the history of Europe during the following two centuries constitutes a testament to the persistence of authoritarian rule. Monarchy remained the preferred mode of rule in Europe and much of the rest of the world, though it gradually became tempered by constitutional limitations on the extent of its power and authority.

Popular Sovereignty

Popular sovereignty, or the concept that ultimate political authority rests with the people, may be a familiar feature of Western politics today, but it was far from familiar to most of the people of the 18th century. Even in the newly established United States, which made popular sovereignty the foundation of its political system, that system was nonetheless dominated by elites. The popular will was distanced from institutions of government through a number of constitutional filters, so this was hardly the type of popular sovereignty to which Americans are accustomed today. Nonetheless, it must be acknowledged that the existence of popular sovereignty in America, however circumscribed, was incredibly significant. While much of the rest of the world still employed some form of unitary rule, the new American nation and the British colonies before it had successfully implemented a type of sovereignty previously considered impossible and illogical.

Particularly in the colonies, the incorporation of political practices based on popular sovereignty, though effective, seemed unusual and unexpected. The idea that the most conspicuous and robust example of popular sovereignty should develop in an uncivilized backwater, which is what the North American continent was at that time, was nothing short of fantastic. However, due to historical circumstances almost uniquely suited to political experimentation, that is exactly what happened. The colonies may have been products of English political culture, but the realities of colonial settlement enabled much wider political participation in America than at home. Especially in the New England colonies, often comprising closely knit Puritan communities, a majority of able-bodied men were involved in some form of local governance. The necessities of town building, food provision, and self-defense in an unfamiliar wilderness produced a population that quickly became accustomed to political participation at all levels.

This should not suggest that social boundaries did not exist or that common people did not defer to community elders, but the kind of social distinctions that severely restricted political participation in England were, for the most part, not present in the American colonies. The upshot is that the nature of politics in the early days of settlement encouraged unprecedented cooperation among commoners and elites, which led to the expectation among future generations that all eligible residents would continue to have a voice in local politics. Even after the development of formal political institutions and the transformation of small settlements into larger towns and cities, most white males in the New England and Middle Atlantic colonies were able to remain involved in local politics. Quite simply, the availability of land and resources in the North American colonies provided most white males with sufficient income and property to meet the qualifications for political participation, whereas wealth and self-sufficiency were confined to a tiny percentage of men in England.

From both an economic and a political perspective, access to land and natural resources offered Americans possibilities that were nonexistent in England, so social conditions that prevailed in England could not be replicated in the colonies. Consequently, an aristocracy never appeared in the American colonies, and the distribution of wealth and income was much, much narrower. Class distinctions did arise, of course, and the colonies developed their own social hierarchies, but disparities between rich and poor were much smaller. By the second half of the 18th century, colonial communities had stabilized along clear socioeconomic patterns, and local elites dominated politics, but the opportunities for political involvement were comparatively high. Economic and financial opportunities in the colonies may have supported various groups of elites and promoted societies that respected status and privilege, but those opportunities also had a leveling effect on politics, so that popular sovereignty was a more logical option for colonial governments than it would have been for the British regime.

The new American republic may have been dominated by an elitist ideology dedicated to social order and tradition, but the willingness to build its future on the rule of the people, no matter how diluted, was peerless. Practically no other Western country, not even Britain, was willing to take such a gamble. Even by the early 19th century, at a time when much of the European continent was being reshaped by progressive ideas, few places were willing to entertain the possibility that the rejection of unitary sovereignty should entail the establishment of rule by the people. The eventual acceptance of popular sovereignty by most Western governments involved not only the denial of unitary sovereignty, but also the recognition that ordinary citizens could be trusted with the possession of political power and authority. Given the aristocratic mentality of Europe's political leaders and their cultural traditions based on social hierarchy, such recognition was neither easy nor warranted. As long as the historical bias in favor of rank, privilege, and status persisted, the transfer of political authority from elites to everyday people would be difficult and impractical.

Despite the long history of aristocratic rule in the West, most European countries did ultimately implement political systems devoted to popular sovereignty. The economic transformations of the 19th century and the brutality of the 20th clearly demonstrated the ineffectiveness of regimes controlled by elites. Furthermore, the dominance of capitalism during the 20th century went hand in hand with the rise of liberal democracy, which depended on popular sovereignty for its survival. As liberal-democratic systems emerged throughout Europe, popular sovereignty became the norm by which the legitimacy of government was judged, and authoritarian regimes based on outdated ideas of unitary sovereignty were dismissed as illegitimate and indefensible. Even the former communist stalwarts of Eastern Europe reconciled themselves to the inevitability of popular sovereignty, as did some of the previously unapologetically authoritarian states of the Middle East, Africa, Asia, and Latin America.

INHERITED CONCEPTIONS OF EXECUTIVE POWER

The idea that an elected civilian should preside over a federal government and function as its head of state may have been new in the 18th century, but the concept of a nonhereditary executive was anything but new. As early as the sixth century B.C., if not before, officers called archons acted as Athenian chief executives and fulfilled many of the responsibilities associated with presidential rule. Likewise, consuls assumed some of the same duties in the Roman republic before the rise of the emperors. During the Renaissance, several of the Italian city-states were headed by nonhereditary princes appointed or elected by local councils. Even in England, one of the historical strongholds of monarchical government, a nonhereditary commonwealth was briefly established after the execution of Charles I in 1649. And, in the American colonies themselves, colonial governors exercised many of the executive functions that the presidency would later assume at the federal level.

Evidently, history offered numerous examples of nonhereditary heads of government and even heads of state for the framers of the Constitution to consider as they tackled questions of executive authority. As it turns out, despite the comparatively unusual complexion of the American presidency among contemporary executives, historical precedent, though limited in this regard, was hardly nonexistent for a nonhereditary or even civilian head of state. So, the pertinent concern regarding the evolution of American executive power is not whether nonhereditary executives had existed prior to the creation of an American republic but which ones were relevant and meaningful to the framers of the Constitution. The framers of the Constitution did not blindly choose the option that appeared the most desirable on paper, but, as was the case with other aspects of the new nation's political system, the framers weighed their experiences against cultural tradition and the lessons of history to design an institution that credibly reconciled the past with present circumstances and future needs.

The Pervasive Influence of History and Western Culture

The story of the birth of the American constitutional republic is largely one of continuity and incremental change rather than revolution and radical transformation. Innovation and adaptation, not invention and disruption, characterized the transition from imperial outpost to independent nation. American Founding Fathers borrowed, inherited, and assimilated relevant aspects of an English political tradition that had become their own. This country's founders embraced familiar political ideals as the foundations of a new government, whose few departures from history were necessary responses to unique circumstances. Novelty was tempered with a steady conservative impulse that promoted political stability and a respect for established societal norms. This is in no way intended to minimize the many groundbreaking accomplishments of the men who penned the American Constitution, but it should underscore the obvious intellectual connections that linked the new republic to its English origins. For better or worse, American political practices were the outgrowth of their English cultural heritage. Although numerous intellectual influences shaped the founders' political mind-set, their decisions about what to do and what not to do were filtered through an English political lens.

The English character of American politics was noticeable in the various structures and procedures that defined government in the early United States. Due process of law, individual rights, political liberty, representative government, the consent of the governed, civic responsibility, and many other aspects of constitutional rule were present in the newly established republic. Its institutions, such as a bicameral legislature comprising an upper and lower chamber, were conspicuous products of America's English past and represented a prudent continuation of colonial politics. Almost everywhere Americans looked, they could see evidence of the English customs that had animated colonial political life. Their recently created federal government, though new and seemingly without historical precedent, was, on the other hand, familiar and, in some important ways, wholly within precedent. To the founding generation, the dual impact of English history and colonial experience was powerful and real, and its logic appeared inescapable.

Nevertheless, that logic could not be reconciled with all features of the American political system, and some parts of it, though necessary and desirable, seemed directly at odds with English precedent. Perhaps the most glaring example is the American presidency, which, according to many, is the most non-English part of the American government. Indeed, the American presidency, despite its similarity to certain political institutions in today's world, was something quite out of the ordinary in the late 18th century. Great Britain and all other major European powers were monarchies, and exceptions of the type contemplated by the framers of the Constitution were, for all intents and purposes, nonexistent. Instances of nonauthoritarian rule could be found in a few places, but none of them resembled what the framers eventually created. This is why many political commentators have concluded that the American presidency lacks not just English roots but, more broadly, identifiable European origins too.

Aside from its superficial appeal, such a conclusion, however, is not supported by the historical record, which includes the intent of the framers of the Constitution. A closer examination of the American presidency reveals affinities with several strains of European political thought and demonstrates close ties to a colonial past that was distinctly English. The intellectual roots of the American presidency are, in fact, very English, from the traditions that formed the core of colonial government to—believe it or not—the habits of monarchical rule that underpinned imperial politics. English influences were combined with classical and Renaissance ideas about leadership into a distinctly American conception of *executive authority*. The American presidency was, in many significant ways, a peerless creation, without obvious intellectual ties to similar contemporary institutions. But that should not diminish its European political lineage, nor should it cloud the fact that English political culture and imperial constitutional practices were indispensable elements of an institution that could not have emerged without them.

Combined with their experiences in colonial government under the British Crown, by far the biggest influence on the framers of the Constitution was their English heritage. By the 18th century, Great Britain had become a constitutional monarchy with a unique respect for political liberty and the rights of citizens. Although it was not progressive by today's standards, it was head and shoulders above its European rivals, the majority of which practiced some form of authoritarian rule, or absolute monarchy. The United States is unusually fortunate to have been colonized by the English and not the French or Spanish, for example. Of course, Spanish and French settlements existed in North America, but their influence over American political development was minimal compared to that of the English (and British more broadly). The fact that the two most stable and progressive governments in the Americas, the American and Canadian, existed as English colonies, either by origin or conquest, is no mere coincidence. The dominance of liberal democracy in the United States and Canada was due, in no small part, to the centuries-long existence of parliamentary government in England.

Had the Atlantic seaboard in North America been settled by an empire with a comparatively authoritarian political culture and not one, such as the English, with an increasing awareness of the constitutional significance of representative government, U.S. history would have been marked by the kind of instability and upheaval that have overwhelmed Latin America for the bulk of the past few centuries. Latin American countries, which sprang from authoritarian environments established by Portuguese and Spanish rule, which was devoid of constitutional freedoms, have only recently begun to adopt liberal principles of government. This is not intended as a criticism of current Latin American regimes, but it merely reflects the fact that American dominance in today's world is as much a product of English political roots as it is of historical developments since 1789. Whether it is seen as fate, blind luck, or just an accident of history, the English settlement of North America and the associated transplantation of English culture to the colonies proved to be the ingredients that made U.S. political evolution so unique and dominant in the Americas.

Classical Examples of Executive Power

Classical concepts about republican government shaped American politics during the crucial decades prior to the American Revolution. American political leaders were greatly affected by the writings of prominent Greek and Roman philosophers, and they often consulted historical sources about the rise and demise of ancient regimes. The framers of the Constitution, men such as James Madison and Alexander Hamilton, were impressed by classical writings and the many political insights they contained. The histories of the republics of Athens and Rome constituted prominent reminders of the possibilities and limitations of the rule of men, and key classical ideals found their way into American theories of government, whose ancient origins are obvious to anyone with even a superficial knowledge of classical politics. Those classical ideals, which exerted such a powerful influence over American political thought, may not have had as much of an impact on English politics, but their contribution to the development of an American political tradition is undeniable. Therefore, a quick review of ancient attitudes concerning executive leadership would be useful for the present discussion.

As indicated above, some of the earliest forms of nonhereditary executive power arose in the ancient world. Following the demise of Athenian kingship, civilian officials eventually gained control of the political apparatus of the Greek city-state. Originally, these civilian officials, known as archons, exercised wide-ranging authority over various internal and external activities and often ruled indefinitely. By the late sixth century B.C., their duties and responsibilities became more narrowly defined and their terms of office were gradually reduced. During the height of Athenian democracy in the fifth century, archons were elected by lot to serve one-year terms from among all but the lowest rung of the Athenian citizenry. Ultimately, as Athens became increasingly exposed through almost ceaseless warfare, generals assumed principal responsibilities as heads of state, but archons remained heads of government for some time. Although archons were typically chosen because of their social breeding, status, and political connections, especially during the sixth and early fifth centuries B.C., these positions were civilian and nonhereditary.

The framers of the American constitution were quite taken with classical Greek politics and philosophy, and they knew the history of ancient Greek city-states, especially Athens. Athenian democracy was one of the principal historical influences on the framers, and they read many of the most prominent Greek philosophical writings. Classical ideas about republican government, civic responsibility, and the allocation of power figured prominently in the Founding Fathers' plans for an American republic. Athenian experiences with democratic government were particularly relevant in their discussions about the form of the emerging American government. The fact that the Athenians had some success with nonhereditary civilian executives was definitely not lost on the framers of the Constitution as they debated the nature of the American presidency.

In addition to Greek sources, the framers relied on contemporary accounts of the Roman republic and philosophical tracts about republican government prior to the advent of imperial rule at the end of the first century B.C. Many American politicians of the late 18th century were obsessed with the rise and subsequent fall of the Roman republic, for they were convinced that its political legacy held the key to an understanding of the birth and death of republican government. Furthermore, the late Roman republic, before the onset of internal strife in the early first century B.C., was viewed by some as a near perfect example of proper governance, so a thorough knowledge of its institutions, ideals, and political practices would have been extremely valuable. Such knowledge was

Photo of a woodcut depicting the triumph of Julius Caesar, with a sign bearing his famous slogan, "Veni, vidi, vici"

frequently gained through familiarity with the works of Cato, Cicero, and even Caesar, whose life and untimely demise offered insights into the reasons that republics decline and eventually die.

Those insights came from careful observations of Roman politics and its institutions, not the least of which was the consulship. The Roman consulship served as a fitting example of nonhereditary executive power, and it provided the framers with information about the legitimate and illegitimate uses of executive authority. The Roman republic had two annually elected consuls with responsibilities that outstripped those of the Athenian archons. Aside from their administrative, law enforcement, and legislative duties and privileges, Roman consuls eventually acquired formidable military authority, and their sphere of influence exceeded those of the Athenian archons and generals combined. Eventually, powerful archons with insatiable military appetites became liabilities rather than assets for Rome, and their personal agendas contributed to the gradual downfall of the republic. Intrigue and political manipulation seemed to be the norm by the second quarter of the first century B.C., and the growing abuses of power by Roman archons fueled the corruption that undermined the republic.

An awareness of that history taught the American founders compelling lessons about the dangers of the accumulation of power within a single institution and the threats posed by an unchecked executive, even a nonhereditary one. The unfortunate undoing of the Roman republic simultaneously demonstrated both the promise and the vulnerability of republican government. To those thinking about the shape of an eventual American presidency, it illustrated the folly of mixing civilian and military leadership and the consequent need to make the military accountable to civilians. Plus, the history of the consulship showed that executive power must be strictly confined to specific areas and that it cannot be permitted to grow arbitrarily. Given their recent experiences with the British parliament, the framers' greatest fear was the abuse of power by any one branch of the government. They wished to avoid the path taken by so many corrupt regimes over the previous centuries, and they were knowledgeable about the fate of the Roman republic in order to escape a similar one.

The Early History of English Executive Power

At the start of the second millennium, the territory that eventually became England was no more than a collection of minor kingdoms that had survived failed attempts at long-term unification. Subject to foreign rule throughout most of the early Middle Ages, England constituted a rag-tag group of fiefdoms administered almost exclusively by local barons, knights, clergy, and other notables. Prior to the 11th century, the country was often under Norse or Danish sovereignty, so native rule could not be established on a consistent basis. After the Norman invasion of 1066, the first English monarchs were Frenchmen with continental allegiances and priorities often times at odds with English political objectives, and they appeased English nobles through concessions that highlighted the Crown's vulnerability. Until the late Middle Ages, English kings were usually more concerned with their possessions on the European continent than with the consolidation of English rule, which promoted the splintering of English politics through local loyalties and the dilution of kingly power. Compared to other European countries, with strong monarchs exerting centralized control, England was controlled by a network of increasingly autonomous barons who competed for power and influence with foreign kings, who were perceived as intruders.

The rise of native, English-born monarchs did not change the balance of power very much, so English kings were forced to share power with the local nobility. The influence and leverage of English barons over their kings was one of the primary factors that led to the rise of a constitutional monarchy. Constitutional curbs on kingly authority became common in England long before other countries were even prepared to contemplate such a development. Unlike their counterparts in other countries, who ruled through royal decrees and relied on centralized administrative networks, English kings had to seek the approval of local nobles and could not impose new legislation and taxes by decree. They became accustomed to working with barons and clergy, albeit grudgingly, and they relied on local officials for the administration of justice throughout England. Thus, by the 14th century, a council had emerged alongside the king, and it advanced the interests of local leaders and their communities through advice, consultation, and debate with the monarch. The nobles and clergy who composed these first parliaments partook in the governing process mostly for selfish reasons, not to represent the interests of any constituents. Nevertheless, their involvement secured the constitutional dilution of executive power by taking the first steps toward a government by consent.

Another factor that contributed to the comparative weakness of English kings was the nature of international politics during the centuries that preceded the English settlement of North America. The emergence of major European empires was accompanied by almost constant warfare among them. The need to consolidate land, establish defensible borders, and produce sustainable wealth fueled competition among Europe's monarchs and fanned the flames of war. Over the centuries, wars grew more complex, larger, and more expensive, draining the resources of even the most economically secure countries. By the 13th and 14th centuries, and definitely beyond, England's wars could no longer be financed from royal coffers alone, so kings repeatedly requested contributions from the English nobility and clergy. Given the relative independence of English nobles, royal demands for money and other resources were subject to continual bargaining and ongoing friction between the Crown and the legislature. Unfortunately for the monarchs, the continued necessity of warfare became linked to the continued necessity of parliamentary government, which ensured that English monarchs would never enjoy the kind of power possessed by their rivals on the European continent.

The Decline of English Executive Power

English kings recognized the need to confer with members of Parliament as a way of obtaining required concessions, but local political leaders realized that a constitutional relationship with the Crown benefited them too. The nobility and clergy quickly became aware that membership in Parliament offered them an opportunity to air grievances and promote their interests before the Crown and that regular interaction with English monarchs only increased their political leverage. Monarchs used Parliament to obtain the cooperation and resources they desperately wanted, while local nobles and clergy used Parliament to protect their privileges and political priorities. Initially, this was a two-way street that promoted mutually beneficial interaction between the Crown and the fledgling legislature, but true balance was never more than an illusion. Although both sides frequently pretended that the established constitutional relationship was good for monarch and legislature alike, mutual jealousies and ongoing mistrust ensured a more or less continuous tug-of-war between two institutions pursuing permanent advantage against each other.

During the 15th and 16th centuries, the Crown appeared to be winning the battle, reclaiming power it had lost during the previous few hundred years and augmenting its leverage over Parliament. However, inept handling of its relationship with Parliament by the Stuart monarchy (1603–49 and 1660–88) and clumsy attempts to seize more power made the Crown susceptible to political attacks from a restless Parliament increasingly aware of its rights and liberties. The actions of Stuart kings coupled with a long history of perceived royal abuses only encouraged a Parliament looking for excuses to confront the Crown over a number of issues. So, during the 17th century, which witnessed a bloody civil war and a revolution, Parliament and its supporters did just that. They confronted Stuart kings time and again until the balance of power began to tip in their favor. Parliament steadily increased its leverage over, not only the Crown, but also other institutions—so much so that by the 18th century, Parliament reigned supreme in Great Britain and outstripped the king in terms of power, authority, and even legitimacy.

From the perspective of executive power, the history of the English Crown during the 16th and 17th centuries played out like a Shakespearean tragedy. The irony of the situation was that the efforts to strengthen its position vis-à-vis the nobility and the clergy proved to be the undoing of the Crown. Its

Engraving of Queen Elizabeth I *(Library of Congress)*

political advantage over Parliament seemed tolerable, or maybe inevitable, to all involved as long as England had strong and capable monarchs, such as Elizabeth I (ruled 1558–1603), who almost ignored Parliament during the last 10 years of her reign. Nevertheless, since Parliament had tasted real authority several times over the previous few centuries, and its members valued their privileges and interests above all, the probability that the status quo would endure was extremely low. The list of grievances against the Crown was long and growing, and any additional mistakes by the monarchy could lead to a political explosion of some magnitude.

Sadly, at least for the monarchy, those mistakes came soon. The explosion was initiated by the Stuarts, a quartet of backward-looking, largely ineffective kings, and the nature of English executive power would never be the same again.

Civil war and revolution accomplished what only a lunatic would have predicted at the start of the 17th century. Although the assumption of the throne by Stuart monarchs created seemingly insurmountable political problems and internal strife of one type or another seemed likely, no one could have imagined the sweeping constitutional changes that occurred in England by the end of the century. The English constitution had been altered forever, and, as a result, the rule of kings was about to disappear. Parliament emerged the undisputed political champion of England, and its authority over kings was finally clear to everyone, as was its constitutional status as the true ruler of the realm. Although British monarchs would continue to hold significant power and influence, especially in foreign affairs, Parliament was the real seat of power in Great Britain from that moment forward. By the second third of the 18th century, parliamentary sovereignty had entrenched itself in Britain, and the rule of kings would never return.

COLONIAL PRECEDENTS

Colonial experiences with executive power and the framers' thoughts on the emerging presidency resonated strongly with certain philosophical currents originating from Great Britain and other parts of Europe. Starting in the late 17th century and continuing throughout the 18th, Europe's intellectual terrain was being transformed by a movement known as the Enlightenment. The Enlightenment was the so-called Age of Reason, and it advocated the scientific examination of human existence through experience and observation. Its followers questioned established truths based on faith or intuition and envisioned humans as agents of progress. They believed that human beings are able to create, re-create, and control their environments by applying the right ideas to corresponding circumstances. Rejecting the concept of a divine right to rule, Enlightenment thinkers argued that human beings, not God or nature, are the architects of society's institutions and that society is ultimately accountable to human laws. Contrary to what had been the case during the previous few thousand years, when political communities were considered reflections of a natural or a divine order, the Enlightenment popularized the notion that those communities, and especially their governments, are products of human design.

The Founders, Contemporary Ideology, and Executive Power

Politically speaking, two Enlightenment influences stood above the rest for the framers of the Constitution. One of these involved the redefinition of an ancient political tradition called republicanism, while the other arose from a new school of thought known as liberalism. Republicanism and liberalism represented the prevailing political ideologies in British North America, and they provided the intellectual basis for the evolution of colonial politics during the 18th century. As an aside, it is imperative to note that these are not the republicanism and liberalism of today, which are very different political species; rather, they are the classical republicanism and liberalism that so heavily shaped the evolution of governments from the 17th to the 19th centuries. In 21st-century America, republicanism refers to the Republican Party, whose largely conservative political and social philosophies share very little with the older school of thought. Likewise, the present form of liberalism, which reflects the left-wing or progressive faction of the Democratic Party, has very little in common with its 18th-century namesake. In fact, they are almost polar opposites, since the present version advocates vigorous and expansive government while classical liberalism calls for strictly limited government whose authority may not exceed a narrowly tailored set of political powers.

Compared to liberalism, republicanism exerted a much stronger pull on the minds of the Founding Fathers, not least because its intellectual lineage was immeasurably longer—it could be traced back to ancient Greece. It first appeared in England during the middle decades of the 17th century and eventually secured widespread acceptance in British North America. English republicanism, also known as commonwealth republicanism, was influenced by Renaissance writings about the ideal structure of republics and emerged in response to contemporary English anxieties over royal authority and absolute government." The residents of British North America were quite impressed by the works of English Whigs (antiroyalist commonwealth writers) and were particularly struck by their responses to the royal abuses of power that led to the Glorious Revolution of 1688.

Whig commentary regarding the English political crises of the 1670s and 1680s had a profound effect on colonial political thought, and it formed a central precedent for colonial protest against the Crown and Parliament during the 1760s and 1770s. By the 18th century, colonial republicanism had become a mixture of classical ideas, Renaissance philosophies, and Whig critiques of executive power. As cutting edge as colonial republicanism may have appeared due to its antiroyalist character and its advocacy of popular sovereignty, it was nonetheless rooted in age-old principles of government that affirmed tradition and ancient order. Republicanism embraced the realization that society comprises natural distinctions of rank and ability, which should be linked to corresponding differences in political power and authority. Simply put, some people are better equipped to rule, while others are more appropriately suited for nonpolitical roles. Thus, the structure of government should reflect the natural hierarchies that exist in a society and should maximize the inherent capabilities of all citizens. Although the Founding Fathers devised a way to reconcile popular rule with such an elitist outlook, their constitutional blueprint was predominantly republican and essentially conservative.

Liberalism, on the other hand, represented a more recent philosophical development built on the foundation stones of the Enlightenment, and it was arguably more relevant to the emergence of the American presidency. Republicanism may have been more relevant to the American political system as a whole, so it prevailed early in this country's history, but liberalism eventually won the day. By the 20th century, the American political system had become thoroughly liberal, despite the framers' original intentions. An American political culture grounded in tradition, order, and hierarchy increasingly dedicated itself to individualism, self-expression, and democratic practices. Over several generations, as elites gradually lost their control of American politics and society, the individualist spirit of liberalism overwhelmed the American people as almost nothing had before it.

Throughout its history, liberalism has upheld four basic principles of government, which are a prominent feature of American politics. First, liberalism emphasizes the significance of the individual and the supremacy of individual rights. Compared to other theories of government, liberalism provides for the greatest amount of individual freedom. Second, liberalism promotes government by consent, or rule by the governed, which means that people must have a role in governing through direct or indirect participation. Third, liberalism is dedicated to the principle of limited government, or the idea that governmental authority must be strictly confined and narrow. Liberals believe that, by its very nature, government has only a handful of legitimate duties and responsibilities, which it cannot exceed or augment in any way, shape, or form. Finally, liberalism demands a separation of law and morality through legal and constitutional neutrality toward citizens and the impartial protection of individuals and their rights.

More than any other aspects of liberalism, the respect for individual rights and the requirement for limited government influenced the design of the American presidency. The need to protect individuals, their property, and their natural freedoms went hand in hand with the desire to keep government small. The framers believed that the best way to secure the rights and liberties of the American people was by preventing the accumulation of too much power by any one branch of the government. As apparent victims of abuses by the British Crown, the American Founding Fathers were keenly aware of the people's susceptibility to a tyrannical executive, so they sought to restrict the scope of executive authority in the United States. Most of the founders were convinced that a nonhereditary civilian executive would be considerably less likely to exceed his authority than a hereditary monarch or a military leader. So, the Constitution provides for a civilian chief executive accountable to the very people whose rights he must enforce.

Royal Authority in British North America
Judging from the grievances in the Declaration of Independence against the British king, an otherwise uninformed reader would be compelled to conclude that the British Crown had been nothing less than tyrannical in its dealings with the American colonists. However, as historians have convincingly demonstrated over the past several decades, the imperial dynamic depicted in the declaration is exaggerated at best. Many of the colonists did indeed believe, albeit wrongly, that a royal conspiracy was afoot against them, and many more also knew that the declaration was an important piece of colonial propaganda. Perceived abuses were magnified for rhetorical effect and to strengthen the justification for rebellion against the king. None of this is intended to imply that the American Founding Fathers were disingenuous or that their motives were impure, but it simply confirms the cold realities of war. In addition, it should alert readers to the fact that the declaration does not tell the complete story of the colonists' experience with royal authority.

For much of their history as possessions of the Crown, the colonies were subjected to minimal interference by either king or Parliament. During the 17th century, colonial settlements in North America were periodically under heightened scrutiny by the mother country, especially in the 1680s, when

England itself suffered from renewed royal meddling. But, after the Glorious Revolution of 1688 and until at least the early 1760s, the American colonies benefited from an unusually casual and permissive relationship with their imperial parent. The bulk of their mature existence as colonies was marked by remarkably loose executive control from Britain and a functional independence that provided colonial governments with considerable discretion over their own affairs. The Crown's attempts to enforce imperial trade laws and revenue measures were almost universally unsuccessful, and its prerogative to appoint administrative officials was often useless. American colonists ignored, circumvented, or only selectively complied with imperial trade and revenue acts, and they expertly manipulated their economic leverage over local officials to thwart royal appointments.

So, by and large, despite some of the sensational claims in the Declaration of Independence, which admittedly applied more to the 1770s than to any other period, American colonists suffered more from neglect than from abuse by the British Crown. As a result, the British inhabitants of North America became accustomed to a comparatively weak imperial executive whose authority over military defense was unchallenged but whose power over internal matters was consistently contested. More than 70 years of colonial autonomy over internal issues ultimately established a dangerous precedent from an imperial perspective, though it was undoubtedly welcome in the colonies. Constitutionally speaking, American colonists gradually embraced the notion that royal executive authority did not legitimately extend beyond a few aspects of foreign policy and imperial trade, so, at least in their minds, the power of the king to regulate internal affairs in British North America had passed to colonial governments. Therefore, contrary to popular lore, the colonies' experience with imperial governance contributed to a tradition of rather weak executive rule, which formed a lasting impression on the men who would eventually design a new American government.

Of course, the British Crown had never surrendered the powers appropriated by its colonies in North America, nor did it recognize a constitutional inability to address internal interests in the colonies. And, following the conclusion of the French and Indian Wars in 1763, which substantially raised the British debt, the imperial government had an opportunity to remind American colonists that all its powers were still intact. For decades, Britain had borne the cost of defending the colonies, and, as indicated above, its attempts to raise revenue from colonial Americans had been ineffective. After several expensive wars to defend and secure the North American colonies, the Crown and Parliament finally decided to exact a fair contribution from them. That decision, justifiable as it was, eventually proved to be the undoing of British rule in the colonies. They had enjoyed a free ride from the British government for decades, and they were not willing to let it end without a fight.

What originally started as a squabble over a few pennies became a bitter brawl regarding the constitutional authority of the Crown and Parliament. Initially, colonists were primarily concerned with maximizing profits from farming, trade, and small-scale manufacturing, so their goal was to keep British fingers out of colonial pots. This was more about selfish interest and greed than constitutional issues of any sort. However, as Crown and Parliament asserted their powers and became increasingly invasive, colonial anxieties about the legitimate authority of the imperial government gradually grew. A series of missteps by the British government failed to ease tensions, and colonial fears quickly developed into paranoia. Some colonial leaders were convinced of an imperial conspiracy to deprive colonial Americans of their rights and property, and they did whatever possible to discredit the actions of the imperial government in London. The resulting friction between colonies and mother country intensified into a constitutional debate of monumental proportions, as more and more colonists threw themselves into what they saw as a struggle against tyranny. The seemingly unconstitutional seizure of power by the British executive triggered a reaction that no one could have foreseen.

King George III *(Library of Congress)*

Colonial Governors in British North America

Although the monarch, as the head of the British government and its empire, was the constitutionally designated chief executive, the colonies were exposed to a second tier of executive rule through their governors. From a strictly constitutional point of view, colonial governors were the king's lieutenants, or surrogates, in North America, representing his interests and executing his duties as emperor of the realm. Aside from enforcing relevant British laws, governors were supposed to serve as heads of government for the colonies, much as British prime ministers did in London starting in the 18th century. At least, that was how the Crown and Parliament envisioned the situation.

Thomas Hutchinson

One of the most tragic figures in American colonial history, Thomas Hutchinson was the ultimate victim of circumstance. Hutchinson was the last civilian governor of the Massachusetts Bay colony prior to the outbreak of war between American colonists and their British rulers. A widely misunderstood figure vilified as the right hand of an increasingly unpopular British regime, Hutchinson became the most visible target of anti-British protest and violence in Boston during the early 1770s. Portrayed as a diehard supporter of British repression against the colonies, Hutchinson was actually a dedicated public servant caught between two sides in an escalating crisis no one seemed capable of managing. Born in Boston with long roots in some of New England's most prominent political families, he had an extensive record of public service before his ascent to the governorship. He served in the colonial legislature for more than a decade, became lieutenant governor in the late 1750s, and was also chief justice of the colony during the 1760s. His views and policies were definitely pro-British, but mainly to the extent that he believed in parliamentary supremacy over the colonies and the legality of British sovereignty.

Misleadingly labeled as a British apologist by contemporaries and historians, Hutchinson bore no ill will against the colonies, nor did he favor their enslavement, as his critics claimed. A conscientious public servant, he was a political conservative devoted to law and order as well as the integrity of the Crown. He may have been a faithful subject of the king and the British monarchy, but most of the American colonists who opposed him had also been loyal at one time. As the governor of Massachusetts Bay and someone with a comparatively patrician background, he favored strong rule and firm control of the colonies, yet, in the end, he was a colonist himself. Unfortunately, his fate was sealed when private correspondence with Brit-

Reality ultimately departed quite considerably from that model, for the governors discovered they could accomplish very little without the cooperation and approval of their colonial legislatures. They were often caught between royal demands and colonial pressures, without recourse to the power and authority they had been promised.

During the first few generations following settlement, colonial governors generally exercised more power than they would subsequently. Facing the exigencies of building and securing viable communities, original settlers and their immediate successors tolerated more active, if not heavy-handed, leadership to ensure survival in an unknown wilderness. What is more, because colonial interests were still closely aligned with those of their sponsors back home, competing priorities between the colonies and their imperial masters

ish officials regarding his political views were made public in 1773 and the writings were used to paint him as a rabid royalist intent on depriving Massachusetts residents of their rights and liberties. Hutchinson's defense of restrictive parliamentary measures in the early 1770s only exacerbated the situation, and, unfortunately, his many years of service in Massachusetts did nothing to change the minds of his numerous detractors. As the political climate in Massachusetts grew more volatile, colonial violence against British property and personnel increased, and angry mobs turned most of their attention to their embattled governor.

A victim of past colonial violence—protesters against the Stamp Act vandalized and looted his home in 1765—Hutchinson knew all too well that he would pay a price for his support of unpopular parliamentary policies. Besieged by an unrelenting mob that viewed him as the handmaiden of a tyrannical British regime and under increasing pressure from the Crown to punish the rebellious colonists, he was caught between a rock and a hard place. As the situation quickly deteriorated, the king sacked Hutchinson and replaced him with a military governor, forcing the lifelong Massachusetts resident into exile. Humiliated and friendless, Thomas Hutchinson retreated to England, where he spent the remainder of his years. Despite his experiences in Massachusetts, he urged the British administration to exercise restraint in its dealing with the colonies, and he counseled against the heavy-handed approach that eventually led to war. Not unexpectedly, Hutchinson did not have a happy life overseas, and he died bitter and disappointed. Never more than a competent and efficient public official, though loyal to a fault, he was not an effective or inspirational leader, which proved to be his downfall. In an age when intellectual charisma and political skill ruled the day, he had neither; Hutchinson was simply a good man, which was not sufficient to save him or his legacy.

were comparatively minimal. As North American communities matured and settlement outposts grew into thriving societies, colonial governments increasingly yielded to local influences. Emerging political cultures in the colonies were strongly shaped by a growing allegiance to popular sovereignty, and political and economic priorities in the colonies began to clash with those in Britain.

By the second third of the 18th century, most British colonies in North America had developed political systems that served their interests and not those of the Crown or its empire. Despite the best efforts of many of the colonial governors, some of whom were directly appointed by the Crown while others were elected by local residents, colonial legislatures successfully marginalized them through various means, which included coercion, bribery, and blackmail. Not surprisingly, colonial governors were largely ineffective as executives, lacking both the independence and the power to fulfill their duties. Therefore, during the formative years of colonial political development, the inhabitants of British North America lived under kings who were weak heads of state and colonial governors who were weak heads of government. On both fronts, the external and the internal, colonial Americans were acclimated to a constitutional structure based on very limited executive authority, which proved to be a lasting influence.

The onset of war in 1775 did not fundamentally alter the equation. Of course, after political ties with Britain were severed, colonial charters had to be transformed into real constitutions so former colonies could officially become independent states. However, the new state governors, though patriotic men with local loyalties, were hardly more effective than the colonial governors they had replaced. In many cases, out-of-control state legislatures, drunk with recently acquired powers, enacted all types of fiscally reckless legislation to appease farmers, merchants, and artisans hit hard by war. During the 1780s, a series of questionable laws catering to very narrow interests proved to skeptics of the American cause that the former colonies could not be trusted with the authority they had inherited. Judging from prevailing political circumstances, the future of a central, or national, executive in America looked bleak.

CONCLUSION

Several decades ago, the famous American historian Daniel Boorstin hinted that the United States was suffering from an excess of democracy. His was not an elitist complaint, for Boorstin was a roundly progressive voice in postwar America, but he merely wished to highlight the inefficiencies and inequities caused by the mass democratization of political and social processes over the previous 100 years. Whether Boorstin's assessment of postwar America was correct is a matter of debate, yet his statement could be applied more appropriately to the newly independent states of North America during the 1780s. By the mid-1780s, the former British colonies of the Atlantic seaboard were suffering, if not dying, from an excess of democracy. Their inhabitants had become so accustomed to popular sovereignty and, consequently, so jealous of competing centers of political authority, that the unwillingness to delegate political power led to executive paralysis and political stagnation, if not corruption. Self-rule appeared to legitimize the selfish promotion of private interest at the expense of public welfare, and, to many, popular sovereignty had run amok.

The novel idea that people should rule themselves is a relative newcomer to government, and, for quite some time, it had to compete against the more popular notion that people should be ruled by those invested with virtually total political power. Since approximately 4000 B.C., or the period when civilization began in the Near East, human beings have been ruled by men who possessed or controlled the ultimate sources of political power. For the bulk of this period, a strict division between ruler and ruled ensured that those without power would be permanently subjugated to those with it. Although the 21st-century world features a number of democratic regimes in which rulers and ruled are one and the same, history has been dominated by regimes that rely on the consolidation of power and authority in one institution—the executive. Fortunately, the people of 18th-century Great Britain and America, as early exceptions to this trend, were willing to consider the dispersion of executive power beyond the executive. Particularly in the British colonies, prevailing theories of government increasingly incorporated defenses of popular sovereignty, which became the force spurring emerging conceptions of American executive power. Since then, popular sovereignty has been the motor driving reform in American politics and the essence of its institutions, including the presidency.

CHAPTER 2

The Constitutional Foundations of the Presidency

Although it was certainly no small matter for those who participated in it, the American Revolution certainly did not attract widespread attention as a transformative event. More ordinary than extraordinary, it was yet another example of imperial strain in an age when far-flung colonies grew intolerant of their political masters. To many outside the North American continent, this revolution was just a rebellion against an imperial sovereign, significant only because it offered an opportunity to destabilize a major empire and, in so doing, shifted the balance of power in Europe. To people in the British colonies, it constituted a risk of monumental proportions, fraught with peril and uncertainty. Sobered by a profound fear of failure against one of the world's most powerful empires, they could not have predicted the outcome of a struggle that threatened their political existence. Hoping to avoid a political move that would seal their destiny, the colonists chose independence after considerable debate about possible alternatives, all of which carried potentially devastating consequences. Their choice made them outlaws, or even traitors, inviting retaliation from Europe's military giant. Nothing would again ever be the same.

Confronting the mighty British Empire was a bold, risky prospect, but revolution had more pervasive effects, and they shattered the colonists' political world. The Declaration of Independence severed imperial links that had defined American political identity for almost two centuries and destroyed the only government the colonists had ever known. What would replace it?

Who would rule? What would happen to 13 colonies whose common bond had been their relationship with the British Crown? Despite regional affinities among some of the newly independent states, social, economic, and political divisions along the Atlantic seaboard were sizable, and the emergence of an American nation seemed unlikely. Economic hardship, political confusion, and social disruption quickly undermined the camaraderie forged by war and made union among the states anything but inevitable, so the fate of central executive authority in North America was unclear. If someone or something would eventually take the place of the British king, Americans had no idea who or what it could be.

Chaotic circumstances demanded quick action, and, unfortunately, the men who signed the Declaration of Independence did not have time to consider long-term options. Deliberations about the ultimate outcome of revolution and the political complexion of postwar America were a luxury they could not afford. No one will ever know the precise intentions of the declaration's authors regarding the political future of the rebellious colonies, but their plans surely did not include a permanent union among the newly independent states, especially not one with a national executive whose authority exceeded that of the British monarch. However, 11 years later, 55 Americans gathered in Philadelphia to create such a union. America's political leaders had undergone a political change of heart by 1787, and they embraced a solution to their political problems believed to have been unnecessary just a short time before. The men who would become known as the framers of the Constitution decided to scrap a confederation that had failed to adequately address the governing needs of 13, loosely united states and design a stronger central government with an elective head of state for the newly independent nation.

THE ROAD TO PHILADELPHIA

The creation of a federal republic in North America with a head of state at least as powerful as the British king contradicted several decades of colonial history and, to many, ignored the causes of revolution against the empire. Americans had traditionally resisted the presence of a centralized executive, so the appearance of a more active presidency in 1787 was rather ironic. The colonies had benefited from a long line of largely powerless and ineffective governors and a correspondingly permissive relationship with the Crown during the 18th century, so Americans had become accustomed to relatively weak chief executives. After the English revolution of 1688, real political power lay with Parliament, so British monarchs exerted decreasing control over their possessions in North America, where residents took freedom from executive interference for granted. Following independence, political experiments at the state level hardly displayed a reversal of the American preference for loose central government, so all signs pointed toward the opposite of what eventually happened in 1787. How, then, did the least likely political outcome in 1776 become the most likely constitutional alternative in 1787?

The Confederation Congress

In 1774, the British colonists of North America convened a Continental Congress to coordinate the colonial response to British measures recently imposed against Massachusetts. Like its predecessor, the Stamp Act Congress of 1765, the Continental Congress was envisioned as a temporary institution created to address a specific problem. It was not intended to be permanent, nor was it designed to handle the duties and responsibilities of government. However, rebellion against Britain changed those intentions, forcing the Continental Congress to aspire to something more formal because Americans needed an institution with the capabilities to prosecute a war. Sadly, it never became more than a legislative body with largely advisory powers, which reflected a tentative stature that was not properly addressed. In addition to its legislative responsibilities, the Continental Congress assumed an executive role that was limited to military oversight and supply, but real executive authority was conspicuously missing. Although its mission had expanded since 1774, its power had not increased accordingly.

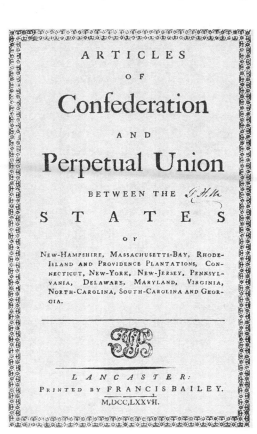

Front page of the Articles of Confederation *(National Archives)*

Nevertheless, as the only viable institution that could act on behalf of all the states, the Continental Congress was the obvious, though reluctant, successor to the British Crown. Some hoped that it would serve as the political center of the former empire and eventually replace the British monarch as its head of state. But the Continental Congress did not possess formal authority over the newly independent states, so its members pushed for the creation of a wartime government that could legitimately handle the tasks at hand. Naturally, the former colonists' main goal was the effective management of the war, so little thought was devoted to long-term objectives—especially to the shape of an eventual peacetime government. Trying to unify 13 different states with varying agendas and create a workable government amid the chaos of war was sufficiently difficult without the burden of addressing a problem, such as peacetime governance, that nobody was ready to tackle. To attract foreign allies and finances and, more important, to pursue the war effort properly, the independent states of North America needed a government capable of meeting current necessities. All in all, the political and military realities of the moment demanded a government of some sort to conduct the war against Britain, but these same realities prevented the emergence of anything more ambitious.

Established as an answer to those political and military realities, the new government operated under the *Articles of Confederation*, which some have viewed as the first American constitution. The Articles of Confederation were adopted in 1778, though they were not ratified until 1781, when the last battles of the Revolutionary War were fought. Handicapped by a lack of political muscle and questionable legitimacy, the Confederation Congress had to beg, borrow, and steal to meet military necessities throughout the war. It was expected to build an effective military force, obtain equipment and supplies, and train a competent officer corps, but it did not have the executive authority to fulfill those tasks. To complicate matters, the Confederation Congress had to ensure that the continental war effort harmonized with the variety of state-based military initiatives that had arisen since the outbreak of hostilities in 1775. Unfortunately, the coordination of state militias with continental forces required organizational capabilities that the new government did not possess, and it ignored the presence of local loyalties that weakened any such approach.

In its dual role as lawmaker and executive, the Confederation Congress had formidable expectations, but it was never able to become either. A legislative body with symbolic powers, it was restricted to an advisory capacity due to its inability to win approval from the states for prospective legislation. When called into action in its role as commander in chief, it was deprived of the resources and institutional legitimacy it needed, and it could not implement its decisions without prolonged bargaining and haggling. Unlike the successor government created in Philadelphia during the summer of 1787, the Confederation Congress did not have the authority to enforce even the few laws it was able to enact. This government had no formal executive branch, so any executive power that it was able to exercise constituted more a function of occasional concession or peculiar circumstance than of institutional authority. Real authority lay with the states, and compromise by these major actors with the central government was difficult to attain. As a matter of course, the states were clearly more powerful than the central government, and they could, and usually did, stymie the ability of the central government to act decisively.

Confederation or No Confederation?

By the mid-1780s, executive power had been reduced to its weakest point, and many Americans were prepared for a change. Decentralized politics through enhanced legislative authority at the state level was running out of steam and quickly losing credibility. The attempt to reconcile a patchwork of local political traditions and promote healthy intercourse among the states without adequate executive authority had failed, and the future governance of the American states required something different. Neither the states nor the central government could maintain stability or exercise political power competently, and the fruits of revolution were being wasted. Increasing numbers of North American residents were eager to find a way out of the resulting constitutional crisis, thereby strengthening the will to invigorate the central government with real power and authority. A critical mass of the population had become convinced that only a constitutional convention could address their grievances appropriately, so delegates were sent to Philadelphia to repair a broken political system.

That the delegates produced a new constitution surprised a number of people. They had been instructed to revise the Articles of Confederation, not to dismantle the existing government entirely. Despite the serious problems that plagued the Confederation government and general agreement that it was ineffective as structured, most people probably believed that it could be salvaged in some way. Indeed, the delegates themselves came to Philadelphia with the intention of doing just that. Some scholars have argued that a number of those who would attend had decided to scrap the Articles of Confederation prior to their arrival in Philadelphia, but such an assumption is difficult if not impossible to prove. Even if individual delegates were strongly prejudiced against the Confederation government and believed that it should not be saved, the men who gathered in Philadelphia were political conservatives, not radicals. They were interested in maintaining political stability, which could have been further jeopardized by a wholesale reversal of constitutional policy. That most of them quickly changed their minds about the future of government under the Articles of Confederation is evidence of the dire political circumstances in which they found themselves, but it does nothing to advance the theory, prominent among many historians, that the delegates conspired to overturn the Confederation government.

All of the reasons and motivations for the change of heart may never be known, but, shortly after their arrival in Philadelphia, the delegates did decide that the Articles of Confederation could not, or should not, be revised. It may not have been the only factor pointing to the creation of a new government, but the lack of a constitutional executive, with the necessary authority to succeed the monarch as head of state, made the Confederation government unworkable. The futility of repairing a nonexistent Confederation executive seemed obvious, as did the folly of a unified American government without a head of state. If continued union among the states was desirable, such a union would have to be equipped with an executive capable of rectifying the failures of governance under the Articles of Confederation. So, as far as the American presidency is concerned, the framers were faced with two options: either no executive and, thus, no union, or union with a properly defined executive. In the end, the choice was clear. The delegates to the convention opted for a new government under a new constitution.

This should not suggest that the establishment of a constitutional executive was the only reason, or even the primary reason, for the emergence of the Constitution. Several issues, some of them just as significant as executive impotence, contributed to the decision to abandon the Articles of Confederation. Nevertheless, had the need for a more formal and vigorous executive not existed, the outcome could have been quite different. Legislative ineptitude could have been addressed through reform at the state level, as could the legal and jurisdictional quagmires that made the interpretation and application of law so cumbersome. Perhaps the cure would have eventually become worse than the disease, rendering permanent union useless, but the mechanisms to confront legislative and judicial problems were present at state and local levels. However, unlike the legislative and judicial vulnerabilities of the Confederation government, the absence of a continental, or central, executive was a matter that state and local governments were powerless to handle. So, as indicated above, the delegates to the convention knew that if they wished to have a head of state presiding over the former colonies, the choice was clear. The recently independent states of North America needed a new government.

The Emergence of the Presidency

Aside from the inability to enforce laws and coordinate national defense, the remaining deficiencies of executive power in the Confederation government were related to foreign affairs. Without a functioning head of state, the Confederation could not effectively interact with foreign regimes, nor could it settle many of the outstanding international issues that confronted it after the war. Commerce with other nations was difficult if not impossible, since the former colonies were incapable of speaking with one voice, and potential trading partners were subjected to several overlapping and frequently contradictory agreements with the individual states. The absence of cooperation among the states and of centralized commercial planning made the former colonies unattractive prospects to other nations, which undermined the international stature of the Confederation government. As such, badly needed financial assistance was slow in coming and ultimately inadequate to alleviate the strain of accumulated foreign debts.

The framers of the Constitution realized that, although a duly constituted executive with adequate authority would not have been able to solve the country's problems singlehandedly, it could have alleviated some of the most serious ones. Therefore, they were committed to creating a presidency with sufficient authority to enforce the country's laws, ensure national security, direct foreign policy, and promote international commerce. These were all areas in which the Confederation government had proven itself impotent and the state governments had demonstrated clear vulnerability, so the framers knew that the American presidency must have sufficient authority and power to handle them. At the same time, those who drafted the Constitution were heedful of their experience with the British Crown and the lessons imparted by history, and they painstakingly avoided granting the new presidency too much power. Together with the rest of the government of which it would be a part, the American presidency would have limited authority, enough to redress the executive deficiencies of the Confederation yet not so powerful as to pose a threat to the people or to their political institutions.

Carefully limiting presidential authority was one way of preventing abuses of power, and making the American executive accountable to the electorate was another. History had proven that hereditary monarchs could not be held directly accountable for their actions and that the resulting friction between monarchs and their subjects fueled instability and corruption. Furthermore, colonial experience had illustrated that an executive based on anything other than popular sovereignty could not be legitimate, so the framers were dedicated to an elective presidency. While failures of executive authority at the state level during the 1780s did demonstrate the susceptibility of elected executives to popular manipulation, the framers of the Constitution nonetheless believed that popular sovereignty, if properly controlled, could serve as be the basis for an effective presidency. None of the political problems of the 1780s, the framers concluded, pointed to the inadequacy of popular sovereignty but merely to the ways in which it was implemented.

The framers' fidelity to popular sovereignty notwithstanding, the constitutional crisis of the 1780s persuaded them that rule by the people must be tightly managed and that its excesses must be avoided. Nothing about their devotion to popular sovereignty indicated a fondness for unrestrained democracy or the unfiltered exercise of the popular will. They were convinced that the voice of the people, though a necessary element of legitimate politics, must be refined or refocused by those inherently more qualified to make political decisions. So, in designing a presidency for the American republic,

Independence Hall in Philadelphia served as the meeting place for the Continental Congress and was the site of the Constitutional Convention in 1787. *(National Archives)*

the framers of the Constitution were determined to insulate the new executive from the kinds of selfish impulses that overwhelmed the governments of the 1770s and 1780s. The state governments, they thought, suffered from too much direct exposure to the politically uninformed masses, which promoted a breakdown of the political process. As a response, the delegates in Philadelphia made sure to protect a presidency based on popular sovereignty from the frailties of the popular will.

A NEW AMERICAN POLITICAL SYSTEM

After the delegates weighed the advantages and disadvantages of preserving the Confederation government, their decision about its future was unambiguous, but the choice of what would replace it was not. A natural or logical successor did not exist, and the delegates were divided, sometimes deeply, over the structure and objectives of a national government. Despite the evident desire of many to create a more active presidency to head a central government with expanded authority, the framers of the Constitution had to balance the support for increased national power against a prevailing allegiance to the sovereignty of the individual states. Most inhabitants were exceedingly proud of their local heritage and considered themselves citizens of their respective states first and Americans a distant second. They were not willing to surrender sovereignty to a central government that could diminish the rights and authority of the several states, yet any sensible plan of union had to provide for a sufficiently powerful national government that would avoid the fate of its predecessor. This was a thorny dilemma for the drafters of the Constitution, and they devoted considerable attention to its resolution. Such a resolution may not have been obvious, but a solution was eventually produced.

Federal Republic

The delegates to the convention in Philadelphia were aware that, regardless of the exact shape of the national government, the states would continue to play an important role in American politics. Therefore, they had to strike the right balance between national and state power. To them, the most sensible solution was federalism, which does not confine the exercise of political power to the national level but relies on the distribution of duties and responsibilities between political center and periphery. As the framers of the Constitution envisioned it, the two would have separate authority and that authority would, for the most part, not overlap though the federal government would have priority concerning those matters, such as defense, foreign policy, interstate commerce, and a few others, that are truly national in scope. On the other hand, the state governments would retain control over a large part of the day-to-day practices of American politics.

For the framers of the Constitution, federalism proved to be a logical response to the need to accommodate preexisting state governments within a new political structure, especially given that the former colonies had developed largely independent of one another. A federal republic was much easier to sell to supporters of state sovereignty than any other arrangement aside from that of no central government at all. The new federal government, and especially the presidency, would be limited in scope, reducing the potential for the abuse of power or the appropriation of the states' political authority. What is more, only federalism could address the diversity of interests in a country as extensive in size as the United States. Although the United States was not nearly as populous at the time of its founding as it would later become, it occupied an expanse of territory unprecedented for a country with only 4 million people, and it contained a population with a mix of cultures and ethnic backgrounds that could easily have overwhelmed the resources of a unitary (no states or other political divisions) government.

Federalism did not solve all problems, but it has served the United States quite well over the past 225 years. It has been unusually responsive to the political objectives of Americans and their localities for generations, and it has promoted political adaptability of the kind not possible in more central-ized regimes. The framers of the Constitution were convinced that a fed-eral structure would be appropriately sensitive to the needs of the American people and also uniquely effective in providing for those needs, and they have been proven right. Of course, during the last 100 years, national authority and the power of the presidency have expanded to a degree that the framers would not have recognized, but federalism has remained a defining feature of American government. The American presidency continues to deal, as it has since its beginnings, with defense, foreign policy, and interstate commerce, but it has also acquired partial or complete control over tax and monetary policy, health care, education, energy, workplace issues, welfare, communica-tions, and countless other aspects of modern life in the United States. And, although the growth of federal power has occasionally come at the expense of local and regional authority, the states have maintained control over a major-ity of the myriad tasks of American governance.

Its accommodation of local and regional needs aside, federalism was not the most conspicuous option for anyone designing a government in the 18th century. No relevant examples of federal rule existed anywhere at the time, nor did history offer much guidance in this regard. Confederations, which were loose associations of sovereign territories unified under largely ceremo-nial leaders, were much more common throughout the history of Western civilizations, so the appearance of a federal republic in North America was truly out of the ordinary. However, confederations were almost exclusively led by kings or princes, who usually assumed the title of emperor, and many of them were even weaker than the American Confederation government of the 1780s. Moreover, confederations would soon be a dying breed. With the rise of nationalism in many European countries and the corresponding disintegration of traditional empires, trends pointed to increased political, cultural, and social consolidation, not the development of regional diversity and decentralized sovereignty, as was the case in the former British colonies.

The absence of historical or contemporary models on which to base an American federal republic was not the only obstacle to a workable design for the new government. Some of the delegates, most notably Alexander Hamilton, were concerned that a two-tier system of politics would promote unhealthy competition and jealousy between the state governments and the government at the national level, thereby reducing federal authority and control. This could have been especially problematic for the new presidency, since its responsibility for national defense and federal law enforcement appeared to overlap with similar gubernatorial duties among the states. In addition, Hamilton worried that a federal structure would impede the execu-tive's implementation of national economic policies by ceding too much power over economic and financial issues to state governments. Hamilton may have preferred a unitary national government free of the jurisdictional ambiguities posed by federalism, but, in the end, the framers successfully created a presidency that alleviated most of Hamilton's concerns. In fact, as one of the principal authors of the *Federalist Papers*, Hamilton became a staunch supporter of the Constitution and the government established under its precepts.

Presidential System

The government established by the Constitution constitutes a presidential system, which means that the American chief executive is an elected president who serves a constitutionally specified term in office. Although a number of the world's countries employ presidential systems, the American regime stands out due to some crucial differences. Contrary to the norm in practically all presidential regimes, the American president is both head of state and head of government. Most of the world's presidents, with important exceptions in Latin America and Africa, serve solely as heads of state and are, as such, responsible for external affairs and self-defense. However, many of them, as the constitutional successors of historically defunct monarchies or dictatorships, such as the Spanish and Italian, are largely confined to ceremonial roles without real power or authority. Even when invested with real power and authority, as in France and Poland, presidents function as commanders in chief, foreign policy bosses, and leaders of their political parties, but their duties do not extend to the day-to-day running of the government or the implementation of domestic policies. The day-to-day business of running the country, which includes the implementation and enforcement of all domestic policies, usually falls to the head of government, or prime minister, who is chosen from among the national legislators.

The framers of the American Constitution, wary of giving the legislature too much power, chose to combine the functions of head of state and head of government in one office. As previously indicated, the framers were particularly anxious about the accumulation of too much power in any one institution of government and the possibility of tyranny, so they took precautions to prevent the abuse of power by government officials. In addition to uniting the roles of head of state and government, those precautions included a number of constitutional impediments to the concentration of power, such as the *separation of powers*, the system of *checks and balances*, limited governmental authority, and the designation of prerequisites for political service. Perhaps the most significant of those prerequisites was based on the conviction that the military must be subordinate to civilian leadership and that, therefore, presidents must be civilians themselves. The founding generation of Americans believed that, as long as the military was strictly accountable to, and separate from, the voters and their civilian public servants, the probability of tyranny would be diminished. The history of Western civilizations had been filled with too many instances of oppression and abuse by military leaders, so the Founding Fathers wanted to ensure that the military would never be used against the American people.

Another important precaution against the abuse of power in the American presidential system has been the practice of limiting time in office. The Constitution defines a specific presidential term, so service cannot be extended indefinitely, but political tradition has placed further constraints on presidential officeholding through the habit of staying no longer than two terms. Despite the fact that many other countries pay lip service to presidential term limits, the United States is one of the few that has consistently restricted the time its presidents should serve. Even before the Constitution was formally amended to limit American presidents to two terms, no president except Franklin Roosevelt ever held office longer. This practice has epitomized a political system in which no individual is greater than the office and one that features the eventual surrender of authority back to the people who delegated it. A president's willingness to turn over authority according to constitutional prescriptions and the public's awareness that his or her service is limited for their benefit are key aspects of a system that preserves the liberty and political power of the people.

Unless removed by Congress for certain types of misconduct, presidents transfer their power and authority, through the American people, to successors chosen at the polls. Over the last several millennia, the transfer of executive power has customarily been secured through the sword, with challengers resorting to assassinations, civil wars, revolutions, or the like against incumbent rulers. Sadly, the peaceful transfer of power has been a historical exception, and, even today, dozens of heads of state around the globe owe their positions to skullduggery of one sort or another. On the other hand, U.S. history has been marked by a peaceful transfer of power among presidents since the inception of the republic, and the nation's dedication to constitutionally legitimate political transitions has been unquestioned. Even after a presidential election as controversial as the one in 2000, when George W. Bush had to await the results of a Supreme Court ruling to proclaim victory, opponents may have continued to protest the results, but no one took to the streets and stormed the capital. (The presidential election of 1860, which put Abraham Lincoln in office, sparked the secession of the South from the Union, but the underlying cause of this action had little if anything to do with presidential succession itself.)

Checks and Balances

One of the many reasons that the United States has experienced peaceful transfers of power throughout its history is that no single individual or party has become more powerful than the institution itself. The exercise of executive authority has been controlled through various means, not the least of which have been constitutional provisions for limited government. In addition to the establishment of distinct boundaries around institutional authority, the Constitution provides for a system of checks and balances that grants powers of oversight to each branch of the government over the other two. The framers' intent in this regard was absolutely clear. By creating a network of mutual relationships that limited institutional power through cross-institutional supervision, they hoped to prevent the unconstitutional exercise of authority by any one institution. In other words, the framers gave each branch a small yet constitutionally significant role in the business of the other two, thereby avoiding the kind of institutional independence and isolation that would undermine accountability.

Thus, besides identifying the essential powers of each branch in three respective articles of the text, the Constitution also acknowledges the duties and responsibilities associated with checks and balances. The net effect of these provisions is the regulation of the separation of powers through a network of institutional controls among the three branches. Ironically, at least to the extent that the separation of powers demands institutional independence, the effectiveness of the controls depends on the continued interaction among the three branches. Over the years, these interactions have produced some interbranch rivalries, especially when checks and balances by one branch have been perceived as intrusions by another, but, odd as it may appear, such friction has actually benefited the American political process and its people. Although the framers of the Constitution did not want a government plagued by internal controversies, some friction among branches is exactly what they intended. Because they wished to avoid the kind of collusion that seemed possible among political institutions in other countries, the authors of the Constitution designed a system that would discourage conspiracies of power among the three branches of government. The last thing the framers desired was a government in which each branch exercised power unopposed or turned a blind eye to the activities of the other two.

By far the most frequent interactions as a consequence of checks and balances have been those between Congress and the executive branch. Although the president was granted some authority over legislative procedures through the veto, thereby preventing a monopoly on legislative power by Congress, most of the cross-institutional controls go the other way. Evidently, the framers wanted to ensure that presidential authority would remain constitutionally limited and that it could not transcend its intended scope. Therefore, the Constitution empowered Congress to regulate the exercise of executive authority in some critical areas. In *foreign policy*, for instance, which is a primary responsibility of the president and his or her *cabinet*, the Senate must ratify all treaties by a super majority of two-thirds. Congressional participation in treaty making was seen as a way of avoiding ill-advised alliances or agreements, particularly those that violate constitutional law or any valid national interests. The Senate must also approve key political appointments to the federal courts, cabinet, regulatory agencies, and armed services, which confines, perhaps even dilutes, presidential influence over principal centers of political activity.

Despite the legislature's supervisory authority over the executive in the above indicated areas, occasional constitutional violations have occurred during the last 225 years, as some executive officials have abused their authority and engaged in misconduct. Although political corruption in the executive branch was a prospect the framers of the Constitution surely did not welcome, they nonetheless anticipated it. Well acquainted with political corruptibility, they were no fools in this regard. The framers realized that the presidency would be occupied by mortals, not gods, susceptible to the same human frailties and vulnerabilities as all ordinary men, so they equipped Congress with the ultimate right to judge the legitimacy of executive actions. Congress was granted the power to legally try and dismiss executive officers who commit constitutional abuses against the people. Specifically, the House of Representatives has the authority to impeach, or submit formal charges against, and subsequently prosecute executive officials, while the Senate has the authority to act as jury in such cases. Through these provisions, the framers ensured that, if they occurred, abuses of power by the executive branch would be punishable in a way that was proportional with the severity of the abuse.

THE PRESIDENCY, FRAMERS' INTENT, AND THE CONSTITUTION

During the past 225 years, the American political system has evolved beyond the original intentions of the men who designed it. American political institutions and the authority they possess have outgrown their expectations, and the three branches of government appear to share almost nothing with their modest and unassuming counterparts of the founding era. Wars, economic progress, and large-scale social transformation have reshaped the function and purpose of politics, and related constitutional alterations have enlarged the scope of acceptable political activity. Of these changes, perhaps none has been as conspicuous as the growth of the American presidency, which now sits at the helm of one of the globe's most influential nations. With its entourage of cabinet departments, regulatory agencies, and advisers, the executive branch of the U.S. government has traveled further from its roots than the other two branches (though the legislature is not far behind).

As impressive as the 21st-century presidency may be, the original from the founding era is still quite significant. The presidency's humble beginnings are not just a historical curiosity but a reflection of its designers' intentions, which still matter today. Since many people are convinced that the framers' intent holds the key to legitimate constitutional development, those beginnings are crucial to gain an adequate familiarity with the executive branch and its legal authority. Any act of constitutional interpretation must begin with the intent of the authors, otherwise it is not interpretation. Without public knowledge of the purposes of the Constitution, its meaning and relevance become lost, so the origins of the American presidency are as pertinent in the 21st century as they were in the 18th. Therefore, with the possible exception of those clauses rendered irrelevant through constitutional amendment, the framers' understanding of the provisions regarding the presidency still holds true.

Electing the President

Every four years, Americans turn out in large numbers to vote for the man or woman they want as their president. The tally from the popular vote is then converted into a vote in the *Electoral College*, and the candidate who secures a majority is inaugurated president of the United States on the 20th day of January. Presidential elections come and go, but this arcane system, based on an institution with which most Americans are utterly unfamiliar, remains. A relic that serves no obvious purpose to many in this country, the Electoral College is a reminder of a time when the popular vote did not determine presidential elections. It was the linchpin of an electoral system that valued social hierarchy and political elitism and a necessary precursor to effective executive governance. The founding generation of Americans depended on it to legitimize an elective presidency and stabilize a society that had emerged from more than a dozen years of political chaos. Regardless of its present role, the Electoral College played an active and indispensable part in the selection of America's chief executives during the early republic, and it addressed a political need that was widely recognized.

These days, the Electoral College could be run by robots, computers, or even well-trained animals, since conversion of the popular vote is purely mechanical, or automatic. The electors themselves are mere puppets, fulfilling a ceremonial function that confirms the obvious. Their "votes" reflect the popular will of the individual states, and they have no discretion or authority to depart from what has been registered. Each state's electoral vote is assigned to the candidate who wins the popular vote, so the electors' votes are redundant. In the late 18th and early 19th centuries, however, the electors' votes were the only ones that mattered. The Electoral College decided presidential elections, and the general public accepted its choices. Like today, the number of electors each state appointed was equal to the sum of its senators and allotted representatives, but, unlike today, electors had full discretion and authority to choose the candidates they, not the public, preferred.

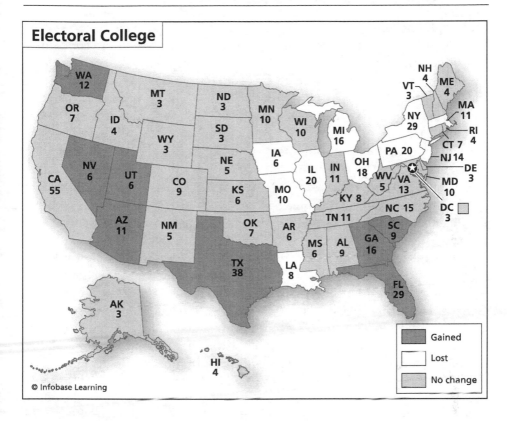

Electoral College

WA 12
OR 7
MT 3
ND 3
MN 10
WI 10
MI 16
NH 4
VT 3
ME 4
MA 11
NY 29
RI 4
CT 7
PA 20
NJ 14
ID 4
WY 3
SD 3
IA 6
IL 20
IN 11
OH 18
NV 6
UT 6
CO 9
NE 5
MO 10
WV 5
VA 13
DE 3
MD 10
CA 55
KS 6
KY 8
NC 15
DC 3
AZ 11
NM 5
OK 7
AR 6
TN 11
SC 9
MS 6
AL 9
GA 16
TX 38
LA 8
FL 29
AK 3
HI 4

Gained
Lost
No change

© Infobase Learning

Wishing to limit the scope of popular sovereignty, the framers of the Constitution created the Electoral College to blunt the impact of political ignorance. As contradictory as it may sound, especially for a government based on rule by the people, the Electoral College was established as a counterweight to democracy by placing the election of the president in the hands of political elites. The framers may have supported rule by the people, but they were not fans of democracy itself, and they did not intend to extend political rights to everyone. To them and their generation, popular sovereignty did not mean direct rule by everyone, nor did it mean that everyone should enjoy the privileges of citizenship. According to America's Founding Fathers, popular sovereignty implied rule by propertied white men, which did not include unqualified white males, women, minorities, or slaves. Popular sovereignty also implied that government should be distanced or shielded from the influence of unrestricted public opinion, even if public opinion reflected only the interests of qualified voters.

Widespread availability of land, resources, and opportunities in the United States translated into an unusually large voter pool, so, compared to other governments, the new American regime could rightly claim to be founded on popular sovereignty. Such a sizable electorate may have enhanced the legitimacy of the recently created republic, but the framers were concerned. Fearing a reprise of the democratic excesses witnessed by state governments during the 1780s, they wanted to protect the nation's highest office from the corrupting tendencies of selfish interest. They believed that, particularly within the executive branch, popular sovereignty must be tempered by appropriate controls and that public opinion must be filtered through political elites. Due to their unfavorable view of Europe's ancient social structure, the framers of the Constitution rejected the possibility of hereditary nobility in America, but they embraced Thomas Jefferson's idea of a "natural aristocracy" made up of those individuals who possessed good birth and breeding, intelligence, experience, proper rank and status, and a respect for the common good of the republic.

This may seem discriminatory to 21st-century Americans, but it was based on the commonsense observation that everyone is not equally equipped to make difficult decisions about complex political issues. The authors of the Constitution knew that a lack of knowledge, intelligence, or proper leadership experience could topple even the most stable governments, so they insulated the newly established republic from the whims and uncertainties of political ignorance. Despite their dedication to popular sovereignty, they questioned the public's ability to translate selfish interests into legitimate political objectives, which is why an institution such as the Electoral College appeared better equipped to select the civilian leader of the republic. Such an acknowledgment may not be politically correct, but it recognizes the political realities and electoral dynamics that can hinder the selection of the best candidate. Therefore, the Electoral College served as an active and critical part of the presidential election process, legitimizing America's chief executives and validating its political objectives.

General versus Limited Authority

The biggest debates about the augmentation of executive authority during the 20th century and the presidency's continued reliance on its expanded powers focus on the so-called vesting clause in Article II of the Constitution. Unlike Article I, whose introduction declares that the "legislative powers [there]in granted shall be vested" in a federal legislature, Article II of the Constitution merely states that the "executive power shall be vested in a President." Judging from the text, the authority of Congress is clearly limited to the specific powers identified in the Constitution, which are known as *enumerated powers*, whereas the constitutional authority of the presidency appears to have no such limits. Advocates of the modern presidency and its accumulation of power over the last several decades, which includes both Democrats and Republicans, have used this clause in Article II as a constitutional loophole to justify the discretionary and ever-increasing activities of the executive branch. They have pointed to the seemingly ambiguous wording of this critical provision and asserted the existence of a general executive authority within the U.S. government.

Unfortunately, at least for those who support what the renowned historian Arthur Schlesinger, Jr., has labeled the imperial presidency, the framers of the Constitution were neither so careless nor so naive to produce a blunder as monumental as a presidency with general, or open-ended, authority without specific constraints. Given the experiences of the Founding Fathers with the British Crown during the 1770s and the painstaking efforts to limit the growth of institutional power in any single branch of the government, not to mention their fear of tyranny, interpreting the vesting clause of Article II as an endorsement of open-ended presidential authority is questionable. Those who possess even a cursory knowledge of the history of the period should realize that this is exactly the opposite of what the authors of the Constitution intended. The overwhelming desire of these men to establish a presidency not susceptible to the corruption and abuses commonly associated with excessive and imprecise executive authority has been well documented, as has their corresponding efforts to create a federal government with limited powers narrowly tailored to specific constitutional needs. The history of the founding era does not lend itself to any argument for open-ended, or general, presidential authority.

Aside from the encounters by the Founding Fathers with apparent abuses of power by the British Crown and historical examples that exposed the folly of unchecked executive authority, 18th-century American political thought cannot be reconciled with claims about the supposed legitimacy of general authority within the executive branch. During the 18th century, ideas of specific governmental powers and limited governmental authority, though impossible to apply to most regimes then in existence, made an indelible mark on American political thought. This central tenet of political liberalism became an indispensable part of American governance in the colonies and eventually provided the logic for a federal constitutional republic. The practice of granting specific powers instead of general authority to governments was anything but common in the West, not least because contemporary theories of sovereignty denied that governmental authority can be curbed in such a way, but it was quite common in the colonies by the mid-18th century. The legitimacy of general political authority was almost universal, and it affirmed the possession of any powers that promoted the realization of governmental objectives.

Constitutional monarchies, such as the British, were no exception. Of all the contributions to American political ideology from a shared English intellectual history, the concept of specific powers, or limited authority, was not

The Bush Presidency

The sadly misunderstood vesting clause in Article II of the Constitution has been the subject of heated debate during the past 40 years or so. As the presidency has acquired increasing authority over various aspects of foreign and domestic policies, many have questioned the constitutionality of its decisions. Some of the most strident controversies have involved national security issues, and perhaps no actions have proven so polarizing as those taken by President George W. Bush in Iraq. During the cold war, the president's powers as commander in chief grew in association with a vigorous and dominant American presence around the globe. Gradually, the notion of limited authority was replaced by the supposedly more relevant concept of general authority, which enabled and legitimized the unprecedented expansions of presidential authority required to support America's postwar international role. No one actually admitted or acknowledged that such a constitutional transformation had occurred, but all were aware both that it had taken place and that it was necessary. Seemingly, everyone accepted the shift from limited to general authority, and the presidency acted accordingly.

So, when the Truman, Eisenhower, and Kennedy administrations seized powers the framers never intended presidents to have, nobody balked. This was just the price of doing business in a precarious world dominated by two competing international giants. However, the consensus began to break down as the abuses and indiscretions of the Johnson and Nixon years became clear, and observers began to register doubts about the presidency's expanded authority. Still, despite the ensuing polemics over the constitutionality and advisability of executive actions in various foreign theaters, worries about constitutionality and legality gave way to real-world concerns about national security and public safety. The Reagan administra-

one of them. It was strictly an American political innovation, born of unique experience and historical circumstance. Constituting partly a continuation of the colonial habit of circumscribing the authority of the Crown and its royal governors and mostly a reaction to perceived imperial abuses against American colonists during the 1760s and 1770s, limited executive authority made eminent sense to a group of men who wished to prevent future tyrannies by creating an American presidency with only specific powers. General executive authority would have offered American presidents greater adaptability and institutional agility, but the last thing the framers of the Constitution wanted to encourage, even with someone as trustworthy as they believed George Washington to be, was political adventurism or constitutional experimentation within the presidency. Even though the creation of

tion was particularly skillful in its efforts to prioritize security over constitutionality, leveraging people's fears about an unstable Soviet Union as none before. The George H.W. Bush and Clinton presidencies benefited from the uncertainty of a post-Soviet environment and the need to formulate a more relevant foreign policy posture, so the public, if not the Washington establishment, became quite accommodating of executive experiments in this regard. Nevertheless, with the George W. Bush presidency, the dam broke, and neither citizens nor their representatives were willing to turn a blind eye to potential abuses of executive power.

Although President Bush did not employ powers denied to his predecessors, many of whom did the very things of which Bush was accused, his administration was the first to defend publicly the concept of general authority. Key Bush personnel, most visibly Vice President Dick Cheney, broke precedent by actively advocating a view of presidential authority that was out of step with the Constitution. Never mind that previous presidents had, in many ways, been just as guilty as Bush; however, they had never openly endorsed a dubious view of executive authority that, no matter how necessary, seemed unconstitutional. Adding insult to injury, Bush administration efforts to legitimize torture of terrorist suspects, military tribunals, the suspension of enemy combatants' rights, and various breaches of international protocol were anything but inclusive and, to some, they were arrogant and imperious. What is more, the claim by Bush that such powers were an inherent part of the general executive authority implied by the vesting clause in Article II appeared patently disingenuous from a president who touted the centrality of the framers' intent. Despite attempts by leading supporters inside and outside the administration to link the expansion of presidential authority to the framers' intent, this clearly violated both the spirit and the letter of what the Founding Fathers had established.

a new government wrought significant political change, the Constitution stood for stability, certainty, and a dedication to tradition that general executive authority would have undermined.

The Scope of Presidential Authority

Without a doubt, then, the presidency draws its powers from a limited, not general, authority granted to it by the people of the United States, and any alternative reading of the second article of the Constitution ignores the intentions of its authors. Admittedly, interpretation of the vesting clause is complicated by what is assumed but not explicitly defined, particularly because most Americans today are not familiar with the intellectual world of the framers. That lack of familiarity with the political ideas that were then current and that still animate the implementation of American constitutional principles obscures a proper understanding of the vesting clause and the entire document of which it is a part. Such an understanding is all the more difficult to achieve through wording in Article II that seems confusing, if not contradictory. Article II of the Constitution actually identifies some powers that belong to the president, but such provisions do not significantly aid interpretation of the vesting clause itself. Since the clause contains no conditional language or references to powers specifically granted later in the article, its purpose is not illuminated by those powers.

Evidently, the structure and language of Article II provide few clues to the real purpose of the vesting clause, which brings the discussion back to the framers' intellectual mind-set. From what was already covered about general versus limited authority, you know that the vesting clause does not tolerate an open-ended executive but that it grants a limited executive authority with only specific powers to fulfill essential duties. The framers were convinced that those duties comprised the only legitimate areas of executive authority, since they reflected the few political tasks Americans were incapable of fulfilling without a federal government. Limited institutional authority, whether in the executive or in the other two branches, was intended to address the basic deficiencies of governance experienced by Americans during the 1770s and 1780s. They included the inability of individuals to guarantee one another's freedoms; the lack of a formal dispute-resolution mechanism of some sort; the absence of an effective system of self-defense; the inability of individuals to carry on relations with foreign governments; and the inability of individuals to facilitate local, regional, or international trade.

Due to these deficiencies, the framers of the Constitution established a federal government for the following purposes: (1) to protect and secure the rights and liberties of its residents; (2) to provide a mechanism for dispute resolution and law enforcement; (3) to establish a system of national defense; (4) to conduct and manage foreign relations; and (5) to coordinate interstate commerce and international trade. The American federal republic was created in direct response to the deficiencies identified above, and the new government was granted only as much authority as was required to redress them—nothing more. The limited authority allocated to the presidency reflected the obvious role of the executive in these five areas, especially the last three, and, for the authors of the Constitution, such authority constituted a natural extension of the powers they had associated with a legitimate head of state during the 18th century. As difficult as it may be for Americans today to believe, the association of legitimate executive authority with no more than these five tasks, and particularly the last three, made the identification of specific powers unnecessary.

Given the framers' theoretical assumptions about executive power and the history of executive authority in British North America, the scope of presidential authority was inherently restricted, regardless of the exact wording of relevant constitutional provisions. None of the Founding Fathers could have imagined a legitimate constitutional structure that facilitated the exercise of executive authority beyond its natural boundaries, so nothing more needed to be said in the vesting clause of Article II. That the "executive power shall be vested in a President of the United States" was sufficient to confirm a constitutional truth that appeared to them to be irrefutable. This conclusion may

Portrait of James Madison, one of the framers of the Constitution *(Wikipedia)*

seem willfully naive or even utterly indefensible to a generation of Americans accustomed to wide-ranging presidential authority, but present-day assumptions about executive power are not pertinent here. The framers may perhaps be faulted for not articulating their generation's assumptions about limited executive authority, but they could not have envisioned a time when their ideas of legitimate executive governance would not be dominant. The authors of the Constitution were not soothsayers, so blaming them for omitting explanations of their assumptions for the benefit of future readers unfamiliar with founding-era politics is ludicrous.

The Founding Fathers were focused on the need to prevent tyrannical government, but they were much less concerned with restricting executive authority than they were with defining the powers of a new federal legislature. They knew that Congress would present a bigger problem than the presidency in terms of limiting political authority, which is why Article I of the Constitution is based on the enumeration of specific powers. After all, the framers had long before accepted the reality that, for better or worse, legislatures are the focus of most governmental activity and that legislative institutions have many more responsibilities than do their judicial and executive counterparts. The framers' worries concerning governmental authority were expressed, therefore, through the precise definition of congressional powers in Article I, but they did not extend to the vesting clause in Article II. Those who drafted of the Constitution evidently believed that the vesting clause in the second article demanded no qualification of any sort.

Enumerated Presidential Powers

The views of the Constitution's authors on executive authority meant that the vesting clause was legally sufficient, yet the second and third sections of Article II identify specific powers that belong to the president. Strictly speaking, this was redundant, because the assumptions supporting the vesting clause made such elaboration unnecessary. Regrettably and unexpectedly, the redundancy in Article II highlighted a weakness in reasoning, or lapse in logic, that did not exist, exposing the Founding Fathers' constitutional principles to misinterpretation and confusion. Since the viability of the vesting clause rested on related assumptions that made further elaboration unnecessary, the identification of individual executive powers later in the second article seemed to compromise its authors' theoretical framework. More seriously, it opened the door to eventual misuse of the vesting clause and the corresponding expansion of executive authority based on a nonexistent constitutional inconsistency.

The exact causes of this apparent inconsistency are not entirely clear, but they have nothing to do with second thoughts or questions regarding limited executive authority. Most likely, as was the case with other sections of the Constitution that exhibited inconsistencies, the framers of the document wanted to guarantee that some details were not left to chance. In other words, particular provisions were so crucial that their inclusion was deemed to be absolutely necessary, even if the Constitution would have been legally sufficient without them. The powers enumerated in the second and third sections of Article II reflect the framers' greatest misgivings about the Confederation government and their principal objections concerning the exercise of power by the Crown prior to independence. The decision to identify those powers in the Constitution, even at the expense of logical consistency, was hardly surprising, not least because one of the primary aims of the Constitutional Convention was to properly define those very powers.

Another issue deserves mention here, and it applies not just to Article II but also to the whole document. The Constitution, which includes the political rhetoric employed in its service and also the ideas it embodies, is impressive on every level. Nevertheless, it is not without its problems, both theoretical and textual. These problems were the by-products of endless compromise, revision, and debate among several dozen individuals with strong opinions and equally strong political objectives, who were under intense pressure to create nothing short of a political miracle in just four months. That such circumstances should have produced a constitution that has endured for over 220 years with only a handful of changes is remarkable. The success of the framers' plan of government is a marvel of history and serves as a tribute to the potential of the human intellect. But, in the end, the Constitution, like any other document, was created by men, who are not perfect but fallible. As is the case with every example of authorship, their weaknesses are as much an element of the Constitution as are their strengths.

The compulsion to explain or understand every textual inconsistency, especially those that cannot be explained or understood, flies in the face of reality and ignores the human capability for error. Some inconsistencies defy every effort to understand them, and, at a certain point, interpreters must move beyond them. Frequently, as in this instance, enough additional evidence exists regarding the issue at hand that the apparent inconsistency is reduced to irrelevance. Because of the various factors at play in Philadelphia during the summer of 1787, Article II of the Constitution is not structured as some would like. Unfortunately, even a perfectly crafted document, and this one comes very close, would have posed obstacles to its interpretation. Whenever authors and readers are separated by as many generations as the Founding Fathers are from Americans today, those obstacles will persist. All in all, readers of the Constitution should remember that interpretation raises numerous questions. Some of those questions have no satisfactory answers, but the absence of those answers should not detract from what is otherwise established as fact.

The fact is that, although the inclusion of enumerated powers alongside a vesting clause that did not need them is a mystery of sorts, the framers' dedication to limited authority through specific powers is not. In that light, those enumerated powers can only help, for they define the presidential duties and responsibilities the framers of the Constitution considered paramount. And, despite the textual redundancy and the interpretive confusion caused by their presence, the enumerated powers do indeed help, as they underscore that the framers largely envisioned the president as head of state and as the top federal law enforcement official. So, aside from the powers to enforce all federal laws and make certain appointments subject to congressional approval, Article II of the Constitution invariably grants or recognizes powers that focus on foreign policy and national defense. The president is designated as commander in chief of the armed forces and the person in charge of the country's dealings with other nations, which includes the power to make treaties. These powers do not in any way exceed the scope of the five purposes of government identified in the previous section of this chapter, and they actually confirm the consistency of the framers' thoughts and intentions regarding limited executive authority.

CONCLUSION

The decision to renounce British sovereignty permanently changed the relationship among 13 newly independent states whose common bond had been their dependence on a British monarch. From a constitutional standpoint, the colonies were cast adrift, and their political status was dubious at best. Because the Declaration of Independence dissolved the existing constitutional structure in British North America, legitimate government disappeared with it. Shorn of a political framework that had defined the relationships of the former colonies to the Crown and to one another, America's Founding Fathers confronted a number of pressing questions that required immediate attention. Foremost among them was the problem of who or what would replace the king as the political center of governance. Past experience provided some clues but no simple solutions, as did almost 2,000 years of Western political history. Wartime circumstances demanded solutions, and a population beset by strife looked for a new system by which to be governed. A decade would elapse before they settled on an appropriate response to fill the gap in executive leadership left by their defeat of rule by British kings. That response was uniquely American.

The American presidency that emerged challenged in a new way the boundaries of intellectual creativity while, at the same time, it bowed to tradition and political precedent. As with everything else the Founding Fathers created, the institution derived from a combination of trial and error, political innovation, and long debates about constitutional alternatives. An acute awareness of history together with a profound intellectual curiosity led the framers to establish an executive unlike any that had existed before. Reflecting a potent mixture of new and old ideas about executive authority, their efforts culminated in a novel approach to political leadership. The framers of the Constitution dispensed with dynastic rule and embraced civilian governance backed by a public mandate, which meant that the new presidency was based not on hereditary privilege but on popular sovereignty. The legitimacy of the presidency rested on constitutionally designated limits to the exercise of power and on acknowledgment that political authority belongs to the people who delegate it. Over the years, it has proven itself the model that others around the world have sought to emulate.

CHAPTER 3

The Political Evolution of the Presidency: The National Security State

Englishman Samuel Johnson (1709–84) once stated that "the road to hell is paved with good intentions." An accomplished and influential 18th-century writer and critic, Johnson did not, in fact, coin this centuries-old adage, but his witty paraphrase certainly struck a chord with contemporary readers. Reflecting a political truth that transcended geography, culture, and history, it seemed to encapsulate a universal human experience. No one who had survived the turmoil of the early modern era could disagree with Johnson, least of all the framers of the U.S. Constitution. Undoubtedly familiar with Johnson's writings, they did not share his political views, but they surely acknowledged the accuracy of his observation. Johnson had been a staunch foe of colonial rebellion in North America, and he symbolized almost everything the framers opposed. To him, the revolutionaries were little more than glorified iconoclasts, while he was a curious anachronism to them. Yet, his sentiments regarding the corruptibility of men and political institutions, captured so succinctly in the above saying, would have encountered little opposition among them.

Despite their Enlightenment attitudes about the perfectibility of man and his institutions, the framers of the Constitution knew firsthand that humans were not perfect. They had seen the consequences of human imperfection for themselves, and they had learned that the best of intentions can be subverted for naked political gain. In an attempt to prevent history from repeating itself, they made their plans concerning the new American republic and its elective presidency very clear. Using the history of executive governance in British North America as both a guide and a warning, the nation's Founding Fathers took every precaution to avoid a repetition of past mistakes and to ensure the longevity of those plans. Their preference for limited executive authority was known to all and preserved through a prolific literature whose wisdom would be available to posterity. The framers of the Constitution consciously strove to create a document with the future in mind in which inevitable changes could be reconciled with the original purposes of that blueprint. Aware of the impossibility of controlling the future, the framers of the Constitution nonetheless hoped their political prescriptions would be honored.

Unfortunately, those hopes, evidenced by the care and precision with which the framers defined their political principles, were dashed by the later transformation of the American presidency. Their intentions may have been good and their political design solid, but, to borrow a phrase from another 18th-century literary giant, unexpected events derail even "the best laid schemes of mice and men." Nothing more aptly describes the fate of the American presidency than these words of the Scottish poet Robert Burns (1759–96), and nothing more forcefully conveys the irony of its evolution. Using the framers' constitutional blueprint as a guide, subsequent generations charted a course the framers would not have recognized or approved and, in so doing, rendered portions of that blueprint irrelevant. This should not imply that the government and its chief executive in existence today are in any way illegitimate, but it does underscore a stark political reality. The development of the modern presidency, with all its power and bureaucratic machinery altered completely the modestly crafted, humble office erected by the framers. Of the three branches of government, the executive has traveled furthest from its origins as the institution that today resembles least the intent of its creators. This chapter and the next will explain how that has occurred.

COMMANDERS IN CHIEF IN THE EARLY REPUBLIC

Truth be told, the presidency was not a substantial prize for most founding-era political contenders, nor was the associated role of commander in chief. Even in an age that was hostile to professional politicians and political ambition, talented public officials had little incentive to seek an office whose risks and uncertainties outweighed the potential benefits. Its prestige was modest at best, its authority narrow, and its resources meager, and, until the political reforms of the 1820s and 1830s, access was restricted to a small circle of elites. In most cases, governors of politically prominent states, such as New York, Massachusetts, and Virginia, wielded more real power and prestige than the nation's presidents, and the executive machinery they could muster under their command dwarfed the restricted capabilities of the federal executive branch. From an international perspective, American heads of state were taken seriously by almost no one, representing a country many thought would perish within a generation. Although American presidents of the early republic were honored and respected by their fellow Americans, not least because of their service and contributions prior to 1789, they occupied an office that was unassuming and limited, especially with respect to national defense and foreign policy, which is just what the framers of the Constitution had intended.

Early Attitudes about the Military, National Defense, and Foreign Policy
The executive branch of the U.S. government has various duties, though none may be as crucial to the life of the republic as national defense. From the standpoint of the day-to-day business of politics, its roles in policy making, legislation, and particularly law enforcement may be indispensable and, thus, more significant, but, without the ability to defend the country from foreign enemies, those would be for naught. The president's powers as commander in chief and the military resources at his or her disposal define the most prominent aspects of executive governance and also influence, if not determine, the overall effectiveness of an administration. The skill and logic with which presidents utilize their military resources affect not only the reception of American diplomatic policies abroad but also, and more important, the consent of their constituents at home. In that regard, the size, shape, and purpose of America's military, both during war and peacetime, must reflect the public's willingness to tolerate the deployment of professional armed forces to achieve political goals. In a democratic regime such as the United States, a nation's military imprint cannot exceed, at least not for long, the people's expectations concerning the legitimacy of military power.

For most of this nation's history, the people's expectations have been unusually modest. Inherently opposed to the existence of professional armies, especially in peacetime, Americans have traditionally supported restrictions on the size and deployment of armed forces. Not until the second third of the 20th century could most Americans even entertain the possibility of a more substantial military presence in the United States. By that point, the executive branch stood on the brink of an unprecedented expansion of responsibility and authority, so it had the means to accommodate a larger military force, which had not been the case during previous generations. In fact, by anyone's standards, the executive branch of the founding-era government was tiny. In addition to the president and the vice president, it included only the Departments of War, State, and Treasury, a few thousand soldiers, and a minor support staff. Modeled strictly according to the framers' intentions and their prescriptions in the Constitution, the executive branch was not the bureaucratic juggernaut it would become in the 20th century.

The diminutive size of the military was particularly striking, even in an age when armed forces were much smaller than they are today. Although the Continental army and navy had swelled in size during the Revolutionary War, their numbers decreased drastically upon its conclusion, leaving the defense of American territory to state militias. This pattern proved typical for most of the next 150 years, as wartime increases in military strength were followed by substantial reductions during peacetime. Prior to World War I, also known as the Great War, America's militias assumed the bulk of its national defense duties, with the federal military responsible for strategic planning, integration of forces, and battlefield command. In addition, federal troops were used for the protection of western territories and all other lands, such as the District of Columbia, under the supervision of the national government. Still, the overall number of federal troops was kept deliberately low, and the absence of a large standing army became a welcome feature of U.S. governance.

The preference for state militias, whose ranks were filled by civilian volunteers, as opposed to professional soldiers, had its origin in colonial precedents and the knowledge that many European governments had used standing armies against their own people. The framers of the Constitution believed that a military reduced in size constituted one of the keys to prevent tyranny, and they worked hard to keep the number of federal troops to a minimum, particularly during peacetime. Americans' bias against standing armies proved longstanding, so the maintenance of no more than a modest federal force continued to enjoy widespread popular support throughout the 19th century. A small standing army also made sense because, unlike today, the federal government had a tiny budget, which meant that it could not afford a substantial peacetime deployment. Because Americans opposed large standing armies and were not willing to pay for them, the size of America's professional military remained insubstantial.

At the same time, reliance on state militias did not diminish. In a nation founded on belief in civilian control of the military and devotion to popular sovereignty, both of which justified the existence of militias, Americans considered militia service to be a patriotic and honorable duty. Knowing that militia members were mere amateurs pressed into temporary service, Americans trusted these citizen-soldiers drawn from local farms, villages, and towns, which was significant at a time when state-centered loyalties still dominated all others. Above all, militias symbolized the virtue of political participation and the fulfillment of civic duty. They were the realization of an ancient Roman ideal epitomized by the farmer Cincinnatus, a historical figure familiar to America's Founding Fathers, who traded his plow for a sword when called on to defend Rome but who returned to his plow immediately after the battle. Made up of planters, artisans, merchants, and other ordinary men who traded the tools of their trade for arms to defend their homes, militias did have professional soldiers or mercenaries. Dedication to their trades and ties to local communities would ensure the men's return to civilian life upon war's end and guarantee freedom from abuse by a standing army. Militias made Americans feel secure, both politically and militarily.

Together with support of militias, 18th and 19th-century Americans were strong advocates of international neutrality. They disliked adventurism abroad and believed that, as long as the nation's military was relatively small, neither the incentive nor the capability for international adventurism would exist. Hoping not to repeat what they believed to be the mistakes of the major European powers, founding-era Americans did not want their government to be lured into foreign entanglements that could destabilize the republic. They had a palpable aversion to involvement in international affairs, especially European diplomatic intrigues and wars, and they frowned on the pursuit of strategic advantage through military gamesmanship. Convinced that foreign entanglements and international activism ultimately cause problems at home, the founding generation concluded that the temptation to meddle in matters abroad could be thwarted by limiting the size of the military. Americans assumed that a limited military capacity necessarily translated into a humble foreign policy and that fewer military means would deprive ambitious executive officials of the resources that they might potentially use for conquest.

War and Diplomacy In the Early Republic
The United States of America may have been a nonentity to the ruling elites of Europe, but it had a pressing international agenda nonetheless. Obstacles to progress and threats to its very existence were apparent immediately, and the United States was confronted with a host of international issues that required attention. One of the biggest problems facing the new nation was that it lacked the international credibility of an established player, so rivals were eager to test its resolve. The major European empires resumed their pursuit of key objectives on the North American continent, hoping to secure long-sought territories that surrounded the young republic. Britain, France, and Spain as well as the various Indian tribes and, later, Mexico all had good reason to provoke the United States, particularly since American gains on the continent had come at their expense. Troubles with France led almost to a war during John Adams's presidency, while unresolved disputes with Great Britain led to an actual war in 1812, as did border controversies with Mexico in 1846. Indian tribes were handled with, in many instances, extreme brutality and intense resolve as American troops drove them beyond the frontier.

During the 19th century, U.S. foreign policy was driven by the urge to acquire land and by the desire to secure the new country's dominance in

North America. Nothing stood in the way of continuous acquisition of territory and the creation of a continental buffer that would protect the United States from potential adversaries. An insatiable drive to obtain agricultural land and the promise of vast riches through the exploitation of minerals and the control of other natural resources lured thousands across the frontier and justified the means necessary to tame the wilderness and expand America's borders. One of the earliest acquisitions was the Louisiana Purchase of 1803, which more than doubled the total square mileage of the United States and stretched its boundary beyond the Mississippi River. Despite doubts about President Thomas Jefferson's constitutional authority to negotiate such a land deal, the Senate approved the treaty, thus seemingly endorsing the growth of presidential power in this area. Although the presidency's constitutional role as caretaker of American territorial expansion was questionable, subsequent occupants of the office eagerly accepted this responsibility.

In the 1820s, with growth in confidence in the powers of the executive as head of state, President James Monroe extended U.S. foreign policy beyond traditional limits by issuing what has become known as the Monroe Doctrine. As much a warning to European nations to stay out of Latin America as a notice to those south of the border, both newly independent

countries and remaining colonial powers, that a new international player had arrived, Monroe's declaration increased, at least on paper, the scope of U.S. authority in foreign affairs. Monroe's international pretense notwithstanding, the primary focus of American expansionism was not south of the border but west of the Mississippi River, where settlers sought new opportunities. Within a few decades, Americans grew convinced that the control of all lands as far west as the Pacific Ocean was the country's *Manifest Destiny*, and they pursued this goal with zestful fervor. A term coined by a patriotic journalist and appropriated by supporters of President James Polk during the 1840s when the

Portrait of James Monroe, the fifth president of the United States *(Wikipedia)*

nation set about annexing Texas, California, and other parts of the continent west of the Mississippi, Manifest Destiny became the rallying cry to justify territorial gains at any price. The term embodied the American spirit, and it served as an apt slogan for a nation with an insatiable hunger for land.

The nation's presidents, though not always of one mind regarding American expansion, defended an assertive continental posture that enabled the realization of territorial objectives even sooner than most had envisioned. By the 1850s, except for Alaska and Hawaii, the United States had acquired most of the land it now comprises, a feat that could not have been accomplished without the backing and encouragement of its chief executives. Of course, the nation's land gains aggravated sectional divisions that, in the end, accelerated the march toward civil war. Aside from the preparation of western territories for eventual statehood, the federal government was forced to confront issues concerning its frontier possessions that it would have preferred to ignore. Facing political pressure to maintain the balance between free and slave states, the national government attempted to manage the issue of slavery in the western territories by pleasing everyone, yet it ultimately satisfied no one. Executive handling of the issue was often clumsy and, at times, nonsensical, contributing to heightening tensions between the North and the South. Northerners opposed the spread of slavery beyond its established base in the South. Southerners feared encirclement by free states hostile to their way of life. Neither side appeared willing to compromise, and the federal government had the unenviable responsibility of defusing a precarious standoff. In the end, compromise proved impossible, and the nation was compelled to wage a brutal civil war.

Thus, presidential duties as head of state were not insubstantial during the early republic. American chief executives were fully occupied in addressing the consequences of expansionist policies, and their powers increased accordingly. Nevertheless, on the eve of the Civil War, the authority of the president as head of state did not differ greatly from that in existence in 1789, as even occasional increases in constitutional authority had not produced a marked deviation from the framers' intentions. Aside from dealing with the consolidation of continental territory and the related issue of slavery, American presidents had comparatively little to do in their capacity as heads of state during the first several decades of the republic's existence. Lack of attention to foreign affairs stemmed largely from the fact of geographic isolation and the political benefits that accrued from that reality. Physically separated from Europe, the young nation had choices that were unavailable to European powers. Free of European entanglements, the United States was able to observe from a safe distance, the diplomatic maneuverings and military actions of the European powers in the 19th century. Its resources could be devoted to the pursuit of domestic objectives. That European interference in North America diminished after the War of 1812 made those objectives even more attainable.

THE ROOTS OF THE NATIONAL SECURITY PRESIDENCY

For at least the first two-thirds of its existence, the United States was not a global superpower. In fact, during much of that time, it could not have qualified as even a minor power. Following the Civil War, however, that began to change. Following the conquest of the North American continent, the nation's attention turned increasingly outward. Seeking markets abroad and eager to enhance its strategic leverage, the United States looked to the world stage for opportunities. Gradually but resolutely, its international involvement grew, and its influence over other countries increased, culminating in the kind of foreign adventurism the Founding Fathers had wished to avoid. By the 1940s, the power of the United States surpassed all previous levels, and the nation was poised to assume the status of the globe's preeminent power. Historians and political scientists have identified what ensued as the emergence of a *national security state*, namely, a nation in which military, economic, and cultural resources were fused for the maintenance of power at home and abroad.

Presidential Authority from the Civil War to the Great War

The last third of the 19th century brought with it a gradual but noticeable change in presidential authority. The two most immediate causes, though many others existed, were the Civil War and the closing of the American frontier. With the creation of a formidable administrative machinery to prosecute the war against the South, the federal executive established constitutional precedents during the Civil War that William McKinley, Theodore Roosevelt, and Woodrow Wilson would later use to justify the promotion of American strategic assets abroad. By the end of the 19th century, American presidents wielded more authority as heads of state than any of their early predecessors, and they eagerly promoted American military and diplomatic interests outside the North American continent. The closing of the frontier went hand in hand with the nation's new military and diplomatic interests, since America's rapidly industrializing economy needed markets for its products. The conquest of the North American continent meant that domestic markets were finite and that future economic growth would rely on foreign consumption of American goods, so strategic penetration abroad would serve national economic priorities.

None of this would have been possible without a presidency capable of accommodating the duties and responsibilities that an increased global presence demanded. Such duties and responsibilities did not appear overnight, but they evolved as a consequence of internal political and economic developments at the end of the 19th century. Some of these developments can be traced to the Civil War and the extreme pressures facing an executive fighting for the survival of the federal union. Relying on powers no other American commander in chief had used, President Abraham Lincoln forever altered the complexion of executive authority in the United States. Although his authority as commander in chief was by no means as extensive as would be that of his 20th-century successors, Lincoln transcended the bounds of what the framers would have considered acceptable and, in so doing, he reshaped the American presidency. His approval of military tribunals, suspension of constitutional rights, and control over the use of industrial resources for war, to say nothing of the emancipation of the slaves, embodied an augmentation of presidential authority that would have been utterly unrecognizable to the founding generation.

Had the Civil War not been such an exhaustive and lengthy conflict and had the United States not stood on the brink of a more active international involvement, perhaps Lincoln's newly acquired powers would have lain dormant and even withered in time. However, the Civil War proved to be a transformational event from which the country could not retreat or hide. It was of sufficient duration and intensity to change the very nature of warfare as well as the relationship between citizens and their military, demanding a nationwide commitment of forces and material from 1861 to 1865 that eclipsed all previous conflicts combined. With a military and administrative staff that far outstripped anything the framers of the Constitution could have foreseen, the sheer size and bureaucratic power of the executive branch were staggering. Union forces numbered in the hundreds of thousands, and the resources at their disposal amounted to a significant proportion of what today's economists call GDP (gross domestic product).

Once victory was achieved, postwar Reconstruction, the federal program initiated to rebuild the South, necessitated similar attention by the executive branch. The occupation, reintegration, and physical repair of the southern states was coordinated by Presidents Andrew Johnson and Ulysses Grant and implemented by an army of executive officials and employees. Reconstruction may have proven itself a political failure by the early 1870s, but it nonetheless required an extensive bureaucratic presence that would provide a meaningful precedent for Woodrow Wilson and Franklin Roosevelt as they addressed the economic and military challenges of their presidencies. Federal troops engaged in what today's commentators call nation building, acting as administrators, engineers, policemen, and engaging in whatever other activities were deemed necessary to create a new postwar society in the South. Scores of new federal agencies appeared almost overnight, confronted with myriad bureaucratic and social tasks and charged with providing basic services to those in the South left destitute by four years of a fratricidal war.

Abraham Lincoln

The history of the Western world has been marked by some unlikely heroes, but arguably none as unlikely as America's 16th president. A humble man with modest ambitions, he never set out to transform a country or revolutionize a presidency, though he did both. Abraham Lincoln was born in a log cabin under unenviable circumstances to uneducated parents in rural Kentucky. Never benefiting from a formal education himself, Lincoln was a self-taught man with keen insights into the human condition and an intellectual curiosity to match. The family moved to Illinois after his 20th birthday, and young Abe subsequently attempted several trades, none of which proved successful. Eventually, politics drew his interest, and, following passage of the bar exam, Lincoln served in the Illinois legislature and also in Congress for several years. After his short stint in the House of Representatives, he returned to Illinois and started a law practice, which engaged his energies for the next several years. With a solid legal career and a family to which he was devoted, Lincoln abandoned politics. In fact, by the early 1850s, politics seemed the furthest thing from his mind, but all that was about to change.

As the friction between North and South increased and the controversy over slavery intensified, Lincoln reengaged in politics, eager to find a solution to the escalating crisis. In 1856, he was the vice-presidential nominee of the newly created Republican Party, and, in 1858, he ran for the U.S. Senate. The Senate campaign, though unsuccessful, greatly enhanced his national reputation, and his skills as an orator were on public display during the famous Lincoln-Douglas debates. His popularity among reformers and his growing political stature provided the foundation for a presidential run in 1860, which proved victorious but hardly resounding. Lincoln won a four-way race that gave him less than 40 percent of the popular vote and no electoral votes in the Deep South. Much to his dismay, his election tore the nation apart. Prior to Lincoln's inauguration, part of the South had already seceded, and the rest was soon to follow, confronting the new president with a political crisis unlike any before. The South forced his hand with the seizure of Fort Sumter by South Carolina forces, and the country would soon be engulfed in war.

Given his meager political résumé, Lincoln seemed ill-prepared to assume the reins as commander in chief, yet he became one of the most effective leaders in the nation's history. Though lacking the practical experience and military knowledge to lead a country into war, he was a quick study and proved to be a decisive chief executive at a time when circumstances required nothing less. Unfortunately, Lincoln was not blessed with a particularly gifted or resolute general staff, which created both strategic and tactical problems throughout the first few years of the war. Probably the most frustrating of his generals was George McClellan, whose extreme

Left to right: Major Allan Pinkerton, President Lincoln, and General John A. McClernand at Antietam, Maryland, in October 1862 *(National Archives)*

caution and penchant for delay bordered on military incompetence, while the successors, until Ulysses S. Grant, were no more capable. As a result, Lincoln was compelled to assume a much more active role in military planning, maintaining hands-on management of the war effort until at least 1863. By 1863, the president found a trustworthy, skilled commander in Grant to take charge of the Union forces, thereby relieving much of his burden. Nevertheless, Lincoln still kept a close watch over his generals to ensure the proper implementation of his overall strategy.

During his term in office, Lincoln expanded the scope of the presidency to a degree beyond any the framers could have imagined, and he consolidated his powers to enable the prosecution of a war of unprecedented

(continues)

(continued)

scale. He marshaled the country's economic and social resources in directing them toward military uses, and he steadily enlarged his authority as commander in chief. Imposing martial law, suspending civil liberties, and appropriating property, Lincoln did whatever he needed to win the war and reunite the Union. In early 1863, he stunned the nation by liberating slaves in the secessionist South through the Emancipation Proclamation, which was a bold but constitutionally questionable measure that renewed the flagging spirits of many who had become disillusioned by the war. Adaptable, self-effacing, and intelligent, President Lincoln had the wherewithal to improvise and innovate during a period when the survival of the nation hung in the balance, and his resiliency and keen awareness of political necessities made him a unique leader. Tragically, his life was cut short by an assassin's bullet, but not before he had defeated the South and cemented his legacy as one of America's greatest commanders in chief.

An expansion of executive administrative capabilities such as this would not be seen again until the Great Depression of the 1930s.

Despite significant increases in executive power during Lincoln's presidency, continued growth of the executive branch was anything but steady or predictable over the next several decades. Lincoln may have redrawn the boundaries of legitimate presidential authority, but the new precedents he established were not embraced by all of his successors. As a result, the executive branch in succeeding decades evolved in fits and starts, its scope waxing and waning according to the varying international ambitions of the men who acted as commander in chief. In terms of foreign policy, two of the most ambitious were William McKinley, the last president who served during the 19th century, and Theodore Roosevelt, who became president upon McKinley's assassination. Considered by some to have been the first modern president, McKinley took the nation into war with Spain in 1898, which resulted in U.S. acquisition of Puerto Rico, the Philippines, and Guam. He was adept at using the press to promote the administration's international objectives and to popularize an assertive foreign policy that announced America's arrival as a global player. If anything, Roosevelt was even more enthusiastic about the country's newfound international status, using his clout to act as a power broker in Asia and Latin America, while eagerly pushing America's economic interests whenever and wherever possible.

Roosevelt was followed by William Howard Taft, a largely ineffective chief executive who made political enemies of Republicans and Democrats alike. Any advances in executive authority would have to await Taft's successor,

Woodrow Wilson, a man with impeccable academic credentials and high ideals at a time when much of the world was engaged in the first of the modern global conflicts. Wilson held a doctorate in political science and often viewed international relations as an exercise in morality through which the world's powers could redress the injustices of the past. Considered naive by some and extremely unrealistic by others, Wilson may have been the least likely of all modern presidents to secure a substantial augmentation of executive authority as commander in chief. Nevertheless, in one of history's great ironies, he did just that. Despite his admitted aversion to imperialism and foreign rule of indigenous peoples, his policies ultimately laid the groundwork for an American global domination that looked very imperial. Military incursions into Latin America to protect local populations and U.S. property interests led to the imposition of American control, and involvement in World War I, though based on Wilson's professed goals of making the world safe for democracy and promoting self-determination for oppressed peoples ensured American financial and military ascendancy in the West.

Wilson may have touted his so-called Fourteen Points, a broad endorsement of political liberty, democratic government, free trade, and civility among nations, as a recipe for global peace and progress, but it was also a platform for the promotion of American interests and political values abroad. Under Wilson's administration, those interests and values were also upheld through active, some would say aggressive, domestic policies that resurrected executive powers not utilized since the Civil War. To secure military victory in Europe, American economic might was harnessed by the administration through agencies such as the War Industries Board (WIB), which, despite its lack of popularity, represented a total commitment to war that eventually transformed U.S. military capabilities. In addition, during the Red Scare of 1919, Attorney General Mitchell Palmer's sweeping use of national police powers to suppress political dissent served notice that the discretionary authority of the executive branch under exigent circumstances would extend beyond standard limits. These ominous developments paved the way for further increases in executive authority as the United States prepared to take a leading role on the world stage.

The End of the Age of Empires and the Dawn of the Superpower Era

Not coincidentally, America's entry onto the world stage coincided with the gradual downfall of European empires that had reigned supreme for centuries. The late 19th and early 20th centuries saw the slow yet inexorable demise of empires that had long dominated the political geography of Europe and its periphery. World War I spelled the end of the Austro-Hungarian and Ottoman Empires and marked the rise of other powers, notably the United States, and Japan. Britain, France, Germany, and Spain faced challenges from within and without that contributed to instability not only in Europe, but also for those nations with colonial possessions around the globe. The end of the Ottomans left a power vacuum in large areas of the Balkans and the Middle East. Italy struggled to resurrect past glories. Russia found itself trapped between past and present as it transitioned from an imperial has-been to a communist powerhouse.

During the first third of the 20th century, as formal empires crumbled, the United States capitalized on international political currents by cementing its stature as a world power and building the economic and military foundation of an informal empire that would ultimately dominate the globe. That domination arose in the wake of two world wars that wreaked vast destruction in parts of the developed world and that relegated others to political oblivion. Such devastation was made possible by a relatively new type of warfare pioneered by some of the great battlefield commanders of the 19th century. Their strategic and tactical innovations ensured that future wars would be bigger, wider, and more destructive than those of the 18th and early 19th centuries, requiring resources that only a nationwide commitment could fulfill. The entire population of nations, not just their professional soldiers, would now wage war, demanding the subordination of economic capabilities to related political objectives and the coordination of social resources toward maximal military strength. This development signaled a new age in which success on the battlefield relied on channeling a country's financial, economic, social, and cultural output into military power.

The military conflicts of the 20th century would thus be so-called total wars, consuming material goods on a previously unthinkable scale, and its participants would ensure the availability of those goods. First employed widely by governments of the French Revolution and by Emperor Napoléon Bonaparte, total war marked a new departure. Gone were the days of professional, small-scale warfare between foes whose armies numbered no more than several thousand combatants fighting seasonal battles according to the rules of honor. Total war brought with it a kind of military conflict that was as exhaustive as it was brutal. Survival hinged on a mass mobilization of personnel, industrial muscle, and cultural wherewithal toward a continuous deployment of armed forces that dwarfed the aristocratic armies of the 18th century. Victory was measured by the destruction of enemy territory and total control of its people, which were facilitated by steady advancements in battlefield weapons. Napoléon's strategic and tactical changes opened the door to global conflicts previously unimaginable, most notably, the two world wars of the 20th century.

The United States experienced total war earlier than some countries, though its introduction to this type of warfare came not through foreign conflict but through a vicious civil war. More than 1 million soldiers served during this bloodiest conflict in American history, much of the South was destroyed, and the social effects were felt for generations. At a cost of more than 660,000 lives, the Civil War demanded an unprecedented mobilization of social and economic resources for four years during which practically every American was affected in some way. As the only modern war fought on American soil, its impact was long-lasting and its lessons would be applied to American military efforts throughout the 20th century. In fighting the Civil War, the United States learned to fight as a world power, and it demonstrated that military effectiveness cannot be achieved without a significant expansion of executive authority. Such expansion proved to be one of the undeniable truths of the 20th century.

America Becomes a Superpower

After World War I, the United States retreated into isolationism for almost two decades, not abandoning its recently won international status altogether but nevertheless distancing itself from further involvement in European problems. The twin pillars of American foreign policy during the early days of the republic, small standing armies and neutrality, resurfaced as Americans became weary of the consequences of foreign entanglements at a time when their future was far from certain. Through the nation's participation in World War I, Americans witnessed the carnage that results from increased militarism, and they were not yet prepared to accommodate a sizable military presence at home. In addition, the economic catastrophe of the 1930s made the American public all the more focused on domestic affairs, and the pursuit of an active international agenda became a luxury they could not afford. Despite substantial gains in authority accruing to the president as commander in chief over the previous few decades, in 1940 that authority lay dormant as President Franklin Roosevelt promised to steer clear of the global war that had erupted a year prior.

As it turned out, Roosevelt could not keep his promise. Circumstances forced his hand in pushing America ever closer to war. After the Japanese attack

This 1941 photograph shows President Franklin D. Roosevelt asking Congress to declare war on Japan the day after the attack on Pearl Harbor. (*Library of Congress*)

on Pearl Harbor on December 7, 1941, he was left no alternatives. Congress declared war on Japan, and Germany declared war on the United States. Recognizing the magnitude and implications of a global conflict fueled by enemies devoted to the extermination of whole populations, Roosevelt's commitment to victory was total. Pledging a mobilization of American resources on a scale never before attempted, the president's expansion of executive authority was quick and decisive, and it proved ultimately irreversible. More than 15 million men and women served in the armed forces in one capacity or another, while tens of millions of others held jobs that supported the war effort. The country's manufacturing potential was channeled into the production of arms, supplies, food, and medicine, required by America's military, while its cultural output was focused on the maintenance of morale. Hollywood, major publishers, and leading radio producers all contributed to the presidency's propaganda machine, churning out movies, books, newspapers, and radio broadcasts that celebrated the superiority of the Allied cause. The power and authority of the executive branch stood at an all-time high.

Upon the conclusion of the war, the United States emerged as one of two principal military powers. Along with the Soviet Union, it was unchallenged as the arbiter of a new world order, no longer in a position to turn back the clock to a simpler era by renouncing its newly won status. Americans realized that World War II had been fundamentally different from all previous conflicts, and they reluctantly accepted that the nation's international role would have to change as a result, even during peacetime. This conflict had killed more than 55 million people, which included almost half a million Americans, destroyed tens of thousands of cities, towns, and villages, and introduced the world to phenomena such as genocide, ethnic cleansing, and nuclear annihilation. Nothing would ever be the same. To prevent further wars of this kind and to protect the West from the growing influence of Soviet communism, Americans and others around the globe needed international leadership from a country with resources and credentials equal to the task. In 1945, the United States was the only possible choice.

Although the desire to avoid another global war constituted an important reason for America's assumption of world leadership and the rapid expansion of executive authority during the late 1940s, the overwhelming factor was the rising power of the Soviet Union. Despite the international agreements ending World War II, which settled obvious geopolitical questions, many European nations were in turmoil. Teetering on the brink of communism, strategically significant countries such as Italy, Greece, and Turkey could not be allowed to fall under Soviet control, which would expand the reach of totalitananism and threaten democratic regimes across Europe. Others, such as France, Austria, and Germany, were susceptible not only to currents from the far left within their borders, but also to extremist elements from the right, which would make postwar rebuilding efforts difficult at best. Even Britain, which had been spared the widespread physical devastation of continental nations, was seriously weakened and faced internal problems that raised considerable political concerns. The Allied victory notwithstanding, Europe's political situation was precarious, and its vulnerability to Soviet aggression was substantial.

The U.S. government and many among the public could read the political tea leaves, and they understood that, absent American leadership in the face of communist threats to the West, the Soviet Union could soon come to dominate vast areas of the world. At this juncture in history, the stakes were much higher than they had been following the Napoleonic Wars or World War I, not least due to the advent of nuclear weapons. The democratic nations of the West resolved to enhance their strength through heightened military preparedness and progressive political reforms. All involved knew that the bulk of the military resources and also the political and economic wherewithal to neutralize Soviet aggression would have to come from the United States. American economic muscle would provide the means to rebuild the European continent, and American political know-how would assist in reforming government, while the U.S. military presence would serve as a deterrent against Soviet expansion.

AMERICA'S NATIONAL SECURITY STATE

During the late 1940s and early 1950s, President Harry Truman consolidated the increased military and diplomatic activities of the previous few decades to promote the establishment of an enhanced executive *bureaucracy* capable of securing the country's status as a superpower. This effort revolutionized American politics by linking the nation's domestic policies to a more assertive global presence and to an ongoing campaign to shape developments abroad. With the goal to maintain America's strategic leverage and protect its diplomatic assets, his successors oversaw an unprecedented growth of military and bureaucratic resources, especially during the *cold war*. Within a few decades, the United States became a military behemoth whose ability to take advantage of its economic might was unrivaled. The stratospheric rise of American influence abroad paralleled a commensurate increase in presidential responsibility and executive duties, allowing the executive branch to extend its reach over not only internal affairs that affected the country's security, but also the lives of ordinary Americans. The scope of legitimate presidential activity widened to a degree beyond any before, and the boundaries of executive power had to be continually renegotiated.

The Cold War Presidency

The cold war never produced a physical conflict between the Unite States and the Soviet Union, but it spawned a number of proxy wars around the globe and a keen political competition that polarized international affairs for more than 40 years. Each superpower was intent on maximizing its sphere of influence by controlling or influencing client states and securing the cooperation of nonaligned countries through political and economic incentives. Domestic tranquility in the war-ravaged countries was deemed essential to maintaining the international status quo, and so trillions of dollars were spent on efforts to restore economic prosperity and on military defense abroad. One such program was the Marshall Plan, under which President Truman ensured the democratic future of Western Europe through a comprehensive aid initiative that paid for the reconstruction of war-ravaged countries and the resurrection of viable economies in these nations. In Germany, Austria, and Japan, the United States remained as an occupying force, undertaking the day-to-day governance of their peoples and overseeing the political structure of their ruling regimes, while elsewhere the promise of American defense forces and U.S. dollars encouraged friendly governments to adopt compliant policies.

Never before had the United States made such a commitment of personnel, resources, and finances. American presidents oversaw the deployment of millions of U.S. military and civilian personnel all over the globe, particularly in Europe. In addition to the powers granted to them by the Constitution and those acquired over the previous several decades, U.S. commanders in chief possessed the authority to dictate, or at the very least guide, the political affairs of other nations. The resources at their disposal were immense. They included hundreds of thousands of soldiers, a vastly reconditioned State Department, a new Department of Defense with an army of support personnel, an intelligence apparatus made up of the Central Intelligence Agency (CIA), National Security Agency (NSA), and a number of other organizations, and a growing complex of military and industrial contractors. The discretion of the president to utilize those resources was largely unchallenged, and the willingness of American commanders in chief to exercise greater and greater authority frequently appeared without limits.

As the world became more dangerous, presidential discretion and authority grew accordingly, while the necessity of military action became inevitable. Support for politically turbulent client states and military insurgencies clashed directly with Soviet interests, which produced "hot" wars in almost every part of the world. The bloodiest and arguably the most prominent were on the Korean Peninsula, in Indochina and Central Asia, particularly Afghanistan, and throughout Latin America, while other incidents between Soviet-sponsored and American-backed forces arose in Europe, the Middle East, and Africa. These international disputes demanded quick action, and they put pressure on American presidents to decrease America's response time to perceived crises. Thus, the frequency and magnitude of American military involvement abroad increased, and the executive branch appropri-

Headquarters of the National Security Agency in Fort Meade, Maryland *(Wikipedia)*

ated most governmental war-making powers. Unfortunately, at least from a constitutional perspective, Congress seemed only too eager to cede its war-making authority to America's commanders in chief, so presidential responsibilities in this area continued to expand without restriction.

The noted political scientist Theodore Lowi is one among many scholars who have argued that, as members of Congress became more concerned with reelection than with making tough decisions over which they could lose votes at home, they willingly relinquished the legislature's power to declare war. America's commanders in chief, for their part, eagerly appropriated a power not granted to them by the Constitution, thereby enhancing their ability to pursue foreign policy objectives without political impediments. Although such a power is strictly prohibited by the Constitution and would have been opposed by the Founding Fathers, it has been affirmed through decades of executive practices. Of the more than 10 conflicts in which the United States has participated since 1945, not one was sanctioned by a congressional declaration of war. In other words, despite the fact that the United States has fought many wars since the end of World War II, the last time Congress invoked its constitutional authority to declare war was in 1941. All subsequent wars have been declared by America's presidents.

This problematic state of affairs was punctuated by what many commentators have understood to be the most cynical foreign policy legislation of the last

50 years, the War Powers Act. Passed in 1973 over President Nixon's veto, it requires America's commanders in chief to consult with Congress prior to the introduction of troops into any military theater, but it simultaneously recognizes a presidential power to respond to exigent circumstances without notification when such notification would compromise the integrity or effectiveness of military action. The net effect of this concession was an acknowledgment in all but word of a presidential power to declare war through a statutory loophole that seems patently unconstitutional. Over the next three decades, Presidents Carter, Reagan, Clinton, both Bushes, and Obama have availed themselves of this loophole to begin or augment American military operations around the globe and secure a presidential power to declare war. From a constitutional standpoint, this has probably been the single most worrisome consequence of the steady expansion of executive authority during the cold war, and it has cast a giant cloud over the legitimacy of American military initiatives.

The Constitutionality of Expanded Presidential Authority

Between 1860 and 1920, the executive branch underwent significant changes, which were ultimately at odds with the framers' conception of it. Presidents Lincoln, McKinley, Roosevelt, and Wilson led the charge toward a more modern presidency capable of accommodating greater authority and expanded resources. Nevertheless, despite some potentially dangerous precedents that affected the future evolution of the presidency, these changes did not yet represent an irreversible breach of constitutional principles or the framers' vision of republican government. During the late 1940s and into the early 1950s, such a breach began to appear. By the 1970s, the American presidency had transcended all of the boundaries of legitimate authority defined by the men who authored the Constitution. Perhaps the most alarming aspect of these developments has been that Americans just stood by and watched. How did the system of checks and balances fail so miserably to prevent, or at least overturn, these constitutional transgressions? Why have the American people tolerated the relentless acquisition of power by America's commanders in chief and the abdication of congressional responsibility and oversight with respect to national defense? More to the point, why has the Supreme Court acquiesced to what has, for all intents and purposes, been a betrayal of the framers' intentions regarding executive authority and republican governance?

These questions have no easy answers. They arise from the same dilemma that resulted in unconstitutional increases in congressional authority over social and economic issues during the last 70 years. Just as Congress acquired powers that went beyond any of those granted to it by the framers to confront the social and economic crises launched by industrialization, the presidency amassed extensive authority to address the military and diplomatic crises spawned by the cold war. In both cases, exigent circumstances required action—not political debate about constitutional amendments—so Americans and their political officials turned a blind eye to what they perceived as the necessary costs of political compromise. The most serious of these costs was an unconstitutional expansion of governmental authority that equipped federal officials with powers that would have been unthinkable just a century before. Since Americans as a whole were complicit in these constitutional changes, neither the will nor the ability to reverse them has been present.

As convincing as such an explanation may be, it tells only half the story. Because the framers of the Constitution were aware of the public's susceptibility to lapses of judgment and because they knew that even majority decisions could be illegitimate, they took precautions against exactly these kinds of situations. They made sure that even in the unlikely event that all of the regular constitutional checks and balances did not work properly a remedy of last resort would compensate for their mistakes. That remedy was the federal judiciary, specifically the Supreme Court of the United States. As the institution charged with interpretation of federal laws and actions that affected the Constitution and determination of the meaning of pertinent constitutional principles, the Supreme Court was established to address constitutional violations and to maintain the integrity of the nation's foundational laws. Although some doubts existed during the early republic about the finality of the Court's broader theories, the founding generation harbored no doubts about the Court's ability to decide the constitutionality of particular acts or the finality of its opinions regarding specific cases.

The Supreme Court's role as a constitutional remedy of last resort notwithstanding, the framers never anticipated the problems that could arise from what Alexander Hamilton understood: The federal judiciary was the "least dangerous branch." Hamilton astutely observed that the judicial branch has "neither force nor will," so, unlike the legislative and executive branches of government, it did not have the authority to implement its rulings or to enforce them. As a result, its actual power was more symbolic than real, resting on its moral credibility and the willingness of the people and their representatives to accept the legitimacy of its decisions. For the founding generation, the seemingly precarious nature of the judiciary's authority vis-à-vis the other two branches was not apparent, since the overall size and scope of federal authority as a whole was relatively small. The framers of the Constitution could not foresee a time, such as the past 100 years, when the "least dangerous branch" would be eclipsed by the formidable power and authority of a federal government that had grown far beyond its intended boundaries. They believed that the federal judiciary's willingness to confront constitutional violations, and especially that of the Supreme Court, would continue to be a function of its moral rectitude, legal responsibilities, and devotion to the Constitution—and nothing else.

By the second third of the 20th century, interbranch dynamics had irretrievably changed, and the judiciary had become not just the least dangerous branch but also the most vulnerable. As the famous legal scholar Alexander Bickel observed a few decades ago, because of this vulnerability, the Supreme Court recognized that it had only a finite amount of political capital to spend before it began to lose support and credibility among the public and its officials. It could not afford to enter every battle, settle every contentious issue, or oppose every questionable policy, so it was forced to pick its fights wisely and carefully. Consequently, the nation's highest court has typically avoided certain types of issues that it does not consider justiciable, that is, capable of being adequately settled through the legal system. Some issues simply cannot be solved by the courts in ways that make sense constitutionally and politically, while others are not sufficiently developed for the courts to intervene. This may be a less than honorable way of deflecting susceptibility to political attack, but it has allowed the Supreme Court to protect its limited authority.

Using justiciability, or the lack thereof, as a standard, the Supreme Court has been able to avoid numerous cases, among which are those that fall under the so-called political questions doctrine. The Court declared as early as the first half of the 19th century that some cases involve questions that should be resolved through the normal political process and should be submitted to the people and their representatives for review and ultimate disposal. These political questions supposedly invoke fundamentally political, as opposed to constitutional, principles whose proper determination belongs to the democratic institutions of government that reflect the popular will. Therefore, the other branches of government are better qualified to address them. Since the distinction between political and constitutional principles is hardly evident, the dividing line between political and constitutional questions has been one of convenience rather than law. Despite the legal ambiguity, the political questions doctrine has become a useful vehicle for the Supreme Court to steer clear of thorny, or inconvenient, political topics.

Foreign policy is one of those topics, so the Supreme Court has traditionally shown considerable deference to the executive branch in its exercise of national security powers. It has not been willing to question the feasibility or legitimacy of presidential actions during the cold war, and it has customarily avoided interference with the conduct of foreign policy and national defense because of the political questions doctrine. Due to its inability to fight the presidency and the public over an issue such as national security that they guard more jealously than perhaps any other, the Supreme Court has reluctantly sidestepped its constitutional responsibilities in this area to preserve its political capital for battles it can win. In addition, as discussed in the last chapter, the wording of Article II of the Constitution, though clear to the founding generation, does not offer much guidance for those who oppose the executive transformations of the last 100 years. The intent of the framers was obvious to their contemporaries, but, to a Supreme Court with limited authority and credibility, intent without specific constitutional elaboration does not constitute sufficient cause to overturn overwhelming public opinion or a powerful executive momentum that has benefited from the terseness of Article II.

The Cold War Military

For a country for which an aversion to standing armies formed the core of its national defense posture for most of its existence, the explosive growth of the military has been nothing short of amazing. As indicated earlier in this chapter, Americans overcame their distrust of a large peacetime military establishment, or, more appropriately, they concluded that, in a post–World War II world filled with nuclear weapons, rogue regimes, and threats from a Soviet empire, their fear of external dangers to the nation's security was greater than their fear of standing armies. Aside from the obvious institutional hurdles to reversing a long and cherished political tradition, the biggest obstacle to a sizable increase in America's permanent military forces had been the public's opposition to standing armies. Therefore, once the American people were onboard in consenting to such a change, military expansion could proceed. The rest was a matter of proper planning, skillful implementation, and adequate funding.

Starting with the National Security Act of 1947, which created the Department of Defense, National Security Council, and Central Intelligence Agency, the federal government demonstrated that its intentions regarding the establishment of greatly enhanced national defense capabilities should be taken seriously by Americans and others around the globe. The new Defense Department, a replacement of the outdated Department of War, symbolized the presidency's dedication to military modernization and a wholesale reorganization of America's fighting capacity and also affirmed the country's goal of security through the permanent deployment of military force. Permanent military deployment was a function of the nation's postwar security needs, and it reflected the international commitments that defined America's recently acquired role as a superpower. The country's traditional rejection of foreign entanglements was resoundingly reversed, exemplified by commitments that included leadership of the North Atlantic Treaty Organization (NATO), an alliance of anti-Soviet states that looked to the United States for military and diplomatic protection from communist aggression, permanent membership on the United Nations' Security Council, association with various other regional anticommunist groups such as the Southeast Asia Treaty Organization (SEATO) and the Baghdad Pact, and membership in nonideological alliances such as the Organization of American States (OAS) and the Organization for Security and Cooperation in Europe (OSCE).

Some alliances, especially NATO, have required a substantial ongoing American military presence, which ensured that peacetime troop levels remained quite high. In some countries, such as West Germany and Japan, the United States handled most if not all national security needs, while in others, such as Turkey and South Korea, American military deployments were more a matter of U.S. strategic advantage than of simple national defense issues. Whatever the rationale, the United States eventually stationed troops and weapons all over the globe, from the Middle East to the Far East, from North America to South America, from the North Sea to the Mediterranean Sea. Active military campaigns, such as the Korean conflict and the Vietnam War, increased the strain on American resources, and domestic security requirements created an additional burden, so the threshold number of professional soldiers in the American military had to be many degrees of magnitude higher than it was early in the nation's history. These demands on military capability made anything but a very large peacetime deployment of American armed forces, both at home and abroad, impossible. The realities of the postwar era negated the possibility of a return to the days of small standing armies and international neutrality.

The large increases in military strength paralleled organizational reforms that enabled American soldiers to fight more effectively and to optimize the use of new weaponry. American soldiers now compose four major services (not including the Coast Guard) with separate purposes and necessities but with the unified goal of defending the United States and its interests abroad. The most recent of those services has been the U.S. Air Force, which was established immediately after World War II as a successor to the Army Air Corps and has served as the principal provider of strategic defense capabilities during the last 60 years. Although its role encompasses various tactical aspects of battlefield support, the air force has made possible advanced diplomatic and military options by leveraging the country's strategic nuclear potential. Operational centers such as the Strategic Air Command (SAC), created following the last world war to coordinate the deployment of the air force's land-based nuclear weapons, constitute fitting examples of the military's elevated regard for the advantages of a properly utilized nuclear arsenal. The North American Aerospace Defense Command, popularly known as NORAD, which is a joint effort between the United States and Canada in providing air-based warning, defense, and attack potential against enemy intruders, is another example of military reorientation that seeks to make the most of the country's aerospace capabilities and its nuclear resources.

North American Aerospace Defense Command (NORAD) blast doors in Colorado *(Wikipedia)*

The U.S. Army, U.S. Navy, and U.S. Marine Corps have benefited from organizational reforms and technological innovations as well. Relying on the destructive power of new armaments, improved tactical training, and the creation of Special Operations Forces such as the navy SEALs, army Rangers, and marine Special Operations Battalion, to name only a few, they carry on a proud tradition of military service that dates back to the 18th century. However, despite the obvious advances in military strength, effectiveness, and preparedness, the increased specialization of military forces and the continued division of loyalties among four major fighting services have produced rivalries and turf battles that have created some redundancies, bureaucratic bloat, and inefficiency, to say nothing of financial waste. Recognizing this problem comparatively early in the nation's emergence as a superpower, President Truman attempted to abolish the boundaries separating the various armed services and establish a unitary force comprising land, air, and sea resources, but, facing fierce political opposition, his plan failed. Interservice rivalries have continued, and mutual jealousies have occasionally compromised battlefield success, so the overall effects of competition among the armed forces have not benefited America's military readiness.

By the 1970s, this competition and the frequent absence of battlefield coordination among the four services captured the attention of key military and political officials, who realized that the situation needed to be actively addressed. Some even pointed to the lack of cooperation among air and land forces in Vietnam as a principal cause of the American defeat, which reinforced the need that something would have to be done soon. During the 1980s, Caspar Weinberger, Ronald Reagan's secretary of defense, working with congressional leaders from both sides of the aisle, implemented reforms that streamlined the chain of command and made battlefield collaboration among the four services more logical and easier. Reagan also presided over the biggest buildup of military resources since World War II, and he vigorously advocated the deployment of space-based anti-Soviet weapons. Although President Reagan's defense policies encountered numerous criticisms, the military reforms and expansion of national security capabilities during his administration produced the most formidable and effective fighting force in the world.

The National Security Bureaucracy
Some years ago, the political scientist Stephen Skowronek, in a book about the rise of what he called a "new American state" during the Gilded Age and *Progressive Era* (roughly 1870 to 1920), described the professionalization of America's bureaucracy. He traced the emergence of a vast civil service, underwriting the expansion of governmental resources and authority to facilitate the industrialization and internationalization of the United States. The processes Skowronek identified were indeed significant and, given their magnitude, without immediate precedent, yet, monumental as they were, they paled in comparison to what began in the 1930s under Franklin D. Roosevelt. Starting in the 1930s as a response to the Great Depression and, a few years later, to World War II and continuing through the cold war, Roosevelt and his successors helped create a bureaucracy of staggering size, which ultimately comprised more than 1 million American soldiers, several million civilian employees and public officials, and thousands of contractors and subcontractors in various industries. It includes the presidency and vice presidency, the White House staff, more than a dozen cabinet departments with their employees, four branches of the military, an extensive intelligence network, and an alphabet soup of regulatory agencies.

From a national security perspective, the growth of the newly created Department of Defense and its staff was every bit as significant as the increases in military resources. With steadily rising budgets, the Defense Department eventually drew on thousands of support personnel working on everything from strategic planning to battlefield tactics, from procurement and design of advanced weapons to provision of the most basic military supplies, from war games to political games. A leadership team of undersecretaries and assistant secretaries, analysts, advisers, and experts joined with the defense secretaries in the preparation of America's military resources, as well as the development of the country's security policies. The Department of Defense is housed within the Pentagon, a gigantic complex located in Arlington, Virginia, which symbolizes, perhaps better than any other institution, the country's status as a superpower. Approximately 25,000 employees walk its halls on any given day, many of them holding access to technological marvels even Hollywood could not imagine that enhance the country's intelligence, assessment, and planning capabilities during an age when information is gold.

As important as the rise of the Department of Defense has been for America's security needs, the creation of the CIA has been just as crucial. Since strategic planning, operational coordination, and tactical execution are only as good as the information on which they are based, intelligence is the linchpin of effective diplomatic and military policy. That is why the existence of the CIA has been so critical over the past several decades and why U.S. presidents have been so dependent on it for their foreign policy successes. The successor to the Office of Strategic Services, which President Roosevelt established in 1942 to gather intelligence for the military services, the CIA is an independent agency that conducts espionage and provides intelligence to various governmental institutions and, most important, to the president. At its headquarters in Langley, Virginia, and at stations throughout the world, the CIA employs between 15,000 and 20,000 people, though the exact number is classified, and the agency serves as more than just a clearinghouse of information.

During the cold war, the CIA routinely engaged in paramilitary operations, provided aid to political groups in various countries, and even helped topple unfriendly regimes, to say nothing of planning or facilitating political assassinations of anti-American officials. Unlike U.S. military forces, which are governed by the transparency of the American political process and operate in conjunction with international conventions and alliances, the CIA carries out many of its activities clandestinely due to the covert nature of its practices. Not bound by regular rules of military engagement or the strictures of diplomatic protocol, CIA operatives have been able to sidestep standard procedures and deal with situations that cannot be handled through normal channels. These solutions have included a disinformation campaign in postwar Italy against communist politicians to help secure the election of pro-Western parties, covert assistance for pro-Western forces in Iran during the early 1950s to achieve the overthrow of an unfriendly government, strategic and tactical aid to military leaders in Chile in the 1960s and 1970s to depose the socialist Allende regime, military resources and financial help for anticommunist contra rebels in Nicaragua, and many other instances of CIA intervention.

The CIA and the Department of Defense are but two of the more dominant institutions created since the end of World War II, but a number of additional ones contribute to the president's ability to conduct foreign policy and protect the national interests of the United States. The National Security Council (NSC), established at the same time as the Defense Department and the CIA, has been one of the more visible organs of national defense and foreign policy. It has provided presidents with advice, information, and support through its ability to coordinate several aspects of national security policy, such as military planning, operational analysis, diplomacy, intelligence, and even economic assessment. Consequently, the president's National Security Advisor has become one of his most trusted allies and has often, particularly during the cold war, played the lead role over other defense or foreign policy officials. Major luminaries in American government have served as National Security Advisor, including Walt Rostow, Henry Kissinger, Zbigniew Brzezinski, Colin Powell, and Brent Scowcroft, which underscores the significance of the post.

Another component of the national defense bureaucracy is the State Department, which has grown immeasurably since its origins as one of three original cabinet posts. Its responsibilities lie almost exclusively within the area of foreign policy, which has brought it into conflict with the Department of Defense on several occasions, whose strategic and operational focus cannot always be reconciled with the aims of diplomacy. Nevertheless, the State Department's large staff, which is deployed around the globe, and its cadre of presidential advisers, headed by the secretary of state, has proven invaluable as the diplomatic arm of the presidency. Due to the public nature of diplomatic activity during the modern era, most secretaries of state have been among the most prominent cabinet members of contemporary administrations, at times even outshining the president himself. George Marshall, John Foster Dulles, Dean Rusk, Henry Kissinger, George Schultz, Colin Powell, and Hillary Rodham Clinton are names their contemporaries would readily recognize.

Finally, the bureaucratic resources available to U.S. commanders in chief consist of a host of officials, advisers, and employees who work for agencies or departments whose primary responsibilities do not deal with defense, intelligence, or diplomacy. However, effective national security policies would not exist without them. First and foremost, certain members of the White House staff, frequently among the president's closest friends, provide ongoing advice, guidance, or insight regarding relevant issues and current policies. Whether formally designated as adviser, aide, counsel, or assistant to the president, these individuals have the president's ear and are often his or her most trusted allies, their importance often surpassing that of members of his or her cabinet. In addition to these officials, members of some domestically oriented cabinet departments serve the presidency's national security requirements by addressing aspects of domestic policy that affect defense and diplomacy. For example, the Justice, Treasury, Energy, Commerce, and Interior Departments all deal with issues that affect national security or foreign policy, and they work with the president and his staff to resolve pressing policy matters.

CONCLUSION

In 1989, the Soviet bloc suddenly disintegrated, and, by 1991, the Soviet Union itself surrendered to the winds of change sweeping across Eastern Europe and itself dramatically broke apart. The cold war was over, and President George H. W. Bush declared the arrival of a "new world order" that extended the promise of a more peaceful and stable future. As the only surviving superpower, the United States looked forward to a post-Soviet world free of communist oppression and geopolitical polarization between East and West. Unfortunately, the optimism unleashed by the fall of the Berlin Wall did not last, as a new kind of war and a new type of instability loomed on the horizon. Ultimately, the cold war, though potentially destructive but characterized by a degree of predictability and equilibrium inherent in its very nature proved to have been more manageable than its aftermath. The demise of the Soviet Union inaugurated developments that no nation, not even the United States, was ready to face. America's new world order stood on the brink of collapse just a few years after its appearance, undermined by enemies that thrived on the unconventional and the unpredictable.

Confronted by amorphous terrorist organizations whose tentacles reach far and wide and by fundamentalist regimes that harbor a hatred of the West, the United States has found itself ill-prepared to adapt a Soviet-era defense capability to post-Soviet circumstances. Americans discovered that fact tragically on September 11, 2001. Amid the questions about America's international status that will be posed in the years to come concerning its ability to meet a new type of international threat, one thing has been clear. Its national security resources will remain formidable at the same time that demands on the nation's military will not abate. Instead of proxy wars in Southeast Asia and Latin America on behalf of foreign client states, the United States now fights wars in Iraq and Afghanistan, which could spread to neighboring states or break out elsewhere. Despite political opposition to President George W. Bush's military initiatives, Americans have reluctantly accepted their country's quest to rid the world of terrorism, and President Barack Obama's administration has recognized the necessity of rigorously opposing this new threat.

Consequently, American bureaucratic capacities have been augmented even further during the past few years, increasing the size of a national defense establishment that already consumed a staggering proportion of U.S. economic and financial resources. The recently created Department of

Homeland Security and a reorganized intelligence network have improved the government's ability to keep watch on individuals suspected of anti-American acts and respond to domestic threats, while improvements in federal oversight of transportation and communication systems have resulted in much greater scrutiny of ordinary Americans. Despite partisan differences over the proper extent of federal surveillance, prevention, and apprehension methods, both Democrats and Republicans have willingly sacrificed additional freedoms for greater security. In the end, the president's role as commander in chief has changed little since the conclusion of the cold war, as the power and authority of the office is, if anything, more substantial now than it was in 1991. Mark Twain once remarked that the only certainties in life are death and taxes. He should have added the accumulation of power. To meet the challenges that lie ahead, American presidents will want more power to deal with the uncertainties of an increasingly interdependent and complex world.

CHAPTER 4

The Political Evolution of the Presidency: The Welfare State

In 1887, Congress created the Interstate Commerce Commission (ICC) to regulate America's railroads. Responding to the public's need for a watchdog agency to oversee the country's quickly growing rail networks, the ICC was the first institution of its kind. An *independent agency* operating under the executive branch, the ICC was a political anomaly. Possessing the authority to legislate, enforce, and adjudicate, it was not bound by customary constitutional constraints such as the separation of powers, nor was it accountable to any particular department in the president's cabinet. In an age when the federal bureaucracy was just emerging, the ICC's power and authority seemed excessive to many, and its ability to operate outside traditional political boundaries disturbed some observers. Yet, by the late 1930s, the kind of power and authority that it wielded had become normal, affirming the presence of a regulatory system made up of several dozen such agencies that had secured a permanent presence within the American government. Over the following 70 years, even more independent agencies appeared, scrutinizing practically every aspect of life in the United States.

Expanded bureaucratic muscle has supplemented the growth of an executive branch whose domestic responsibilities have multiplied over the course of time. In addition to more than 50 independent agencies and government corporations, various cabinet departments handle everyday matters that the founding generation believed to be none of the government's business. The American presidency was never intended to have such sprawling resources

81

at its disposal. Article II of the Constitution did not envision an executive capable of regulating the economic, social, or cultural activities of its citizens, nor did it authorize the acquisition of authority in the domestic sphere such as the past century has witnessed. Be that as it may, few people are willing to contest the presidency's gains, and even fewer are sufficiently bold to demand their reversal. At this point, almost no one questions the status quo. For better or worse, the American public stopped asking questions some time ago, choosing instead to acquiesce in the existence of an executive branch that, for all its intrusions, eases the pressures and blunts the discomforts of a modern, increasingly complex society.

DOMESTIC AUTHORITY OF THE PRESIDENCY BEFORE FDR

Commentators on *domestic policy* often divide American history into two eras, one prior to the Great Depression and the other beginning with Franklin Roosevelt's *New Deal*. They view the FDR administration as a watershed, believing it fundamentally transformed American politics through an activist government that became the nation's social and economic watchdog. Indeed, the New Deal and its famous president have been recognized by Democrats and Republicans alike for invaluable contributions to the emergence of a modern bureaucracy that successfully manages the world's largest economy. However, as momentous as the New Deal and its consequences may have been, this traditional interpretation of America's past minimizes the importance of what came before the New Deal. The separation of American history into pre– and post–New Deal periods relegates the early years of the republic to a minor footnote in the rise of a domestic bureaucracy and ignores seminal changes in the way government responded to the Industrial Revolution. Those early years played a critical role in the development of the presidency, and they served as a foundation for the expansion of its domestic authority.

Economic and Social Powers of the Early Presidency

Today's domestic bureaucracy does many things in many arenas, but it exists for one major reason. It exists in response to economic conditions that arose at the end of the 19th century, and the growth of the presidency's domestic authority is largely a function of those conditions. Prior to the emergence of an executive bureaucracy meant to deal with the consequences of industrial capitalism, the presidency's domestic portfolio was extremely limited, not least because the overwhelming majority of public business was conducted at state and local levels. The social and economic needs of the American people centered on an economy still dominated by agriculture and small business, and the federal government had no cause to interject itself into the day-to-day lives of workers, minorities, the poor, or other groups that were later to be so significantly affected by industrial progress. Before the end of the 19th century, when Congress empowered the executive branch with regulatory authority through the Sherman Antitrust Act (1890) and the Interstate Commerce Act, the presidency practiced a hands-off approach to the market. Just as the Founding Fathers expected, the executive branch did not intervene in the economy, nor did it attempt to redistribute its fruits in any way.

Above all, the absence of executive control over the economy reflected loyalty to the framers' vision of an unfettered marketplace, but it also responded to contemporary economic circumstances. The Industrial Revolution may have been changing the manner in which goods were produced and distributed, but, during the first part of the 19th century, it had not yet led to a rupture with past practices. It produced small-scale manufacturing, advances in agriculture, and the emergence of a professional class without disturbing an essentially agrarian economy. Furthermore, the early decades of the Industrial Revolution never seriously tested the states' ability to address social changes, and economic opportunity consistently trumped temporary deprivations. Despite the growth of regional markets, innovations in steam and rail power, and the associated construction of roads, rail lines, and canals, the appearance of a truly national marketplace with extensive exchange capabilities remained a distant prospect. In the end, America's industrial activity, though steadily increasing, hardly required federal supervision.

Still, the executive branch was entrusted with some economic responsibilities, specifically the collection of tariffs and various other taxes, the creation of a national financial infrastructure, the maintenance of transportation and communication networks, and the management of federal lands. Alexander Hamilton, George Washington's treasury secretary, lobbied for the establishment of a national bank and the consolidation of the national debt, which aroused considerable resistance. Many believed his efforts exceeded the constitutional authority of the presidency, but Hamilton ultimately had his way, though the national bank remained a source of contention for more than 30 years. Andrew Jackson, a vehement foe of the bank and federal financial authority in general, triumphantly derailed the renewal of the second Bank of the United States in 1832. The consolidation of the national debt fared better, however, serving as a foundation for financial markets that grew throughout the next two centuries and underwrote America's economic transformation.

Aside from the presidency's comparatively minor economic responsibilities, much of its energy was consumed in dealing with the issue of slavery. Presidents may not have had much constitutional authority over slavery or any real power to control it, but, during the first two-thirds of the 19th century, their attention was increasingly focused on it. By the 1830s, if not sooner, slavery had begun to affect almost every aspect of domestic politics, and America's presidents tried to broker political deals that would relieve the growing tension between North and South. Some, such as John Tyler,

Cartoon satirizing President Jackson's battle with the Bank of the United States *(Library of Congress)*

openly made decisions that exacerbated existing problems, pushing for the annexation of territories that disturbed a delicate balance of free and slave states. Mostly, however, America's antebellum presidents were not willing to acknowledge the extent of the political dysfunction caused by slavery, either hoping for a resolution that never came or praying that the growing national powder keg would not explode on their watch.

Presiding over a series of congressional compromises that proved unworkable, America's chief executives often chose the path of least resistance, which offered a tempting way out of an apparently insoluble situation. Predictably, because these measures—the Missouri Compromise, the Compromise of 1850, and the Kansas-Nebraska Act—failed to resolve the political dilemma posed by slavery, wishful thinking and circumstantial tinkering only made matters worse. As the crisis deepened, the country did not benefit from skillful leadership in the executive branch, which was hampered by a clear lack of political savvy and strategic vision, not to mention bipartisanship, among the holders of the presidency. Choosing party above union, or politics above principle, Millard Fillmore, Franklin Pierce, and James Buchanan, the last three presidents prior to the Civil War, were weak leaders utterly unwilling or incapable of dealing with the growing sectional crisis in the 1850s.

By the time Abraham Lincoln, a capable leader willing to tackle the issues that threatened the federal union, arrived in Washington, the political environment had become unmanageable, and no amount of presidential skill or goodwill could avert a civil war that would ensue following the secession of southern states.

The Age of Mass Industry

The Industrial Revolution, which began in the United States toward the end of the 19th century, changed life dramatically during the ensuing 150 years. Distinguished by two major phases of economic development, it transformed a rural society made up of farmers, artisans, and local merchants into a nation of urban communities in which industrial workers, white-collar employees, and service professionals came to predominate. The first phase, covering roughly 60 to 70 years, introduced standardization, the division of labor, and basic mechanization to labor-intensive industries and led to increased levels of efficiency and productivity. Inaugurated by the invention of the cotton gin and the steam engine, the Industrial Revolution relied on technology and human creativity as the engines that drove continued economic progress. During its early days, it involved a gradual process of urbanization accompanied by the establishment of small factories in New England towns and the extension of trading networks throughout the North and what is today the Midwest.

Some of the earliest workplace innovations took place in the clothing, textiles, and shoemaking trades, spearheading industrial advances that soon spread to other areas. Skilled artisans slowly but inexorably relinquished their hold over specialized trades such as shipbuilding, construction, and woodworking, to name a few, succumbing to entrepreneurs capable of leveraging more favorable economies of scale. Unskilled and semi-skilled workers were replacing America's craftsmen, and its communities, once inhabited by independent producers, now were peopled with paid employees. At the same time, a middle class was emerging, which created a broader market for luxury goods and led to the production of a range of household products and personal accessories available only to elites just a generation before. As the supply of manufactured goods increased and markets continued to grow, more sophisticated capitalization efforts enhanced a quickly maturing financial infrastructure. Furthermore, improvements in transportation enabled manufacturers to reach an ever-increasing number of consumers, and the resettlement of Americans to the frontier fueled the expansion.

Within a few decades, the economic makeup of the United States changed irreversibly, and the country was about to embark on the most transformative phase of its development. By the last quarter of the 19th century, most of the prerequisites for mass industrialization were present, at least in the North and West. The application of technology to workplace processes had been extensive, and the reorganization of human effort had been just as sweeping. America's cities were teeming with workers, while its smaller towns were becoming connected to each other through vast transportation networks. The ability of manufacturers to move goods hundreds of miles at any time of the year greased the wheels of commerce by meeting rising consumer demand and creating efficient markets where none had existed before. Increasing supply meant larger and larger factories, as America's industrial facilities dwarfed the workshops of the early 19th century. Large-scale, resource-intensive industries, such as steel, mining, and railroads, grew more prevalent, and many saw them as symbols of a new age.

Only one thing had been missing up to that point. America's businesses, though very big by historical standards, still lacked the means to overcome the structural constraints that had limited their ultimate size. During the first three-quarters of the 19th century, those businesses had been run by the families who founded them, so proprietors themselves assumed the combined burdens of ownership and management. This confined potential growth by concentrating risk and simultaneously restricting available investment capital. Therefore, the next phase of American economic development would depend on creating the means to transcend traditional financial and legal limitations, enabling U.S. businesses to leverage greater amounts of capital and manpower. It would involve a mechanism that separated management from ownership and transferred liabilities from individual owners to businesses themselves. Furthermore, ownership would be dispersed among dozens or maybe hundreds, eventually thousands, of shareholders with the combined power to provide almost unlimited investment capital. As it turned out, such a mechanism was the modern corporation, which was officially acknowledged by the courts toward the end of the 19th century.

The advent of the modern corporation launched what the economic historian Alfred Chandler called a managerial revolution, culminating in the creation of today's multinational conglomerates. Among other things, the managerial revolution produced a white-collar class, consisting of business professionals who perfected the art of running America's corporations. No longer burdened by the risks of ownership, America's new management experts turned business administration into a science, transforming the corporation into a well-oiled machine capable of maximizing profits. They introduced to the world marketing, strategic planning, corporate finance, organizational leadership, corporate welfare, and many other fields of management that had been unknown to earlier generations. Made up of senior executives, midlevel managers, and throngs of support personnel and office staff, the nation's emerging white-collar class stimulated, implemented, and maintained the development of the modern corporation and, thus, paved the way for the emergence of industrial capitalism in the United States.

The Federal Response to Industrialization

Although industrialization in the United States was comparatively benign, leaving behind in dire poverty far fewer people than was the case in most European countries, it was not without its problems. Economists and other social scientists noticed that an industrial economy poses unique structural challenges, which are fundamentally different from anything faced by an agrarian society. The magnitude and duration of economic dislocations in an industrial economy appeared much greater and the risks to workers more substantial. Economic activity in general seemed more volatile, and recovery following recessionary periods was not guaranteed. Indices such as unemployment, inflation, and national income were suddenly very important, and the ability to control the business cycle seemed paramount. Employees were much more vulnerable than the producers of an earlier time had been, and their susceptibility to workplace uncertainties undermined financial security. As a result, poverty became an ever-present prospect, as did the inability to meet basic needs such as food and clothing, housing, health care, and education.

Prior to the late 19th century, concepts such as unemployment were irrelevant. Entrenched minorities permanently displaced by an industrial economy did not exist, nor did the conditions to create them. Poverty was definitely present, but, with abundant resources and widespread property ownership, it was not permanent. Social dislocations were adequately addressed through local governments and private charities, so federal involvement was unnecessary. Besides, the Constitution would not have permitted a more active federal role. Even if American presidents had wished to monitor or regulate the national economy, prevailing constitutional doctrines would have proscribed doing so. Furthermore, the American public frowned on government action that promoted the interests of one group over another, whether it was disadvantaged or not. Still driven by the political ideals of the Founding Fathers, Americans expected their presidents to play a neutral role, particularly with respect to the economy, treating consumers and producers alike. Class-based bias or preference of any kind was deemed to be illegitimate, regardless of its reasons.

By the end of the 19th century and the beginning of the 20th, however, a growing number of experts realized that the consequences of mass industrialization are felt disproportionately by specific groups and that the federal government could no longer sit on the sidelines. Contrary to what had been the case during the early stages of the Industrial Revolution, the very nature of industrial capitalism relied on, or at least assumed the existence of, permanent dislocations. An industrialized society causes long-term disruptions that create what economists call a basal, or minimal, level of economic deprivation. For better or worse, it tolerates the presence of those who are unemployed, disabled, or injured as well as those who are unable to care for themselves, impoverished, or hurt in any other way by the realities of the economic system. This does not mean that the more fortunate welcome or promote these consequences or that they intentionally exclude the less fortunate. It merely reflects the inescapable fact that an industrialized economy creates winners and losers in a way that an agrarian one does not. The stakes are simply much higher.

By the early 20th century, after state efforts to confront various issues connected to industrialization had failed, a growing wave of social pressure for federal remedies pushed Congress into action. It had already created the ICC to regulate railroads and passed the Sherman Act to arm the Justice Department with trust-busting authority. But it was ready to go even further by providing the executive branch with unprecedented powers. Before 1920, the executive branch came to include a new Department of Labor charged with the oversight of employee-employer relations, a federal-reserve system intended to stabilize the nation's banking system, an expanded Internal Revenue Service to supervise the newly instituted federal income tax, the Federal Trade Commission to prevent anticompetitive practices, the Food and Drug Administration, and other executive institutions whose powers enhanced the president's authority over the American economy. As was the case with the presidency's national security powers, its domestic powers were growing quickly and irrevocably, buttressing a modern executive branch that seemed intent on accumulating authority the framers of the Constitution did not provide.

THE RISE OF AMERICA'S WELFARE STATE AND REGULATORY BUREAUCRACY

The United States is a capitalist society with a liberal system of politics, which means it is devoted to free markets and private ownership under minimal government interference. As the modern world's first liberal democracy, it has customarily valued freedom above control and individualism above collectivism. Other liberal democratic regimes have used it as a model, but none has succeeded in ensuring the apparent balance between liberty and authority achieved under the American governing system. Despite the many reforms during the last half century that have weakened the influence of socialist institutions in Europe and brought European and American economic practices ever closer, capitalism in the United States remains different from its counterparts across the Atlantic, still less fettered by government restraints. Although European governments have increasingly come to question the financial viability of the so-called *welfare state*, which refers to the bureaucratic machinery that emerged in many European countries during the second third of the 20th century to provide numerous social services, the principle of cradle-to-grave socioeconomic protection continues to enjoy widespread support. The United States, on the other hand, has never had a welfare state. The belief has been general that its people would never tolerate it, nor can its political system accommodate one. Maybe, maybe not.

One of the great myths concerning the American political system is that it is inherently incompatible with any and all socialist principles. This myth is rooted in American exceptionalism, a belief stressing the intrinsic uniqueness and superiority of American political culture, and such a sentiment underscores the legitimacy of the American system of government. Necessary, albeit misleading, it reinforces the American public's continued support of questionable political changes such as those discussed in the previous chapter and serves as a source of national pride. Since World War II, the United States has dedicated so much effort in combating communism around the globe that the credibility of the entire American way of life seems to rest, at least partly, on a successful rejection of socialist-based ideas. Nevertheless, myth or no myth, the welfare state is alive and thriving in the United States. It has been dispensing social services to Americans for more than 70 years, and ignoring its presence will not alter the facts. That does not make the United States socialist, far from it. The existence of a welfare state in America simply underlines the reality of managing a capitalist economy in the industrialized world.

FDR and the First New Deal

As the 1920s unfolded and the period historians have labeled the Progressive Era drew to a close, Americans had a renewed sense of hope. With the end of World War I, they anticipated a "return to normalcy," as President Warren Harding put it, looking forward to economic progress at home and peace abroad. Relieved that the turbulence of recent years had ended, they had good reason to be optimistic. Despite continuing discontent among radical labor groups and communist sympathizers, the United States seemed poised to overcome the structural obstacles to ongoing industrialization and make the most of its international financial strength. President Harding's wish for business as usual appeared vindicated by positive economic trends, as growing numbers of Americans enjoyed increasing access to the consumer products that accompanied industrial capitalism. They moved into new homes and bought cars, appliances, and other big-ticket items on credit as well as enjoying a host of new leisure activities. The economic fate of the American people was improving, and the future looked brighter than at any point in the previous several years.

Tragically, it was all a mirage. In 1929, the economy imploded as markets disintegrated. Like the 1990s and the early years of the 21st century, the decade after World War I was characterized by excess and greed fed by limitless credit. Unlike today, the economic collapse took place on an unprecedented

This classic photograph, *Migrant Mother, Nipomo, California* (1936), was taken by Dorothea Lange for the Farm Security Administration. *(Library of Congress)*

scale and few government tools existed to combat the crisis. During the Great Depression, unemployment reached 25 percent, the national income (GDP) declined by almost a third, inflation soared, and net investment in the economy decreased year after year. Banks collapsed, businesses disappeared, people lost their homes, and farms lay fallow. Faced with a national disaster, President Franklin Delano Roosevelt asked for authority to confront the crisis and pushed Congress into decisive action in 1933. Within a few months of taking office, Roosevelt secured a package of measures covering a broad array of social services and expanding the regulatory authority of the executive branch over workers, employers, farmers, utilities, banks, consumer prices, wages, natural resources, and much more. The power of the presidency to control the economic fallout from the depression was without precedent.

Roosevelt's Federal Emergency Relief Administration (FERA) distributed hundreds of millions of dollars to the poor, while the Civil Works Administration (CWA) provided construction jobs for several million unemployed. The nation's young people were offered relief through service in the Civilian Conservation Corps (CCC), an agency set up to tackle environmental restoration, particularly reforestation, while at the same time imbuing the younger generation with a public spirit. A number of southern states benefited from the Tennessee Valley Authority (TVA), which was created to construct dams and provide electricity in the Tennessee River valley, as well as address degradation and squalor in local communities. The farming crisis was handled through Roosevelt's Agricultural Adjustment Administration, whose authority to reduce production, set commodity prices, and subsidize farmers set significant precedents for the next seven decades. The National Recovery Administration (NRA), created to supervise America's manufacturing industries had wide powers to fix wages and set maximum working hours, and even the price of goods, while the new Securities and Exchange Commission (SEC) policed the stock market in an effort to pursue allegedly unfair practices.

The Second New Deal

Despite steadfast support from progressives close to the administration, social activists and intellectuals, and the many people helped by New Deal programs, the flurry of executive action during Roosevelt's first several years in the White House attracted more than its share of opposition. Industrialists grew tired of government interference, small businesses claimed unfair treatment by regulatory agencies, and many politicians grew skeptical of the administration's concentration of power, which led to a buildup in momentum against Roosevelt's policies. In addition, as impressive as Roosevelt's efforts to ease the plight of ordinary Americans were, the New Deal was doing very little to improve overall economic performance. People may have been feeling better about themselves as a result of government work programs, but basic economic indicators were not encouraging. On top of that, the Supreme Court's refusal to sanction the president's expanded authority worried policy makers, and the Court's reversal of key New Deal measures dealt the president a serious setback.

Nearing the half-way point of his first term, Roosevelt realized that continued endorsement of his policies was not guaranteed, so he modified his tactics. He consolidated his gains from the so-called first New Deal and reoriented the administration's focus toward consumer demand. The first New Deal had been both a success and a failure, but FDR was committed to unqualified victory in launching the second New Deal. Lasting from approximately 1933 to 1935, the first New Deal largely concentrated on the supply of goods and commodities through regulation of production. It provided relief to consumers through work programs, subsidies, and direct aid, but its principal target was what economists call the supply side of the economy. The second New Deal, on the other hand, aimed to address the demand side of the economy by increasing the purchasing potential of consumers through initiatives for dislocated minorities, industrial workers, retired persons, and others disproportionately affected by the depression. For the first time in American history, the implementation of a federal income tax in 1913 notwithstanding, the government would become involved in the redistribution of wealth and income to achieve a degree of social and economic equity.

Early in 1935, the administration launched the Works Progress Administration (WPA), one of the nation's largest relief agencies and a lasting icon of New Deal ingenuity. With more than 30 percent of the country's unemployed among its ranks, it tackled public works projects throughout the United States and provided various kinds of aid to families hit hardest by the depression. Its impact especially significant in rural America and the West, the WPA built schools, libraries, roads, bridges, and other public structures and offered food, clothing, and shelter in communities starved for resources. America's industrial workers benefited from the National Labor Relations Board (NLRB), inaugurated to promote the rights of unskilled and semi-skilled workers in mining and manufacturing and protect organized labor against abusive employers. The NLRB became a national mainstay, ensuring the integrity of collective bargaining procedures and supervising unionization drives in hostile industries. Deemed crucial to the survival of organized labor, the NLRB was viewed by labor as its white knight, and the congressional act that created it was considered one of the New Deal's premier achievements.

The NLRB, WPA, CCC, CWA, NRA, TVA, FERA, and numerous other New Deal agencies became well known to contemporary Americans. Some of them, and not just the ones that have survived, remained significant for future generations. For the majority of Americans, one program stands above the rest. No initiative has been as closely associated with the New Deal as that of the Social Security Act, which formally established America's welfare state by recognizing the federal government as the provider of basic social services. All subsequent welfare initiatives would take their inspiration and draw their political momentum from the Social Security Act, which set a precedent from which future efforts to increase the domestic authority of the executive branch would be launched. Passed in 1935 as the centerpiece of the second New Deal, the law created a guaranteed federal pension for the elderly, unemployment compensation, aid for dependent children, additional support for unwed mothers and their children, and related minor services. All in all, it reinvented American government and forever changed its relationship with the American people.

The Road to the Great Society

As is often the case with such high-profile political strategies, the second New Deal ultimately ended with a whimper, despite its accomplishments and enormous legacy. The flurry of legislation and creative activity witnessed during Roosevelt's first few years in office succumbed to economic and political realities beyond FDR's control. After bullying—some would say blackmailing—the Supreme Court into legitimizing the federal government's new role as social and economic watchdog, the president's welfare and regulatory policies, though not necessarily complete, had run their course. Opposition to the administration's heavy-handedness resurfaced among business leaders and political opponents, and foreign affairs required increasing attention. Moreover, the president's dedicated efforts to resuscitate the economy through federal intervention had mixed results, so continued tolerance of costly attempts to fight the depression was not likely. While helping to arrest the decline and stabilizing the economy, none of the Roosevelt administration's economic policies ever succeeded in putting an end to the depression. In the end, World War II did what the New Deal could not. The nation's entry into the war lifted it out of the depression and launched one of the longest economic recoveries of the 20th century.

Nevertheless, the die had been cast. The New Deal may not have been successful as an antidote to economic depression, but the Social Security Act had done for domestic policy what the National Security Act did for foreign policy several years later. By validating the existence of America's welfare state, the Social Security Act paved the way for a modern presidency whose domestic authority would eventually reach every corner of the economy. This may not be what the framers of the Constitution intended, but it reflects what the American people have wanted over the past 70 years. They have consented to an increasingly powerful regulatory apparatus in place alongside the country's welfare bureaucracy, and they have accepted the readiness of presidents to intervene in market activities, endorsing wage and price controls, production quotas, subsidies, and other measures. Indeed, when President Harry Truman seized the country's steel mills in the early 1950s, many Americans supported this bold expansion of authority. The Supreme Court invalidated the president's action, but that setback did not deter future chief executives from similar efforts.

Truman also exerted economic control through the Wage Stabilization Board, but, overall, the Truman administration and that of his successor, the war hero Dwight Eisenhower, concentrated their attention on national security matters. These were critical years in the unfolding cold war, and Truman and Eisenhower devoted considerable energy to the consolidation of America's strategic assets and the promotion of friendly regimes abroad. Much of their domestic policy rested on security-related initiatives, which occasionally threatened Americans' rights of free expression and association, but a steadily expanding postwar economy decreased the need for greater economic intervention. Further gains in executive authority over the economy, through enhancements of both services and regulation, would have to await the Johnson years, which outstripped the accomplishments of the New Deal and enlarged America's welfare state well beyond FDR's vision. By the mid-1960s, Johnson's *Great Society*, as his reform policy was called, covered the poor, the elderly, America's youth, political minorities, mothers, the workplace, schools, housing, the nation's cities, and much, much more.

Lyndon Baines Johnson assumed the presidency on the assassination of John F. Kennedy, an American president who was idolized by many contemporary Americans in representing the promise of the 1960s and the hope of a better future. Kennedy's supporters and the legions of political fans

International Monetary Fund

The International Monetary Fund (IMF) and its sister organizations emerged out of the Bretton Woods Conference, which sought to address the financial instabilities and economic deficiencies of national, regional, and global systems that produced the depression of the 1930s. Held in 1944, the conference was convened to address the dislocations caused by mass industrialization and the consequent need to confront the inadequacies of pre–welfare state efforts to address industrialization. The agreements produced at the conference embodied the belief that conflict can be avoided through the facilitation of international economic cooperation, which would promote prosperity across the globe, and that, therefore, the removal or gradual reduction of barriers to free trade and stable exchange rate is paramount. Despite the overarching economic objectives that animated Bretton Woods negotiations, the primary reasons for the existence of the IMF itself were financial; other organizations, such as the World Bank, answered broader economic needs. The primary purpose of the IMF was to provide a mechanism for financial stability and cooperation through currency stabilization. Obviously, it was established to support the goals of the participants, namely, goals of free trade and economic liberalization, but its practical focus has been confined to the oversight, management, and regulation of currencies and the control of factors that ensure currency viability and financial stability.

From a day-to-day perspective, the IMF's responsibilities include financial supervision and assessment of the capabilities, effectiveness, and performance of member and nonmember states; lending and structural aid through currency support programs and financial liberalization efforts; and technical facilitation through training, knowledge management, and infrastructural development of many kinds. The IMF is a large organiza-

he attracted in the years following his death believed, wrongly as it turns out, that he would have been the one to achieve what Johnson ultimately did. Lacking Johnson's passion for social issues and also his will to confront domestic opponents at a time of growing international crisis, Kennedy was never committed to such sweeping changes as his successor. Johnson, on the other hand, though an unlikely hero given that he did not possess Kennedy's charisma and political magnetism, was even more dedicated to progressive reform than FDR had been. Whereas Roosevelt's motivation had been largely paternalistic and, to an extent, opportunistic, Johnson's was mostly idealistic. Irascible and insecure, Johnson was nevertheless a formidable politician, who was intent on completing what FDR had started some 30 years before.

tion with its headquarters in Washington, D.C., and a current membership of 185 states, each of which has a seat on the board of governors. It is headed by a managing director, who serves a five-year term and answers to a 24-member executive board. Because of the relative size of the American membership quota and the resulting clout the United States has over other members, managing directors have been viewed as the handpicked representatives of the U.S. government, although no American has ever served as the managing director of the IMF. Despite evident U.S. influence over IMF policy and its organizational governance, the extent and effectiveness of American pressure on other members has been overstated by the IMF's critics.

The IMF frequently works very closely with the World Bank and other development-based organizations, but its mandate is limited to the stabilization of currencies and financial systems. Through loans and other forms of assistance to countries with substantial financial problems, the IMF attempts to restore, establish, or maintain sustainable, feasible, and equitable exchange rates in international markets. It monitors economic relationships among member states and facilitates favorable balance of trade in regional and global markets. Although its lending programs and currency measures constitute financial activities, intervention and assistance are contingent on economic reforms in target countries. As has been true of the World Bank, the IMF has underwritten projects across the globe, especially in regions that are underdeveloped or experiencing serious structural difficulties. It has been labeled by some critics as a tool of Western expansionism and as an institutional tool of the industrialized world to exploit developing countries. However, when the IMF disburses financial aid on condition that recipients put in place economic and monetary reforms, it does so not to perpetuate Western domination but to compel economic reforms that will ensure long-term economic stability.

Acknowledging Johnson's dedication to social reform may ruffle the feathers of JFK admirers, but it is not intended as a political slight. It may not bolster the Kennedy myth, but it does accurately reflect the two men's priorities. In addition, though Kennedy was a strong and resolute commander in chief backed by a legislature as intent on vigorously waging the cold war than he was, he faced stiff opposition to his domestic policies from congressional leaders who did not take the young president seriously. Like Bill Clinton some 30 years later, JFK was acutely aware of public opinion and the prevailing political winds in Washington, and he knew that confronting Congress over controversial domestic policies would weaken his national security credentials, which was a risk that he was not willing to take. However, LBJ found himself in distinctly different circumstances, reaping the rewards of substantial Democratic gains in Congress after the 1964 elections and benefiting from a long career in Congress that made him intimately familiar with legislative politics. Also, JFK's assassination infused Johnson's policies with an urgency recognized by federal legislators, providing added momentum for the passage of Great Society proposals.

Entitlements, Civil Rights, and the War on Poverty

Perhaps the most visible aspect of LBJ's Great Society was his War on Poverty, whose lofty goal was to abolish want through public programs that lifted the long-term prospects of America's destitute. Leading the attack was LBJ's new Office of Economic Opportunity (OEO), modeled on its New Deal predecessors to coordinate the implementation of relevant policies. OEO and its agencies provided job training, housing assistance, educational enrichment through initiatives such as Head Start, food and clothing subsidies, basic health care, resources for neighborhood improvement, and other services. The War on Poverty was supplemented by related reforms, many of them in education, that vastly increased the amount of money available to states and local communities. Measures targeting elementary and secondary schools, as well as colleges and universities, distributed billions of dollars for facilities, teachers, supplies, and training and created federal financial aid programs for needy students. The executive bureaucracy expanded further through the newly created Department of Housing and Urban Development (HUD), charged with the revitalization of America's cities through building projects, renovations, and enhanced public transportation. Given the profound problems facing America's urban poor and the crippling social divisions in most big cities, HUD quickly assumed a major role in the implementation of LBJ's domestic policies.

HUD, OEO, and other Great Society institutions occupied the front lines of the president's War on Poverty, but the landmark achievements of Johnson's administration, at least concerning the welfare state, were Medicare and Medicaid. These two programs were to LBJ's Great Society what the Social Security Act had been to FDR's New Deal. The Great Society proved relentless in its efforts to eradicate poverty and alleviate other social and economic hardships, but it will be remembered most especially for providing health insurance to the elderly and dislocated. Medicare focused on the nation's retirees, offering them health-care benefits that included hospital treatment, nursing home subsidies, and physician care, while Medicaid, which was to be managed in cooperation with the states, would service the poor, disabled, elderly not eligible for Medicare, dependent children and unwed mothers, and others identified as needy by the federal or state governments. These were not simple accomplishments; rather, they represent the capstone of more than 30 years of political struggle to provide a degree

President Johnson meeting with civil rights leaders in the Oval Office, from left to right: Martin Luther King, Jr., President Johnson, Whitney Young, and James Farmer, Jr., 1964 *(Photographed by Yoichi R. Okamoto; Lyndon Baines Johnson Library)*

of national health insurance for the needy, and, in many ways, they served as a springboard for further reforms, especially since Medicare and Medicaid left millions uninsured.

LBJ's social policies did not end with attempts to redress economic inequities. Believing that cultural advancement goes hand in hand with enhanced economic opportunities, Johnson lobbied for increases in government-sponsored research and funding for various cultural activities. The National Endowment for the Humanities (NEH), created in 1965, disbursed grants to libraries, museums, universities, schools, foundations, archives, broadcasters, and qualified individuals for projects that promote historical awareness and community enrichment. Its sister organization, the National Endowment for the Arts (NEA), also launched in 1965, distributed money for painting and sculpture, dance, theater, film, music, photography, and other artistic pursuits, often extending assistance to groups or individuals unable to obtain exposure in mainstream outlets. Although both organizations have attracted a degree of opposition over the years for apparent funding biases, the NEA has become the more notorious, acting as a lightning rod for criticism of the government's support of controversial artists. Still, regardless of the long-term fallout, the NEH and the NEA solidified LBJ's cultural contributions and further cemented his legacy.

In addition to the accomplishments described above, Johnson's legacy includes pivotal civil rights reforms and the related growth of federal authority to combat discrimination. Although the passage of the Civil Rights Act of 1964 and the Voting Rights Act of the following year speak more to the spread of congressional powers to areas the Constitution did not envision, this legislation served as the basis for a radical reorientation of executive resources with respect to racial inequities. Enacted by the Johnson administration to protect not only racial minorities but also women, the elderly, ethnic minorities, the poor, and other disaffected groups from economic, social, and political discrimination, these measures were drawn on by the administration and those that followed largely to address racial discrimination. Moreover, the executive branch, not willing to limit itself solely to the enforcement responsibilities that derive from those acts, has pursued a proactive approach to the protection of minority rights and the promotion of minority interests.

The president's authority to enforce compliance with the Civil Rights Act may have been limited to public establishments and federal contracts, but Johnson served notice of his intent to apply his powers very broadly with creation of the Office of Federal Contract Compliance (OFCC). Established to eliminate discrimination among firms doing business with the federal government, the OFCC was used by LBJ in signaling in executive focus in instituting affirmative action initiatives. Believing that a level playing field for the nation's black community could be secured only through a system of racial preferences, Johnson relied on his authority and whatever public credibility he could muster in light of controversies over the Vietnam War to push affirmative action in constituting at least a partial solution to America's racial tensions and injustices. Despite partisan differences, his immediate successors did not back away from affirmative action programs, especially after the Supreme Court validated several of the early attempts to fight discrimination through racial preferences. Until Ronald Reagan's election, America's presidents did not seriously challenge the viability of affirmative action, preferring to save their political capital for less contentious issues.

THE END OF REFORM AND THE AGE OF CYNICISM

Johnson's additions to the domestic bureaucracy were lasting, and they still define the legitimate boundaries of federal authority for many Democrats and Republicans, but the reformist zeal of the 1960s did not last. Antiwar agitation, social unrest in America's cities, and a growing sense of pessimism after three political assassinations in less than a decade produced widespread cynicism and apathy. An economic downturn coupled with a growing energy crisis reduced the government's ability to respond, and the Watergate scandal diverted much of the public's attention from more pressing issues. Disillusionment became rife in the 1970s. The country was reeling from its first military defeat in history, its politicians seemed to be lying to everyone, police corruption in America's cities was systemic, drug abuse and alcoholism were growing at alarming rates, racial friction was on the rise, and an economic recession was hurting people's pocketbooks. President Richard Nixon's resignation in August 1974 added to the national malaise and restrained the idealism formerly professed by many.

Skepticism, Corruption, and Ineffective Leadership

All was not lost, but many Americans had reached their limit. By the late 1960s, LBJ had accumulated a number of domestic policy successes, but on other fronts he grew increasingly besieged. Vietnam turned out to be his undoing, undermining his public approval and derailing his presidency by exposing what became known as a credibility gap. The countless promises about impending victory and misleading accounts of military progress did not match the reports coming from America's journalists and television anchormen about a deepening quagmire in Southeast Asia. Americans began to realize that U.S. military casualties were escalating and that a solution to the conflict in Vietnam was not on the horizon. Faced with what it believed were lies from the administration about the Vietnam War and increased political agitation on the streets of U.S. cities, the American public began to abandon LBJ. Protest and social unrest throughout the country made the president's position increasingly precarious, as riots broke out in more than 150 American cities and towns from 1965 to 1968. By spring 1968, Johnson had had enough, proclaiming his intention not to seek a second full term as president.

Not long after Johnson's withdrawal from the race, the civil rights leader Martin Luther King, Jr., and the Democratic presidential candidate Robert Kennedy were assassinated, further deflating the idealistic hopes of a disheartened electorate. Into this climate entered America's next president, a man whom many believed seemed better suited for any career other than one in the national spotlight. Intelligent, well-qualified, and politically capable, Richard Nixon was also paranoid, secretive, and visibly uncomfortable in public. He is remembered as the only president ever to resign, but that fact should not obscure his success in achieving a number of domestic and foreign policy goals. As a former vice president, Nixon certainly had the necessary experience to be chief executive, but his personality handicapped his administration from the outset. Some of the most influential Republican personalities in Washington, such as Henry Kissinger, Richard Cheney, Donald Rumsfeld, Patrick Buchanan, and George H. W. Bush, to name a few, earned their credentials under Nixon, so he was undoubtedly able to attract top political talent. Still, in the end, his personal foibles proved his undoing.

Amid the considerable pessimism and political confusion of the post–LBJ years, President Nixon did manage some enduring achievements. An unlikely advocate for conservation and ecological preservation, he was able to secure approval for the Environmental Protection Agency (EPA), which was created to punish polluters, set environmental standards, and ensure compliance with pertinent federal legislation. That a Republican president should establish an intrusive regulatory agency intended, among other things, to oversee industrial polluters might come as a surprise to many, but Nixon was not a small-government conservative of the type that is prominent today. He secured increased benefits for dependent children, Social Security recipients, and minorities, and he defended deficit spending as a way to relieve unemployment, inflation, and economic contraction. Anything but predictable, Nixon was an activist president saddled by a lackluster public image, and the real tragedy of the Nixon presidency is that Watergate overshadowed some significant domestic and international accomplishments.

Upon Nixon's resignation, his vice president, Gerald Ford, assumed the presidency. The only president not to be elected to the office or to the vice presidency, Ford appeared to be the exact opposite of Nixon. Genial, unassuming, and approachable, he had neither his predecessor's psychological baggage nor the single-minded ambition of most who have reached the nation's highest office. Not exceptional in any way, aside from his political

President Richard Nixon leaving the White House after resigning in the wake of the Watergate scandal *(Getty Images)*

integrity, Ford might have served longer than the 30 months remaining in Nixon's second term had he not pardoned his former boss. The pardon cost him dearly, as an electorate intent on punishing the disgraced Nixon ultimately punished Ford at the polls. Saddled by problems beyond its control, the Ford administration failed to achieve any domestic breakthroughs. Hoping to alleviate growing economic pressures, Ford used the bully pulpit to encourage Americans, often resorting to catchy sloganeering, such as WIN (Whip Inflation Now), which became fodder for comedians and the late-night talk-show circuit. Hampered by his clumsy demeanor and labored communication style, he was arguably too ordinary to be remembered as anyone more than the man who pardoned Richard Nixon.

The man who followed Gerald Ford into the White House would have been more appropriate for the 1870s than the 1970s. Favoring unfettered markets and unobtrusive government, President Jimmy Carter was not a typical Democrat. Deeply religious and profoundly idealistic, this farmer from the South was also one of the most intelligent American presidents. Unfortunately, his intelligence did not contribute to making him an effective chief executive, and it may have even hindered his efforts, contributing to an overly analytical and meandering leadership style that lacked focus and cohesion. Carter was not at his best managing people or delegating authority, and his administration was one of the most poorly organized in the modern era, often giving the impression that the president was not in charge. He did, however, achieve several domestic successes prior to leaving Washington after the 1980 election. Most notably, despite intense opposition from members of his own party, Carter deregulated both the airline and trucking industries, enabling carriers, especially among the airlines, to set routes and fares freely without government interference. These actions would serve as critical precedents for further relaxation of government regulatory powers during the Reagan years.

The Reagan Revolution and Fiscal Imbalance

If Nixon epitomized the 1970s, Ronald Reagan was a perfect symbol of the 1980s. Confident, charismatic, and proudly patriotic, America's 40th chief executive presided over a decade that would be famous for mergers, acquisitions, and hostile takeovers that remade the nation's economy. Scorned by academics and left-wing intellectuals, the grandfatherly Reagan was widely admired and supported by many among the public who customarily voted Democratic. The quintessential right man at the right time, he appeared as the answer to the public's yearning for a national hero after a period that witnessed military embarrassment abroad and economic setbacks at home. By 1980, American pride stood at a low point, and the country's international standing was questioned for the first time in almost 40 years. Reagan promised to restore national dignity by freeing the market of unnecessary government intrusions and reaffirming U.S. military and diplomatic leadership across the globe. A former actor, he was uniquely suited for the role, which required political skill and stage management in equal parts. One of the most controversial presidents of the modern era, Reagan was also one of the most significant.

Capitalizing on the political disillusionment of the preceding years, Reagan blamed big government for the country's social and economic ills. His message that a bloated executive bureaucracy and a meddlesome Congress with too much power had led to economic gridlock and had sapped American competitiveness struck a chord with an electorate that increasingly viewed government as the enemy. However, despite his antigovernment reputation, Reagan was a walking contradiction. While he doggedly fought to trim federal regulatory powers, thereby promoting a leaner domestic bureaucracy, Reagan simultaneously presided over the largest military expansion in American history. The Reagan administration relaxed bureaucratic control of the private sector by promoting a hands-off approach to agencies such as the FTC, SEC, and NLRB, even threatening to eliminate the Small Business Administration, which was originally created to help America's entrepreneurs. Convinced that the federal government was wasting taxpayer dollars on dubious social programs, the administration restricted funding and subsidies for an array of services and lowered disbursements to state and local governments for health care, education, poverty prevention, and other concerns.

From an economic perspective, Reagan's approach was strikingly similar to that of the framers. Reagan believed as did the drafters of the Constitution that the government had no right to interfere with the market or to redress the perceived inequities that result from free competition. In this regard, he would have been quite at home among 19th-century conservatives who advocated something called laissez-faire economics, which simply meant that markets should be self-regulating and not subject to political controls of any type. A self-made man from humble beginnings who believed that government involvement in promotion stifled competition and personal motivation, Reagan abhorred preference-based systems for the elimination of discrimination and, thus, fought against affirmative action in the public and private sectors. Wishing to abolish the NEA at one point and critical of research priorities at the NEH, he expressed no great fondness for intellectuals who pushed for multiculturalism at the expense of cultural assimilation, nor did he tolerate what he believed to be creeping anti-Americanism infecting education and the arts.

At the same time, Reagan was not at all troubled by massive increases in the size of the military establishment, nor was he worried about the presi-

OMB director David A. Stockman briefs President Reagan in the Oval Office, October 6, 1981.

dency's ever-growing national security authority. Ultimately and maybe even ironically, Reagan's defense buildup proved that big government was not sustainable. The man who set out to show Americans that the modern executive bureaucracy would bankrupt the country succeeded in doing just that through an unprecedented expansion of federal resources. Reagan's augmentation of national security capabilities, though effective as a cold war ploy against the Soviets, produced record deficits that eventually burdened the American economy. However, blaming Reagan alone for the fiscal mismanagement that resulted from decades of executive growth would be grossly inaccurate and unfair. Aside from increases in defense spending, the cost of America's welfare state has been the principal reason for its financial difficulties. During approximately the last 20 years, the world has realized that more so than any other single part of government, the welfare state is unsustainable. This is why European governments have become more fiscally conservative and why even socialist regimes have backed away from the lavish cradle-to-grave protections that became common across Europe. Not only have Great Britain and Germany been compelled to make changes, but also bastions of social democracy such as the Scandinavian countries.

Retrenchment, Expansion, or the Status Quo?

Crediting the outgoing Reagan administration with a sustained economic recovery and not at all impressed by the Democratic nominee Michael Dukakis, Americans elected Vice President George H. W. Bush to the presidency in 1988. Quite possibly, no other candidate was ever as qualified as Bush to serve as America's chief executive, but, unfortunately, his qualifications did not always translate into an effective leadership style in the White House. His administration did not lack talent, assembling one of the most seasoned executive teams in recent years, and his political agenda was not particularly controversial. Given his wide-ranging foreign policy experience, Bush's greatest achievements were in the national security arena, with successes in Eastern Europe, Latin America, and the Middle East. On the domestic side, he was not so lucky, despite his advocacy of a key bill to protect disabled Americans. The Americans with Disabilities Act (ADA) of 1990 was a personal triumph for Bush, who, believing discrimination against the handicapped to be clearly wrong, was little concerned that the ADA enlarged an ever expanding executive bureaucracy. The ADA notwithstanding, Bush's presidency was weakened by a slumping economy in the last year of his term and the reversal of a campaign pledge not to raise taxes. In many regards the anti-Reagan, lacking the former president's charm, eloquence, and public stature, Bush could not overcome a two-pronged attack from Bill Clinton and Ross Perot in the 1992 presidential election.

In his first State of the Union address to Congress in early 1993, President Bill Clinton promised to "end welfare as we know it." His comment drew hearty applause from both sides of the aisle and praise from political pundits on every news network. Of course, President Clinton was not referring to the welfare system as a whole but to just the portion commonly associated with the word *welfare*, which was formally known as Aid to Families with Dependent Children (AFDC). AFDC had become a favorite target of conservative critics, libertarians, and other opponents of big government because the support it extended to needy children was perceived as encouraging their parents to remain on federal assistance indefinitely. As a percentage of federal expenditures on social services, AFDC was relatively modest, but it served as a symbol of a dysfunctional welfare state straining the financial resources of the American government. Over the previous dozen years or so, Americans and their public officials had begun to accept that America's welfare state posed a serious threat to the nation's financial stability, and the Clinton administration was definitely aware of that.

Tapping into the public's rising discontent over the government's apparent financial incompetence, Clinton's welfare reform initiative gave evidence of a new kind of Democrat. Perhaps the greatest politician ever to occupy the presidency, Clinton was representative of a trend that transcended U.S.

borders. Like Britain's Labour Party and Germany's Social Democrats, both of which were left of center parties, the Democrats in the United States were adapting their platform to changing times. Traditional support of large welfare states was surrendering to the fiscal realities of the late 20th century, and pragmatic Democrats such as Clinton reoriented their policies accordingly. However, as the British prime minister Tony Blair and the German chancellor Gerhard Schroeder both eventually discovered, historical momentum is not easily reversed. Clinton's welfare reform was finally passed in 1996, and his vice president, Al Gore, spearheaded an effort to streamline the executive bureaucracy, but, on other fronts, the Clinton administration expanded social services and regulatory activities. The administration's health-care proposals, though ultimately defeated, were vilified for promoting too much government. And they illustrated that Clinton's commitment to reducing the domestic bureaucracy was not universal.

CONCLUSION

Bill Clinton was caught between a rock and a hard place, and he was no less successful at decreasing the size of government than his Republican counterparts had been. Clinton and his successors, George W. Bush and Barack Obama, have all recognized that spending on social services has grown out of hand, but they have been trapped by the lack of political will to confront an issue the public would rather ignore. Reforming government entitlements is an explosive prospect that threatens political careers and makes the American people uneasy, so, over the last 20 years, the nation's politicians have only tinkered with the welfare system, deferring the responsibility of crafting real solutions to future generations. As a result, America's welfare state has become a political grenade. Everyone acknowledges that left to itself it can be destructive and that, therefore, it must be defused, but no one wants to touch it. Like its predecessors, the Obama administration now faces a fiscal problem that could eventually derail the U.S. government. Ballooning entitlement costs along with an aging population that demands an ever-greater share of the nation's resources are turning what was once the world's most formidable creditor into its largest debtor, which is not good for anyone.

Recent economic conditions have only served to exacerbate the nation's financial burdens, as government interventions by the Bush and Obama administrations pushed deficit spending to new heights. Surprising and even infuriating many of his conservative brethren, George W. Bush orchestrated a massive government bailout of the automobile, insurance, and banking industries, leaving Barack Obama with little choice but to open federal coffers further. Rightly or wrongly, the Obama administration supplemented federal subsidies to ailing corporations with strict management oversight, which moved the government deeper into the market than at any point since the

New Deal. Furthermore, as has been the case with the airlines, railroads, and steel, not to mention farming, the auto industry initiative will invariably pull the government into successive efforts to rescue the Big Three automakers. Market purists convincingly argue that federal support of failing businesses is counterproductive and inefficient and that it distorts the fundamental dynamic between supply and demand, but an America irrationally committed to its Fords, Chevys, and Chryslers will not listen to logic. For better or worse, as long as domestic industrial priorities are a function of patriotism and nostalgia, the electorate will continue to endorse questionable economic policies by both parties.

CHAPTER 5

Political Parties, Electoral Politics, and the Public Presidency

In early 1789, as a new nation awaited confirmation of the obvious, the 69 members of the Electoral College met in their respective states to pick George Washington as the first president of the United States. With no primaries, political parties, or formal nominees, to say nothing of a popular vote, their choice was no less legitimate than the results of general elections today. Having little say in the selection of electors, the public was not directly involved in the process, which is exactly what the framers of the Constitution intended. Over the next eight presidential elections, America's chief executives would owe their jobs to a cloistered, if not secretive, system designed to maintain leadership by political elites. Congressmen would meet behind closed doors to name official candidates whose fate would then rest with the Electoral College. For a generation, the popular will, though politically relevant in other ways, would be largely irrelevant during presidential elections. Backed by tradition and a deferential citizenry, America's "natural aristocracy," as Jefferson referred to the nation's elite class, would continue to dominate the presidency until at least 1824.

Despite the framers' intentions to preserve this pattern, changing political circumstances ultimately produced significant deviations. The duties and responsibilities of the presidency have evolved, and so have the procedures by which its occupants have been chosen. Over the years, America's presidents have become more representative of the public at large, not least because the public has played an increasing part in presidential politics. Today, Americans take their role for granted, assured that general elections will determine the electoral vote and that common citizens, not political elites, will dominate the presidency. No longer handpicked by a natural aristocracy, the president embodies the cultural diversity of a nation with 300 million people from all walks of life and all backgrounds. In fact, most of America's modern presidents have been ordinary men whose rise would have been prevented by the very hierarchies that promoted the careers of its early ones. The presidency may no longer reflect the framers' intent, but, for better or worse, it does reflect the public's intent.

In 2009, Barack Obama, a black man of Kenyan heritage, became president, which some commentators have seen as the culmination of a process of electoral reform that began in 1828 with the election of Andrew Jackson. Jackson was the first common man to occupy the presidency, and many others have followed. Astute and keenly aware of changing trends, Jackson realized that popularity would help win elections in a democratic America. The coming of the television age approximately 130 years later made popularity and public approval the cornerstones of a public presidency that set the stage for the 21st century. Armed with broadcast media, print media, the Internet, and emerging technologies, today's presidents can reach the electorate instantly, continually, and consistently. Their administrations can tap into the popular will through polling, focus groups, and countless analyses, furthering a connection to the American people that is unbreakable. Although the framers of the Constitution could not have foreseen its emergence, the public presidency symbolizes everything they worked so hard to prevent. Perhaps they would have considered it illegitimate, but the public presidency is here to stay.

THE PRIVATE PRESIDENCY

The American political system is commonly called a liberal democracy. Although both parts of the term *liberal democracy* underscore the centrality of popular sovereignty in American government, it was neither very liberal nor very democratic at the outset. Certain aspects of liberalism have always been important, especially the prevalence of individual rights, yet others, such as government by consent, were deliberately diluted by the framers of the Constitution. Not actually democratic, founding-era government was more antidemocratic. Democratic ideals, despite their present-day appeal, were the preserve of the silly, naive, or even crazy, and democracy was customarily equated with mob rule. Indeed, the Founding Fathers habitually referred to democracy as "mobocracy" and believed that direct rule by the people was foolish and ineffective. Convinced that the common masses were unqualified to take part in governance, the framers of the Constitution established mechanisms to filter the popular will through those qualified by social rank, political experience, wealth, and education. The indirect election of America's presidents by electors accountable to elites was one of those mechanisms, and the electoral laws of the early republic clearly reflected the framers' intent to distance political decision making from the general public.

Presidents, Politicians, and Political Parties before 1828

The framers did not view the presidential election process or the elitist nature of American politics as regressive or inequitable. To the contrary, the system of government they designed was uniquely progressive. Based on popular sovereignty and tolerating a degree of public participation unknown anywhere else, it was generations ahead of its counterparts on the European continent. Still, that system was a product of its times and the political culture that prevailed at the end of the 18th century. The truth is that, despite their allegiance to popular rule, the framers were not utopian fools dedicated to the eradication of social hierarchies that preserve political stability. They did not allow popular sovereignty to override common sense and experience, nor did they have any evidence that the abolition of political control by elites would benefit the American republic. A political system managed by America's natural aristocracy offered the greatest probability of political success, as did a social structure governed by paternalism, deference, and order.

Aside from their fear that common people were too ignorant and preoccupied to be entrusted with direct control of government, the framers worried that the popularization, or democratization, of politics would undermine the integrity of public service. Believing that a political system based on mass appeal would lead to the emergence of permanent factions and professional politicians, they did everything in their power to avoid such a fate. To the founding generation, public service precluded the existence of professional politicians and political parties, both of which would cheapen and degrade American governance. The framers of the Constitution were convinced that professional politics was a symbol of corruption and decay and that public officials should have nonpolitical careers. Responsible public officials served temporarily and, upon the conclusion of a relatively short term of office, returned to their private careers. The notion that public servants should aspire to become professional politicians and train for a career in politics, as is the case today, would have been considered ludicrous or even offensive at the time.

As long as public servants maintained careers and possessed goals that transcended politics, their priorities would coincide with those of the American people. However, because professional politicians have careers and goals within politics, their priorities would coincide with those of their party or political cause. The presence of professional politicians would create an interest in opposition to the people, because those politicians would no longer identify with private citizens, so they would protect their stake in politics to the detriment of their stake in legitimate government. Obviously, since professional politics leads to the creation of permanent factions, political parties were not welcome either. By discrediting political parties and fostering conditions to prevent their emergence, the Founding Fathers hoped to preserve a unified citizenry and honest governance. Having witnessed the rivalries and jealousies between British Tories and Whigs as colonial subjects, they equated parties with lasting political divisions that would undermine the cooperation, compromise, and fairness required in a nation as diverse as the United States. Consequently, the men who authored the Constitution were determined to keep political parties out of American government.

Nevertheless, reality dictates that no two people, to say nothing of the more than 4 million who populated the newly created republic, will share identical beliefs, so public officials divided themselves according to contemporary constitutional differences. Like the rest, the two main groups, known as Republicans (later Democratic Republicans) and Federalists, were loosely organized coalitions of intellectual elites who traced their roots to the ratification debates of 1787 and 1788. The former included supporters of weaker federal government, states' rights, and an agrarian economy and, as such, they included many of those who had opposed ratification of the Constitution. The Federalists, on the other hand, were advocates of strong federal government, the establishment of a national bank, assumption of state war debts by the federal treasury, and industrial expansion. Most had backed ratification of the Constitution. However, despite the partisan rhetoric and spirited controversy, Federalists and Republicans were not the professionally managed and well-funded organizations that would eventually dominate national politics. Lacking the formal structure and independent existence of political parties, to say nothing of the wherewithal to promote the careers of affiliated public officials, Federalists and Republicans more closely resembled debating societies than they did real political parties.

The Revolution of 1800

The nation's fourth presidential election was also one of its most fascinating, replete with controversy and a cast of characters that would make Hollywood screenwriters envious. Immortalized as the Revolution of 1800, it has been remembered more for what did not occur than what actually did. A revolution evokes images of bloodshed, violence, and political upheaval, yet this particular revolution had none of these, and that is exactly what made it so revolutionary. The incumbent president, John Adams, was a Federalist with impressive social credentials and a patrician outlook on politics that seemed better suited to the past than the future. His advocacy and enforcement of the reviled Alien and Sedition Acts, which suppressed free speech and attracted bitter opposition against one of America's most beloved revolutionary heroes, made him an easy target for critics. Moreover, his preference for Britain over France in foreign affairs enraged Republicans, who believed the French Revolution had remade America's former ally into a free republic. Disillusioned with the embattled president's agenda, the Republicans hoped to replace Adams with Thomas Jefferson, their intellectual standard-bearer. They also nominated Aaron Burr, a combustible New Yorker viewed by many as the quintessential political troublemaker, in the belief that he would be elected vice president.

When the votes were counted, the fact that Adams failed to secure a second term did not come as a surprise, but the electoral draw between Jefferson and Burr was. Republicans assumed that Jefferson, as the most popular and best qualified candidate, would undoubtedly win the presidency. Unfortunately, since each elector voted for two candidates without distinguishing between a presidential and vice-presidential choice, the resulting confusion easily produced a tie. Ultimately, as the Constitution prescribed, the draw was resolved in the House of Representatives, whose members picked Jefferson as the third president of the United States. In the process, the election became all the more contentious due to the politicking and horse-trading necessary to ensure Jefferson's victory in the House. Adding insult to injury,

Adams made a number of federal appointments in the dying hours of his presidency, which hardly pleased the incoming administration and its supporters. To an outside observer, the situation would have appeared dire.

However, despite the ill-will and political turbulence, the animosity between Federalists and Republicans, and the contested electoral vote, the system and the country survived, which is what made the election of 1800 so revolutionary. It may not seem momentous to 21st-century Americans, accustomed as they are to peaceful transitions after elections, that the change from one administration to the next occurred without incident, but, in the context of contemporary politics, it was

Portrait of Thomas Jefferson, the third president of the United States *(Wikipedia)*

a major feat. At that time, transfers of power between rival regimes were anything but peaceful, so, when an outgoing head of state willingly relinquished power to one of his fiercest political opponents and the country simply acquiesced, the world noticed. People did not riot in the streets as had happened recently in France, nor did the followers of the defeated head of state take up arms in his defense as had been the case in late 17th-century England. Respecting the constitutional legitimacy of the election results and willing to abide by them for that reason, the American people never thought twice about the right thing to do. In the end, the nation endured because the Constitution worked.

Starting with the election of 1800, the Republicans dominated national politics for some time. The Federalists may have produced the first two presidents, but they faded into historical anonymity shortly thereafter. During the first three decades of the 19th century, the Republicans, who became known as the Democratic Republicans, had the field to themselves, controlling the federal legislature and the presidency without much opposition. They nominated presidential candidates in congressional meetings called caucuses and presented lists of candidates to electors. Prior to 1824, only a small minority of qualified voters participated in general elections, and the public accepted the electors' decisions without reservation. During the first four presidential elections (1789, 1792, 1796, and 1800), each elector voted for two candidates without differentiating between a president and vice president, with the top two recipients claiming those two offices, respectively. The Twelfth Amendment to the Constitution, ratified in 1804, simplified the process, compelling electors to distinguish between presidential and vice-presidential candidates. Americans hoped this would eliminate any further confusion.

The Corrupt Bargain of 1824

As it turned out, the Twelfth Amendment by itself could not prevent renewed confusion or debate about the electoral system. Although the Republican ascendancy dampened ideological wrangling, other obstacles to political uniformity eventually arose. Briefly, however, especially following the War of 1812 against Britain, all seemed well, and unity prevailed. Buoyed by a second victory over the world's mightiest empire in just 30 years, Americans turned their attention to more immediate concerns such as industrial innovation and the expansion of the frontier. The nation's textile and clothing industries kicked into high gear as the second decade of the 19th century drew to a close, and improvements in transportation presented new possibilities for producers, consumers, and settlers on the move westward. The postwar consolidation of political gains by the Republicans was punctuated by the so-called Era of Good Feelings during the presidency of James Monroe

(1817 to 1825), so many Americans hoped for sustained progress and political tranquility.

Unfortunately, the good feelings did not last, as an economic recession in 1819 and disagreement over slavery engendered by Missouri's application for statehood deepened existing cracks in the political landscape. Divisions among Republicans between those who advocated a federal role in banking, promotion of domestic manufacturing, and infrastructural improvements, on the one hand, and states' rights traditionalists, on the other, eventually split them into National and Democratic camps, with the Democratic Republicans morphing into the Democratic Party by 1828. Sectional rivalry reached a zenith during deliberations over the Missouri Compromise, which admitted Maine as a free state and Missouri as a slave state, and generational differences between those committed to the framers' vision and young politicians pushing for democratic reforms began to appear. By 1824, as Monroe's second term neared its conclusion, the status quo, which the founding generation had tried so diligently to maintain, was no longer sufficient for many Americans, and change seemed inevitable.

The presidential election of 1824 may not have produced the change some had anticipated, but it proved to be the final gasp of a system that looked hopelessly outdated. Andrew Jackson, the hero of the War of 1812 and arguably the most revered military figure since George Washington, won a plurality of both popular and electoral votes but failed to secure a majority, so, as had been the case in 1800, the election was thrown into the House of Representatives. After what Jackson labeled a "corrupt bargain" among his political opponents, the House chose John Quincy Adams, the son of the country's second president, as the next chief executive. Charges of collusion against Adams and his supporters were difficult to substantiate, but Henry Clay's appointment as secretary of state appeared as nothing more than outright compensation for delivering Kentucky's vote for Adams in the House. Whatever the truth may have been, the result tainted a process that a growing number of Americans felt was unrepresentative, unfair, and even illegitimate.

The corrupt bargain of 1824 constituted the last nail in the proverbial coffin, and presidential elections would never be the same again. Gone were the closed-door nominating sessions and independent electoral votes, as was the idea that American politics should be the preserve of its social elites. Andrew Jackson spent the bulk of the next four years politicking and campaigning to reverse the loss he suffered, ensuring that history would not repeat itself in 1828. Inspired and also incensed by recent events, Jackson's supporters, advocates of reform, and a younger generation of public servants who increasingly looked to politics as a career and not an avocation built the foundations of professional organizations whose purpose would be to promote the candidacies of popular men with mass appeal. In this context, Adams was an anachronism, a political dinosaur whose formidable political pedigree could not overcome his perceived failings as a symbol of an irrelevant past. He represented a reclusive presidency whose occupants were more comfortable in a private chamber with political elites than in a public arena. Owing his career to the very system Americans wished to replace, Adams seemed regressive at a time when the nation wanted to be progressive.

THE TRANSITIONAL PRESIDENCY

As the first generation of political leaders passed the baton to a younger group of politicians who came of age under different circumstances and as the Industrial Revolution fueled the growth of an American middle class, founding-era electoral constraints became obsolete. A more democratic electoral system would soon emerge, drastically reducing the power of elites and offering political access to ordinary men such as Andrew Jackson and Abraham Lincoln. The personification of the American dream, these men never benefited from social privilege or family status, and they had more in common with average Americans than did those who had controlled politics during the early republic. They symbolized a newly established ideal that appeared to be gaining increased credibility. A democratic spirit was sweeping the nation and transforming the way Americans approached politics and what they expected from their public servants. For the next 125 years or so, electoral politics and the presidencies it produced would be in transition, slowly completing a process that the election of Andrew Jackson had begun.

By the time Andrew Jackson assumed the nation's highest office, the elitist political culture into which he had been born was under siege. A new political reality greeted America's public officials, brushing aside all vestiges of elitism and intellectual aloofness and linking its future to an equally striking economic reality. Political reformers opened the electoral process to middle- and lower-income voters, eased restrictions on officeholding, and promoted public service based on electability and not social class. As founding-era misgivings about political careers gave way to faith in political expertise, constituents increasingly backed candidates who possessed the requisite savvy and skill to address local needs. Into this climate, the professional politician was born, and he took center stage in the country in short order. Unlike early public servants, the professional politician was a self-made man whose connection with average Americans established his political credentials and public appeal. Spending his time on the stump, in meeting halls, and with his constituents, he alone could muster the practical knowledge, resources, and contacts necessary for political success in a democratizing society.

The Spoils System

Nothing more aptly describes the period inaugurated by Andrew Jackson's election to the presidency than Senator William Marcy's declaration "to the victor belong the spoils." The victor in this case was less the president than the Democrats themselves, who through what become known as the *spoils system* distributed the fruits of political victory as shrewdly as a pirate divides prizes at sea. Equipped with money, power, and influence, 19th-century political parties dominated electoral politics. Adept at placing their candidates and supporters in various government posts, these organizations became the proving grounds for aspiring politicians at the local, state, and federal levels. Campaigns, elections, and even service in office were controlled through extensive party networks that permeated every institution. Aside from popularity, party loyalty served as a chief measure of success, and political gifts and favors were the currency of exchange. Public service became synonymous with partisanship, and political appointments rewarded contributors, supporters, and key aides, while solidarity and ideological conformity reinforced party discipline. These were the foundations of a modern party system that would survive until the present day.

Vilified by the framers but lauded by their successors, political parties arose from circumstances the founding generation neither understood nor anticipated. They changed the nation's political landscape irrevocably and facilitated the democratization of its institutions. Since the 1820s, numerous national, regional, and local parties have affected the political development of the United States, though only a few have endured. America has had workers' parties, socialist parties, agrarian parties, conservative parties, progressive parties, antislavery parties, pro-slavery parties, religious parties, anti-religious parties, and many, many more. Their members have included radicals, reactionaries, anarchists, reformers, xenophobes, evangelicals, atheists, capitalists, communists, peaceniks, conservationists, and myriads of others. Representing the broadest spectrum of political views and differing in their approaches to American politics, they shared a conviction that parties facilitate legitimate governance and promote electoral equity. Perhaps most significant, modern parties changed America's political institutions, the most prominent of which is the presidency.

The first modern party in the United States was the Democratic, which absorbed the remnants of the old Democratic Republican coalition. Its initial rival was the Whig Party, which was founded in 1834 to formalize opposition to the Jackson administration and prevent the election of Democrat Martin Van Buren in 1836. Although Van Buren won the presidential vote, the Whigs did capture the presidency in 1840 and 1848 with two widely admired war veterans, William Henry Harrison and Zachary Taylor, respectively. Coincidentally, both Harrison and Taylor died early in their first terms, leaving

President Martin Van Buren *(Library of Congress)*

the presidency to two of its most lackluster occupants. Taylor's death proved an omen, as the Whigs suffered their own demise by 1854. Some former Whigs along with a number of northern Democrats and members of various smaller parties then formed the Republican Party, which has survived until today. Despite changes in outlook and affiliation since the 19th century, Democrats and Republicans have controlled presidential politics over the years without significant challenges from third parties. Unable to compete consistently with the two major parties, minor parties have nonetheless persisted and have even occasionally threatened to upset the balance of power between Republicans and Democrats, such as during the 1912, 1992, and 2000 presidential elections.

Starting with the 1832 election, political parties managed the presidential selection process at every step. Although the popular vote determined the electoral tally by the 1830s, party functionaries dominated everything from nominations to the appointment of electors. This is by no means intended to minimize the sweeping electoral reforms of the 19th century, but parties developed as much influence over elections as elites had possessed during the early republic. Nominations, for example, instead of coming out of the closed-door environment of founding-era congressional caucuses, resulted from elaborate conventions attended by hundreds of party loyalists, yet the public had little say over the outcomes. The time, place, and manner of general elections, despite some guidance from Congress, were set according to party dictates, so the popular vote was often affected by the manipulation of polling conditions by local party bosses. Presidential candidates had substantially more public exposure prior to general elections than had been the case at the beginning of the 19th century, and the popularization of the electoral process necessitated active national campaigns, but political parties choreographed practically everything. Still, presidential elections were considerably more open than they had ever been, and the American people exerted influence that they did not have prior to 1828.

The method of electing America's presidents became increasingly more open to the public as the 19th century unfolded. However, aside from its more common or ordinary occupants, the presidency did not. Newspaper reporters had greater access to the White House and presidents were generally more visible, but their activities and interactions were confined to a handful of institutions and officials in Washington. Their political relationships could hardly be labeled exclusive or secretive in the same way that those of America's early leaders were, and their policies faced public scrutiny through greater transparency at every level. At the same time, presidential communication strategies and tactics changed little, as did the willingness of America's chief executives to maintain a dialogue with the people while in office. In many ways, theirs was still a cloistered existence within an office that needed to keep the people at arm's length to preserve its privacy, and, despite progressive reforms that made the presidency more democratic, America's presidents were not yet sufficiently comfortable as public leaders to overcome that privacy completely.

The insularity of the office was mostly a function of constitutional design, but it also stemmed from the fact that 19th-century presidents were overshadowed by Congress. Abraham Lincoln notwithstanding, America's chief executives did not have nearly as much impact on the development and implementation of policies as the federal legislature. Most federal activity was centered in Congress, which usually set the country's political agenda. In addition, and this may have been due to the nature of the presidency itself, 19th-century presidents frequently appeared awkward, unassertive, and indecisive, while representatives and senators of that era were some of the more illustrious and memorable characters in American history. Except for Lincoln, before the McKinley administration, strong leadership customarily originated from Congress, not the presidency. To make matters worse, the reputation of the nation's highest office was occasionally tarnished by scandal, particularly during the presidencies of Andrew Johnson, who was impeached by the House in 1868, and Ulysses Grant, whose administration was one of the most corrupt, if not inept, of the century. The dubious election of Grant's successor Rutherford Hayes, decided by an electoral commission and sealed through a political deal known as the Compromise of 1877, hardly helped. The following two decades witnessed one of the country's longest economic downturns, which continued in place as the 19th century came to an end.

A New Presidency for a New Century

Appearances aside, the last two decades of the 19th century were not all doom and gloom. As discussed in the previous chapter, the federal government began to confront mass industrialization through progressive measures that aided the economically dislocated, and the United States began to flex its international muscle. Grover Cleveland, the only chief executive to serve two nonconsecutive terms, helped restore credibility to the presidency through hard work and personal integrity, while Congress finally addressed the political corruption that had infiltrated Washington. With considerable aid from the Hayes and Cleveland administrations, federal legislators enacted civil service reforms that undermined the partisan patronage of the spoils system by instituting merit-based performance and hiring criteria for all but cabinet-level bureaucratic jobs. After several decades of unregulated growth, U.S. political parties realized that the days of staffing the government bureaucracy with party functionaries were numbered. Civil service legislation may not have directly pertained to political parties, but it severely curtailed their ability to peddle influence through government appointments. Moreover, it highlighted the need for greater transparency and accountability within political parties, which continued to exert pressure for electoral reform.

The end of the century brought with it international ambitions and a new kind of president, one more adept at using the media to his advantage, less awkward before the public, and decidedly more assertive vis-à-vis Congress. How much of this was simple historical coincidence as opposed to cause and effect is difficult to determine, though changes in foreign policy were certainly related to corresponding changes among America's presidents. William McKinley and especially Theodore Roosevelt were clearly more charismatic, self-assured in public, and politically resolute than most of their predecessors, and they welcomed, if not courted, the media attention previous presidents had shunned. Roosevelt was the first occupant of the White House who consistently and without reservation submitted key policies before the people through newspapers and speeches, and one of his aides even held regular press briefings, which was a practice resumed by Woodrow Wilson from 1913 to 1921. Wilson also started the practice of presidential press conferences, formalizing the relationship between the presidency and the news media. With some exceptions, presidential politics would unfold as much in public as behind closed doors over the ensuing decades, so the emergence of an extroverted presidency during the waning years of the 19th century and the beginning of the 20th, whether coincidental or otherwise, was a seminal development.

As has been the case with similar changes throughout the history of the American republic, the presidency's reorientation at the beginning of the 20th century was coupled to equally important trends in the news media. McKinley's tenure as chief executive coincided with the advent of so-called yellow journalism, a phenomenon originating from the newspaper wars between the publishers Joseph Pulitzer and William Randolph Hearst of New York. In the strictest sense, yellow journalism referred to the less than ethical reporting tactics used by the two men's newspapers to increase circulation through exaggerated stories that relied on equal parts fact and fiction. Motivated by profit and convinced that newsworthiness and sensationalism go hand in hand, Pulitzer and Hearst produced the forerunners of today's tabloids but presented them as respectable publications. In a broader sense, the term *yellow journalism* transcended the Pulitzer-Hearst feud and its immediate environment and applied to the transformation of the news media during the Gilded Age and Progressive Era. As such, it symbolized the commercialization of news driven by the emergence of America's media empires.

This does not suggest that newspaper publishers of the past were not concerned with profit or increasing circulation, but it emphasizes the relationship

Portrait of Theodore Roosevelt, the 26th president of the United States *(Wikipedia)*

between big business and journalism that arose at the end of the 19th-century. Prior to that, journalism was driven more by community needs and vocational calling than by the dynamics of supply and demand, rendering news reporting a public service of sorts. Founding-era newspapers were largely propaganda outlets for Federalists and Republicans, fulfilling the ideological objectives of contemporary elites and maintaining dialogue about relevant issues, while the bulk of later 19th-century publications were modest entrepreneurial ventures that addressed the public's curiosity regarding local happenings. Unlike the last several decades, which feature news outlets owned by diversified corporations or families with practically limitless assets, large media companies did not yet exist, nor did the close link between journalism and profit. Until publishers adopted the corporate innovations and economies of scale that revolutionized manufacturing, the nation's newspapers remained independent and comparatively small.

Mass industrialization, however, swept everything in its path, and newspapers were no exception. As publishers applied management principles to their businesses and responded to a growing demand for entertainment among readers with increasing leisure time, the marketing of news became as significant as, if not more significant than, the news itself. Suddenly, how the news was packaged attracted more attention from editors and publishers than it ever had in the past, and everyone, including journalists, seemed aware of the need to sell the news and not merely report it. News publication was being absorbed by a fledgling entertainment industry that would eventually control the production and distribution of news in this country. Entertainment had traditionally been the preserve of the wealthy, but the emergence of a middle class made it available to all and, consequently, turned it into an unprecedented opportunity. Professional sports, films, photography, and mass-market publications fed the public's demand for inexpensive entertainment, as the nature of news coverage changed forever.

The Watershed Years

McKinley, Roosevelt, Wilson, and America's other presidents during the early decades of the 20th century took note of the evolving media industry and used it with varying effectiveness. Roosevelt and Wilson were among the most successful, though, after the president's stroke, the Wilson administration learned that an extroverted presidency was also more vulnerable because of increased exposure. As the nation's highest office gradually opened itself to the press, its occupants were decreasingly capable of hiding potentially compromising information from the public. By the 1920s, the proverbial genie had been out of the bottle for some time, and no one could restore the more private relationship between presidents and the American people that had previously prevailed. Most likely, very few would have wanted to do so in any case. After the introduction of commercial radio broadcasts in the 1920s, the die was cast, cementing the connection between presidents and the media and enhancing the people's access to the presidency. Radio may have exposed the presidency to a new kind of scrutiny, but, more critically, it provided the country's chief executives with a unique tool for shaping not only their own agendas, but also public opinion.

The nation's airwaves offered unsurpassed immediacy and the broadest possible range, giving presidents access to America's homes, businesses, and public establishments. Broadcasting extended the presidency's reach beyond any the Founding Fathers could have imagined, and it encouraged executive officials to act with greater purpose, alacrity, and precision. At the same time, radio enabled an increasing portion of the electorate to witness and perhaps monitor the activities of its presidents, drawing the public and the presidency ever closer. One of America's most popular presidents, Franklin Delano Roosevelt, was keenly aware of this and took advantage of radio's potential to the fullest. Leveraging the power of live broadcasts, FDR held a series of "fireside chats" throughout his presidency, garnering support for his domestic and foreign policies through trust and confidence forged over the airwaves. FDR's speeches, public addresses, and press conferences have become legendary, and his ability to inspire and befriend the American people still serves as a benchmark for many elected officials. To FDR, the political benefits of involving the public in presidential policy making through live broadcasts were obvious, as were the ultimate windfalls at the ballot box.

Like many of America's more eloquent presidents, FDR was less an innovator than he was a superbly adaptive politician. With respect to technological and structural advances in the media industry, he could not have appeared on the scene at a more fortuitous moment. As had been true of Andrew Jackson, Teddy Roosevelt, and Woodrow Wilson, FDR proved to be the right man at the right time. This observation should not detract from the fact that he was a tremendously skillful communicator, but it once again demonstrates that coincidence of personality and circumstance, rather than design and purpose, often results in momentous institutional change. The emergence of radio appeared ideally suited to this unusually articulate chief executive who exuded fatherly authority and patrician charm, attributes of which the president and his advisers were fully aware and which they used very effectively. Unlike his immediate predecessors, Herbert Hoover and Calvin Coolidge, FDR successfully exploited the new medium. During a time of distress, his comforting style and steady approach blended with the medium of radio, much as John Kennedy's natural charisma seemed optimal for television several decades later.

From the perspective of the president's relationships with the news media and the American people, these truly were watershed years. Poised between the institutional formality of the past and the unpredictable fluidity of the future, FDR's presidency was not yet the public office of JFK and his successors, yet it had surpassed those of McKinley, Teddy Roosevelt, and Wilson. For better or worse, the presidency FDR bequeathed to those who followed was committed to public communication and greater exposure, and its credibility rested on an apparently unbreakable link with the media. However, greater exposure meant increased transparency and accountability, which made presidents susceptible to public criticism as never before. As a result, FDR and especially his successors during the television age depended on communications management of a type that was completely new to the presidency. Suddenly, presidents and their advisers became acutely conscious of communication strategies as well as public approval, and, with an eye on their legacies, controlling the news cycle and maximizing popularity, while minimizing damage from unpopular policies, became top priorities.

Despite these changes, the FDR presidency was transitional rather than transformative. It had passed a point of no return, but, with one foot still in

Franklin Delano Roosevelt *(Library of Congress)*

the past, its debt to tradition was evident. Whereas the public presidency today is part of a media-driven environment that enables real dialogue between the nation's chief executives and its people, FDR's dialogue with Americans, though progressive and open by historical standards, was choreographed by means of a paternalistic approach in which the administration maintained the upper hand over the news media. Like his predecessors, though not as extensively, FDR maintained a buffer between himself and the people, and his communication with them was neither continuous nor mutual. Perhaps the true genius of FDR as communicator lay in his ability to create the illusion of unrestricted dialogue through carefully staged monologue. In the end, however, the president was not nearly as accessible to the public as would be the case just a few decades later. Similarly, despite the increased frequency of interactions by the president with journalists and broadcasters, media access was tightly managed and controlled, and the relationship could hardly be labeled equal.

Aside from its guarded turn outward, FDR's presidency was transitional in another regard. He and his 20th-century predecessors changed the relationship with their political parties. As the public visibility and popularity of the presidency grew, the comparative power of political parties gradually diminished. This does not mean that parties lost their political influence or relinquished control of the electoral process, but their power relative to presidential candidates definitely decreased. During the 19th century, parties clearly overshadowed their presidential candidates, with voters picking presidents primarily based on their party affiliation and paying less attention to other qualifications. Notable exceptions aside, such as Abraham Lincoln, many candidates receded almost into anonymity alongside party organizations that dominated electoral politics. As presidents became more assertive and benefited from increased media exposure, public attention began to shift from parties to personalities. Party dynamics acquired greater balance, and the electorate started focusing on personalities as much as they did parties.

THE PUBLIC PRESIDENCY

So much has already been said about a *public presidency* in this chapter that it begs the obvious question: What is it? To begin with, it combines two characteristics identified by the political scientists Jeffrey Tulis and Samuel Kernell. In his writings, Tulis has described a rhetorical aspect of the modern presidency that reflects the willingness and ability to engage people directly through substantive dialogue, as opposed to the formal, perfunctory, and strictly limited contact with the public characteristic of presidencies during the 19th century. He traces it to the early decades of the 20th century, particularly to McKinley, Roosevelt, and Wilson, stressing the latter's efforts in promoting progressive initiatives. In this respect, the president became the communicator in chief, serving as the point man for direct interaction with the American people and a key source of political rhetoric. Building on Tulis's idea of a rhetorical presidency, Kernell has added the concept of "going public," which refers to the increasingly common presidential habit of bypassing Congress and the policy-making bureaucracy by appealing directly to the American people for support. The net effect is an unmediated dialogue between presidents and the public that circumvents the Washington political establishment.

As significant as Tulis and Kernell's contributions have been, they alone are not sufficient as determinants of a public presidency. Additional factors have been just as important, and one of the most critical is the American public's awareness not only of its role as an equal participant, but also its own power and influence. During the FDR years, for example, the presidency's relationship with the people was paternalistic and carefully staged, whereas, by the 1960s, Americans expected that relationship to be mutual, spontaneous, and relatively unrestricted. Another factor is an independent press whose allegiance to the people is greater than its fear of the presidency and whose credibility is not threatened by presidential authority, the capitalist nature of the news media notwithstanding. Finally, the public presidency is also based on the awareness that presidential success and effective leadership are related to public approval. Nineteenth-century chief executives and even those of the early 20th century did not worry as much about public acceptance because their presidencies did not play out in public, but those of the last several decades have. In the end, the public presidency, while an evolving institution whose attributes are always in flux, is defined by features that make it unique and that distinguish it from the presidencies of prior eras.

The Television Age

From a substantive standpoint, John Fitzgerald Kennedy was not a transformative president. In office for only a thousand days, his policy achievements were not remarkable by modern standards. His assassination prematurely ended a promising presidency, and his short tenure produced as many failures as it did successes. However, in one respect, he changed the presidency as no one before. A consummate public figure with aplomb and youthful appeal, JFK made the institution he occupied truly public. Unlike his last two predecessors, he was at home in front of the camera and utterly at ease with the press. He embraced television and and invited America into the White House to witness presidential politics firsthand. Aided by a skillful team of advisers and an effective press secretary, JFK used television and an intimate relationship with the print media to create an open dialogue between the presidency and the public, ultimately undermining the remaining barriers that separated presidents from the American electorate.

Radio modified political communication, but television completely redefined it. Visual effects now accompanied familiar voices, and Americans' familiarity with their public officials increased as a result. Ordinary people

The Bully Pulpit

The origins of the rhetorical presidency and the president's use of the bully pulpit are credited to Theodore Roosevelt. He promoted the president's role as the national leader of public opinion and used his rhetorical skills to increase the power of the presidency through popular support. Roosevelt believed that the president was the steward of the people and that weak presidential leadership during the 19th century had left the American system of government open to the harmful influence of special interests. He adopted an approach to expand presidential authority by interpreting the Constitution as allowing the chief executive to draw on broad discretionary powers, the first president to do so during peacetime, as opposed to adhering to a more conservative and literal reading of presidential powers as defined by the Constitution. Roosevelt's "Stewardship Doctrine" mandated presidential reliance on popular support of the people, and it also raised the public's expectation of the man and the office. He often appealed directly to the American public through his active use of what became known as the bully pulpit to gain support of his legislative agenda in an attempt to place public pressure on Congress. He referred to his speaking tours around the country as "swings around the circle." Roosevelt's use of the presidency as a bully pulpit changed American's view of the office and helped to shift power from the legislative to executive branch during the 20th century.

Later presidents, though not all, would follow Roosevelt's strategy of relying on the bully pulpit to elevate the power of the office in an attempt to lead democratically as the chief spokesperson for the American public. Woodrow Wilson contributed to a more prominent role for the presidency

began to associate faces with names and judged the effectiveness of political speech by the appearance of the speakers. Image was becoming as important as substance, and success was measured by popular appeal. The new medium was not just immediate and pervasive; it seemed palpable and even real. It presented the sufficiently talented with endless possibilities for self-promotion at the same time that it held tangible dangers. While radio could mask social awkwardness and public discomfort, television revealed everything. It offered its subjects no places to hide and made first impressions difficult to overcome. The advantages of television were simultaneously its disadvantages, and politicians would use it or avoid it at their peril. Kennedy appeared acutely aware of these facts, and he will be remembered as America's first public president of the television age.

It is tempting to say that JFK was to television what FDR was to radio, but that understates the transformational relationship between the Kennedy

through his use of the bully pulpit, and he broke with a 113-year tradition by becoming the first president since John Adams to deliver his State of the Union address in person before Congress in 1913. Through his rhetorical skills, especially during World War I, Wilson established the presidency as an office of strong leadership at both the national and the international level. Franklin D. Roosevelt relied heavily on the bully pulpit, particularly through his use of radio, to persuade the American public to support his New Deal policies during the 1930s and rally the nation in World War II during the 1940s.

Use of the bully pulpit has become especially important since the start of the television age, when a president's overall success or failure as a leader can be determined by his rhetorical skills and public influence. Since the 1950s, four presidents stand out as more successful in their use of the bully pulpit than others—John F. Kennedy, Ronald Reagan, Bill Clinton, and Barack Obama—due to their frequent use of speeches to explain public policy and to express, often in eloquent terms, their visions for the country. Kennedy talked of a "New Frontier" and motivated many Americans to become active in public service. Reagan considered the bully pulpit to be one of the president's most important tools, and, relying on his communication skills as an actor, he provided a strong image of moral leadership that restored Americans' faith in government institutions. Clinton's talent as an orator, and his ability to speak in an extemporaneous and empathetic manner, aided his leadership on some, if not all, of his legislative priorities, such as affirmative action and education. Obama's oratorical skill, particularly in large, formal settings, helped to elevate his candidacy in 2008, and it remains one of his most useful public relations tools as president.

administration and the news media. As indicated above, FDR's use of radio was groundbreaking, but he nonetheless kept the media at arm's length and, in so doing, preserved leverage over the purveyors of news. On the other hand, due to television's greater intimacy and the increasing assertiveness of the press, JFK made the news media partners in presidential politics. Despite, or perhaps because of, personal influence and family leverage over the press, he accepted the media not as its superior but as its equal. This does not mean that, like most modern presidents, JFK did not also manipulate, mislead, or even bully the press when it suited his purposes, but the news media's relative independence and enhanced power had eroded the inherent advantage and imbalance FDR had enjoyed. And though the media did not reveal JFK's personal indiscretions or investigate his private life as they have done with more recent presidents, not doing so was largely a function of institutional boundaries, professional ethics, and consumer demand rather than a favorable balance of power for the young president.

JFK's short tenure did not unfold in a vacuum, and, as always, historical circumstances played their part in the changes affecting the presidency. The 1960s proved to be one of the most turbulent decades in modern history, both domestically and internationally, and television offered Americans front-row seats to dramas that Hollywood could not have scripted. The showdown with the Soviets in Berlin, the Cuban missile crisis, and the Vietnam War were but three of the many international events that drew Americans to their televisions during the Kennedy and LBJ years, while race riots, antiwar protests, and assassinations at home also kept them watching. By providing coverage of these events, television broadcasters permanently ingratiated themselves with tens of millions of Americans, and traditional print outlets rode television's coattails by expanding their own reporting. As a result, the power and influence of the news media increased over the succeeding years, especially relative to the presidency and other governing institutions. The news media fed the people's curiosity and gave them access to information that had been hidden or out of reach just a few years before, and the link between the public as consumer and the media as supplier of information was cemented.

As indicated earlier in this chapter, a presidency open to the public was both a curse and a blessing, since greater exposure posed risks as well as benefits. During the 1960s and 1970s, it was frequently a curse, as the risks ultimately undermined two presidencies. The LBJ administration was plagued by a credibility gap that resulted from media coverage of the Vietnam War, forcing the president to withdraw from the 1968 election, and Richard Nixon was exposed as a liar by a press corps searching relentlessly for clues of wrongdoing. Their successors, though honest and well meaning, learned the hard way that the television age would not be kind to those who lacked natural grace and charisma and that style was just as important as substance in a media-driven political environment. Neither Gerald Ford nor Jimmy Carter had much charm or photogenic appeal, and their presidencies were harmed by public awkwardness and an inability to engage their audiences. These were the realities of the public presidency.

The Public Presidency and the Electorate

As obvious as it may be, the public presidency could not exist without the public, which means it depends on people who can actively participate in the political processes that necessitate communication with the presidency and whose rights as voters are guaranteed. Aside from prevailing ideas regarding government by elites, one of the reasons the early presidency remained private was a relatively narrow electorate. While a far greater number of Americans were eligible to vote than was the case elsewhere, most people were still barred from the franchise. Nonpropertied white men, women, slaves, Native Americans, and many others did not have the franchise, so a true public dialogue between political leaders and their people would not have been possible even if presidential practices had been different. Political reform thus coincided with electoral reform, and, as the electorate expanded, so did the rhetorical scope of the presidency.

Prior to the 20th century, the Reconstruction amendments were the most crucial electoral reform initiatives since the 1820s and 1830s, with the Fourteenth Amendment serving as the basis for the eventual inclusion of minorities in the electorate. During the 20th century, important electoral changes enabled political participation by an ever larger proportion of the population, as previously disenfranchised groups gained constitutional recognition. The Nineteenth Amendment, ratified in 1920, extended the vote to women, and, several decades later, the Twenty-Sixth Amendment lowered the eligible voting age from 21 to 18. Next to the Nineteenth Amendment, by far the most significant electoral reform measure was the Voting Rights Act of 1965, which LBJ ushered through Congress following the passage of landmark Great Society legislation. The Voting Rights Act finally gave teeth to the Fourteenth and Fifteenth Amendments, removing barriers created through generations of discriminatory practices by state and local governments.

The enfranchisement and political empowerment of voices that had lain silent throughout most of American history altered the dynamic between presidents and the public, not least because the upper middle-class priorities of the white Protestant majority that had controlled public opinion was not representative of a more inclusive electorate. During the last 40 years, the presidency's dialogue with the public has been more complex as a result, reflecting increased electoral diversity and the growing influence of minorities and women. The proliferation of media outlets that cater to specialized audiences has facilitated the continuing incorporation of previously disaffected groups and enhanced public access to presidential politics. As the years have passed, those groups have become more or less equal partners with other members of the electorate, and they have demonstrated their growing power by securing a foothold among the major political parties.

The ongoing democratization of the electorate has translated into the further popularization of presidential politics. Some presidents and presidential candidates have responded by attempting to be all things to all people, while others have courted only the support of a fervent majority. Either way, elections have become beauty contests among candidates attempting to leverage their popularity and personal assets. Likewise, presidents seek to maintain popularity and minimize opposition in order to sustain high public approval, thereby ensuring reelection or a favorable legacy, or both. Measuring popularity has become a science, or perhaps an art, as presidential advisers gather data from polls, surveys, and focus groups, and communication experts shape and reshape presidential rhetoric to maximize its effectiveness and ensure mass appeal. In such a setting, press secretaries are no longer sufficient, so the modern presidency is equipped with a communications director whose staff formulates proactive communication strategies that convey policy objectives by optimizing presidential popularity. With the myriad interests represented by public opinion, nothing is left to chance.

Presidential Elections, Primaries, and Candidate-Centered Politics

The continued popularization of presidential politics has produced corresponding changes in the elections process. Throughout the 20th century, the power of presidential candidates relative to their political parties increased steadily, especially as candidates attracted ever-greater attention from the media and the public. With the advent of the public presidency and the assertion of influence by the electorate, party-centered nominating procedures came under fire, and pressure steadily mounted for the democratization of the process by which candidates were selected. By the 1960s, a number of states were holding primary elections, whose purpose was to shift power away from party delegates to the voters themselves. As national disillusionment with government and public officials grew, particularly during the late 1960s and early 1970s, reformist momentum culminated in changes that permanently altered the balance of power between parties and candidates. During the 1972 presidential election, most states held primaries to determine delegate votes, and, in 1976, every state had either a primary election or a caucus, thereby ending the long period of party domination.

From these changes emerged a system of *candidate-centered politics* in which parties, though still important, play a subsidiary role as fundraising organizations for nominees, providing the infrastructure and support network necessary to run successful campaigns. Candidates emerged as the clear winners, making strategic decisions and managing campaigns according to personal priorities and not party dictates. This does not mean that political parties no longer matter to the electorate, because party loyalty has remained a formidable factor in elections, but voters increasingly pay attention to candidates as individuals, and their choices reflect a preoccupation with personalities rather than party platforms. Presidential campaigns have become elaborate and extensive as candidates spend substantial sums and mobilize armies of volunteers and staff to market themselves throughout the United States. In just a few years, presidential elections were transformed from a bureaucratic process run by the major political parties into a public spectacle fueled by the news media and revolving around individual personalities.

More than anything else, campaigns of this sort require money, and successful campaigns demand a great deal of money. During the last 30 years, since the shift to candidate-centered elections, presidential campaigns have consumed ever-increasing amounts of money. What at one point cost millions of dollars became tens of millions, then hundreds of millions, and has recently crossed into the billions. Critics have consistently argued that all this money has skewed presidential politics, creating a system that caters to the wealthy and produces presidents who are beholden to the wealthy. They have repeatedly attempted to redress the apparent inequities through campaign-finance reform, which has not always survived constitutional scrutiny. The Supreme Court has upheld contribution limits but has invalidated spending limits as violations of free-speech guarantees in the First Amendment, and presidents have been loath to bite the hand that feeds them, being less then persistent in seeking further curbs. Efforts to eradicate so-called soft money, which refers to unregulated contributions made directly to parties instead of candidates, led to moves to simply reroute such funds through other channels, demonstrating further that spending limits are difficult to establish and enforce. They cannot successfully overcome First Amendment hurdles, nor can they change the fact that candidate-centered elections for a public presidency are invariably capital intensive.

Elections in the United States today are expensive for all sorts of reasons, not the least of which is the cost of advertising and marketing in a what has become a veritable media circus. Media coverage is continuous, unrelenting, and ubiquitous. With the Internet, network television, cable television, radio, and traditional print outlets driving tens of thousands of media sources that operate nonstop, what is considered comprehensive or even representative? How do presidential candidates decide where to spend their advertising dollars? Saturation is impossible to attain, but those with sufficient funds have tried. And once candidates become presidents, how do they address the unending media barrage to which they are subjected day after day? These questions offer no easy answers, but they underscore a political certainty in today's world. While the news media emerged as equal partners in the public presidency of the 1960s, they have gained the upper hand over presidents during the past several years, occasionally setting their agendas and, at times, even bullying them. The irony is that America's presidents, not the news media, opened this Pandora's box. Where it will all end is anybody's guess.

CONCLUSION

Of course, Americans need not pity their presidents, because the reality is not as dire as it appears. The news media may have unprecedented power, influence, and access, but so too do the nation's chief executives. On the whole, they have responded effectively to institutional challenges and the shifting boundaries between government and the press. Admittedly, some recent occupants of the White House have not been as successful as others, but they have accepted the public presidency for better or worse. Without a doubt, the most remarkable public presidents have been Ronald Reagan and Bill Clinton. Their differences greatly outweighed their similarities, but they were both superlative communicators. They enhanced the rhetorical potential of the presidency and set standards for others to follow. Together, and each in his own way, Reagan and Clinton demonstrated the adaptability of the presidency and its ability to confront the television age. Most important,

President Barack Obama speaks with former president Bill Clinton and senior adviser Valerie Jarrett in the Roosevelt Room of the White House on July 14, 2010. *(Wikipedia)*

by embracing its extroverted nature and using it to their advantage, they personified the public presidency and secured its relationship with the American people. That relationship has not been uniform or predictable, but it has been democratic and mutual. Reagan was a fatherly figure who, unlike FDR, proved that public presidents can be paternal but not paternalistic. Clinton, on the other hand, illustrated that empathy and neighborly charisma are the right vehicles for intellect and knowledge and that public presidents rule from within and not from without. President Barack Obama, though not as smooth or silver-tongued as either Reagan or Clinton, has learned from both of his predecessors. As the first president who came of age during the computer age, he is as qualified as anyone to prepare the public presidency for an unpredictable future in the media spotlight.

CHAPTER 6

Vice Presidents, Presidential Advisers, and America's First Ladies

History is a strange business. Its purpose is to explain the past by revealing what really happened. Unlike its sister disciplines in the humanities and social sciences, it supposedly tells the whole story. While political science, economics, anthropology, and sociology concentrate on specific aspects of the human condition, history presents the big picture. Most scholars look at individual parts, but historians put those parts together. Yet, though the aim of history is completeness, the results are often the opposite. To be comprehensive, historians must be selective; to illustrate complexity, they must simplify. Paradoxically, to be complete, history must be incomplete. In the end, historians are nothing more than impressionist painters, recreating the past in a way that highlights its most prominent features but that often blurs the details. They hope readers will get the big picture, convinced that nothing crucial was omitted or sacrificed for the benefit of the whole. For clarification of those parts of the story insufficiently or entirely unexplained, readers must look to a different kind of artist.

Like it or not, completeness is an elusive goal. Unfortunately, something is always lost in its pursuit, and, just as unfortunately, the magnitude and significance of those losses may be considerable. Take the presidency. Typical accounts of its development focus almost exclusively on the presidents themselves, leaving the impression that they singlehandedly ran the country. Some of their most illustrious advisers often play important roles, but the complex operation of the institution is not addressed. Except for a few of the more notorious examples, vice presidents certainly are not very conspicuous, and neither are chiefs of staff, or budget directors, secretaries of transportation, speechwriters, or any of thousands of other public officials and employees that make the presidency what it is. Without a doubt, the presidency is the president's domain, and the president is its most powerful member, but it is able to function only because of the armies of executive appointees and support staff. This chapter focuses on those armies. They are often neglected by historians and other scholars, but their role is critical nonetheless.

THE VICE PRESIDENCY

Perhaps the most thankless position in Washington, the vice presidency has been the butt of jokes since its creation. Lacking the respect accorded the presidency, not even its occupants have been impressed by it. John Adams, the first to hold the office, referred to it as the most insignificant political institution in history, Harry Truman complained that he did nothing but attend weddings and funerals; Lyndon Johnson quipped that it was the worst job he ever had, while many others claimed the vice president simply waits for the president to die. Since only four out of 44 presidents died in office, four were assassinated, and one resigned, are the American people to believe that all but nine vice presidents have served for naught? Clearly, the vice presidency lacks both the prestige and the power of the presidency, and it may not be the post to which most politicians aspire, but, surely, it cannot be as trivial as all that. As was the case with all of the offices that they created, the framers of the Constitution must have had sound reasons for establishing it, and its duties must be more substantial than its detractors commonly assert.

Historically speaking, the vice presidency is unusual. Created to meet the unique demands of a presidential system of government, it was an institution without precedent in the late 18th century. The American colonies had some experience with

John Adams, the first vice president and second president of the United States *(Library of Congress)*

lieutenant governors, but these officers had been a completely different species of public official. The vice presidency was an experiment, if not a gamble, that eventually succeeded, but it was not necessarily the most logical option at the time. The outcome of efforts to create a political system without kings and preserve stability in a society without hereditary succession, the vice presidency was not the most prominent institution created by the framers of the Constitution. Nevertheless, contrary to John Adams's sarcastic characterization, it was not intended to be the least significant. From a modern perspective, despite long periods of inactivity or comparative obscurity, the vice presidency has become one of the more essential.

The Vice Presidency and the Dilemma of the Framers' Intent

Students of founding-era political history can search far and wide, but they will find only a few references to the vice presidency in contemporary literature. Of the hundreds of pamphlets, essays, and letters generated by American writers about the Constitution, not one focuses on the vice presidency itself. Alexander Hamilton devoted two paragraphs to it in Federalist 68, but his comments offer no insight into the primary purposes of the institution. Although a number of other documents reflect the concerns of the Anti-Federalists over the vice president's role in the Senate, they reveal nothing about the nature of the office, nor do they shed any light on its theoretical foundations. If the framers of the Constitution had anything but minor interest in the vice presidency, the historical record seems to provide no proof of it. Indeed, judging from the lack of contemporary information about the vice presidency, assertions regarding its insignificance appear all the more credible, and issues such as the framers' intent become irrelevant.

The problem with this conclusion is that it contradicts everything scholars know about the framers and their dedication to intellectual consistency and coherence. It is not probable that they would have saddled the executive branch with an institution about which they knew little and cared even less. Some provisions in the Constitution, as evident products of compromise, are somewhat ambiguous, while others are obsolete, but not one was trivial or superfluous at the time of adoption, so to assume that the vice presidency was an afterthought is nonsensical. Most likely, because it elicited minimal debate during the ratification process, it attracted little attention from contemporary writers. In addition, as illustrated in the first two chapters, much of what scholars have discovered about the executive branch in general has been a product less of explicit explanations left by the framers than of inferences drawn from related writings. As we know, Article II of the Constitution is short on detail, and other documents do not successfully resolve the consequent ambiguities, which only compounds existing problems of interpretation concerning the vice presidency. Finally, though the vice presidency was far from insignificant to the framers, it was not as critical as some of the other institutions, especially those that had so obviously failed under the Confederation government.

Aside from references in founding-era writings and scholarly inferences, the best single source about the vice presidency is the record of the Constitutional Convention. In the early 20th century, Max Farrand compiled all relevant documents into a four-volume set that is still used today and remains the most authoritative collection of primary materials on the convention, but it is not without its shortcomings. The bulk of the material relies on James Madison's notes on the convention's proceedings, which were not published until 50 years after the adoption of the Constitution and which Madison amended several times during the intervening decades. Much other information, valuable as it may be, is compromised by inconsistency of reporting and the inherent biases of its authors, so, on the whole, the published record of the convention must be examined carefully. This does not mean that it is useless; rather, its utility as a reflection of contemporary beliefs about the Constitution and its provisions is questionable.

Farrand's compilation has clear value, but its accuracy and completeness are sufficiently compromised to pose serious doubts about its status as the authoritative source on the convention. The best guide to the framers' intentions about the vice presidency is the late 18th-century political environment itself. Only a thorough understanding of contemporary politics, prevailing political philosophies, and the framers' constitutional motivations can yield an enhanced familiarity with the original purposes of the vice presidency. Unfortunately, even many among the most informed today have no more than a passing acquaintance with such issues, and this institution has been widely susceptible to manipulation and misapprehension. Claims regarding the framers' intent are often dubious, even more so than those concerning the presidency, so expansions of power and authority seem limited only by the competing egos and ambitions of America's presidents. As the prestige and stature of the office have grown, culminating in the unprecedented vice presidency of Dick Cheney, its natural boundaries appear difficult, if not impossible, to define. Therefore, knowledge of founding-era political practices and ideologies is all the more critical. Without it, those boundaries will remain irrelevant and meaningless.

The constitutional record on the vice presidency may be meager at the same time that Western history is hardly more illuminating on the topic. It provides few compelling clues about the intended nature of the office, since the concept of a second in command is largely a modern invention. Unlike almost everything else in the Constitution, the vice presidency lacked connection to relevant classical or Renaissance examples. It did not have the intellectual lineage of other political institutions, which was highlighted by the absence of useful Athenian, Roman, or Florentine precedents. With most other aspects of the new American government, the framers looked to the past for assurance and warnings about the probability of success, but they found little regarding the vice presidency. Even the presidency, which was a new creation, rested on an intellectual foundation built over two millennia. The closest analogy to the vice presidency would have been the Roman practice of naming two consuls, who were the chief magistrates of the republic. Frequently but not exclusively, one consul would dominate the other, acting as a de facto head of state, while his co-consul assumed a subordinate role. Nonetheless, this was almost uniformly the result of individual differences in personality and not institutional design, so the situations are not really analogous.

Two Models of Vice-Presidential Authority

The most informative historical examples are actually more recent and lay much closer to home, and they addressed the framers' two principal concerns about the office of vice presidency. Not unexpectedly, both concerns stemmed from the broader need to replace the British Crown with an adequate and appropriate nonhereditary executive. The first of these was the issue of succession. A nonhereditary executive entailed no obvious or inherent mechanism of succession, whether upon the death of a president, his inability or unwillingness to serve additional terms, or the electorate's decision to replace him. That fact accordingly increased instability and uncertainty, both of which had undermined regimes throughout Western history. For all its drawbacks, hereditary monarchy had one conspicuous advantage over republican government. Since succession was determined, or fixed, automatically by the very nature of dynastic rule, monarchy promoted stability and continuity at a regime's most vulnerable juncture—political transition. To the 18th-century mind, and this was not confined to the framers of the Constitution, stability and continuity were the key objectives of legitimate governance, so a reliable mechanism of political succession was a critical requirement. Therefore, the framers had to provide the new government with a feasible means of political succession that minimized disruption and unpredictability yet preserved popular sovereignty.

Second, the framers were concerned about the nature of the relationship between the president and the vice president in the new republic. In that regard, the British Crown offered almost no insights as a relevant example, for monarchies have been typically intolerant of pretenders to the throne. While a second in command is unnecessary to secure succession in a hereditary regime because succession is automatic, such a result contradicts the logic of monarchical government itself. A monarch's authority was considered indivisible, and it could not accommodate a vice monarch of some sort.

Aside from these theoretical considerations, personal dynamics also played a role in preventing the division of executive authority, no matter how unequal, between a monarch and a vice monarch. Most, if not all, hereditary rulers guarded their sovereignty jealously and were unwilling to share it voluntarily, and they undoubtedly would not have tolerated constitutional rivals within their regimes.

The British monarchy may not have offered much inspiration with respect to the prospective relationship between presidents and vice presidents, but colonial experience definitely did. Most colonial governments had a lieutenant governor who served under a governor appointed by the Crown. Some of these lieutenant governors, such as in Massachusetts, were relatively active and possessed considerable powers, performing legislative, executive, and judicial duties. They truly were the second in command, assuming leadership during gubernatorial absences and managing the day-to-day governance of their colonies. In Massachusetts, because lieutenant governors were directly accountable to the colonists themselves, they were more visible and might enjoy more popular support than the governors, and they became an indispensable part of colonial governance. The relationship between governors and lieutenant governors was often unpredictable and might be strained and the relationship could be exacerbated by the colonists' political manipulation of it. In the end, for the framers of the Constitution, it served more as an example of what they ought not to do than of what they should do.

Nevertheless, colonial experience suggested two options for an American vice presidency: a weak and a strong model. The strong model envisioned an active vice president sharing executive authority with the president and, like some of the more powerful colonial governors, acting as a head of government. Viewed from a modern perspective, the strong model assumed a relationship between president and vice president that is akin to that between a commanding officer (CO) and his executive officer (XO) in today's military, with the CO in charge of policy, strategic planning, and overall leadership and the XO handling the day-to-day management of the troops and the implementation of policy objectives. On the other hand, the weak model offered more or less what emerged from the Constitutional Convention, which confined the vice presidency to a clearly restricted and subordinate role within the executive branch, with limited authority focusing almost exclusively on succession. This option minimized friction between the vice presidency and the presidency and relegated the former to ceremonial functions within presidential administrations.

The strong model, however compelling, proved not feasible for several reasons, the most prominent of which was the scope of the new presidency. Because the framers restricted the authority of the presidency, a relatively vigorous vice presidency would not have been compatible with their design. As it was, the intended duties and responsibilities of the president of the republic were rather narrow, so dividing them would have unnecessarily diluted the powers of an office that had few tasks to begin with. By extension, a strong vice presidency alongside a limited presidency would encourage rivalries that could threaten the stability and unity of executive authority, which was exactly what the framers wished to avoid. They could not have foreseen the expansion of executive authority that has occurred during the last 100 years, so they never entertained the possibility that a more active vice presidency could actually be beneficial or desirable. The fact that the vice presidency of Dick Cheney secured the ultimate triumph of the strong model, which the framers had rejected out of hand, underscored one of history's more glaring ironies.

The Political Evolution of the Vice Presidency

The framers' choice of the weak model does not in any way imply that they sought to establish the vice presidency as an insignificant office. Although they created a vice presidency endowed with largely ceremonial authority, the framers believed it was one of the most important political institutions in the new government. Its establishment spoke directly to the first concern identified in the previous section, namely, the issue of succession, and was considered to be an indispensable prerequisite for stable governance in the new republic. From a purely procedural standpoint, the vice presidency provided for continuity in solving the political dilemma posed by the possibility of presidential death or incapacity, but its real value for the framers lay in what it represented. Through the electoral system originally defined in the Constitution, the framers hoped to turn the vice presidency into, for lack of a better term, a presidency in waiting, thereby eliminating the uncertainty, rivalry, and contention associated with political transitions.

By accommodating the predictability of hereditary rule within a system of popular sovereignty, they believed they would secure the best of both worlds. Per their intentions, the Constitution required electors to vote for two undifferentiated candidates during presidential elections, which was supposed to produce a president and his presumed successor and, in so doing, preserve the unity and thus the stability of the presidency. As such, the framers hoped vice presidents would be among their presidents' closest advisers, supporting presidential policy making and getting on-the-job training for the nation's highest office. Unfortunately, the framers' plans never materialized, as personal incompatibilities soon undermined original intent, relegating the vice presidency to a back seat in executive politics. The Twelfth Amendment solved the difficulty by formally acknowledging the inferiority of the vice presidency and subordinating it to the presidency in a way the framers had never intended. The resulting reduction in status handicapped the vice presidency for some time to come, and it would not recover a more substantial role until the latter part of the 20th century.

Aside from their constitutional role as presiding officers of the Senate, 19th-century vice presidents had no real power or authority. John Tyler, Millard Fillmore, Andrew Johnson, and Chester Arthur ascended to the presidency upon the deaths of William Henry Harrison, Zachary Taylor, Abraham Lincoln, and James Garfield, respectively, but their contributions as presidents did nothing to enhance the reputation of the vice presidency. None of the four distinguished himself in the White House, at least not in a positive way. Competent and conscientious, Arthur was the most effective of the four, doing nothing to disgrace the office. Fillmore displayed overt partisanship and a lack of leadership ability, while Tyler and Johnson had a special talent for making political enemies. Johnson's impeachment merely added to the impression of incompetence, confirming widespread skepticism regarding the quality of the nation's vice presidents. The 19th century was without a doubt the vice presidency's time in the wilderness.

The assassination of William McKinley and the succession of Theodore Roosevelt to the presidency in 1901 began a slow albeit intermittent rehabilitation of the vice presidency. Roosevelt was a vocal and comparatively assertive vice president, and he became one of America's most admired chief executives, whose effectiveness in the presidency alerted observers to the potential importance of a historically neglected office. As is so often the case, Roosevelt was also helped by a unique confluence of events that turned the ordinary into the extraordinary. McKinley's death at a critical juncture in America's emergence as an international power offered Roosevelt a tailor-made opportunity to showcase his skills. However, despite Roosevelt's accomplishments, the expansion of vice-presidential power and authority thereafter was gradual at best. A hundred years of political momentum would not be reversed so easily, and, over the following four decades, the vice presidency largely languished. The death of yet another president, Warren Harding, did not prove as fortuitous for his successor, not least because Calvin Coolidge was no Teddy Roosevelt.

In 1945, as in 1901, an unusual set of circumstances produced another opportunity for someone who, from a historical but not a contemporary perspective, seemed handpicked for the occasion. At the time, no one could have predicted that Harry Truman, an unassuming clothier from Missouri, would become the architect of America's national security state and one of its most formidable commanders in chief. Compared unfavorably to FDR in almost every possible way by the public, Truman was expected to fade into anonymity with the rest of America's vice presidents. FDR's death in April 1945 shattered those expectations and served as the springboard for an exceptionally effective tenure, especially with respect to foreign policy. Unlike in 1901, the Washington establishment and also the public in 1945, aware of the realities confronting a world that faced the challenge left in the wake of a global war, recognized the significance of a properly qualified and adequately experienced vice president. At a time when U.S.-Soviet tensions were escalating and nuclear war presented a tangible threat, the possible repercussions of a less than competent presidency due to the succession of an unqualified vice president were staggering. Quite conceivably, the fate of the United States could rest with the vice presidency, so vice presidents needed to assume a more prominent role in presidential politics.

The Modern Vice Presidency

Dwight Eisenhower was as aware as anyone of the changing political realities in postwar America, and his vice president, Richard Nixon, played a more active role than had any of his predecessors. As a clear symbol of his elevated status, Nixon was the first vice president to be given an office in the White House, and he participated regularly in cabinet meetings and other high-level deliberations. Most of his authority centered on foreign policy responsibilities, as Eisenhower relied on Nixon's expertise in this area. Vice President Nixon represented the administration on several foreign trips, increasing the visibility of an institution that had been relatively anonymous throughout the previous 150 years. With Nixon, the vice presidency changed forever, undergoing a gradual but inexorable expansion during the following 50 years. While it never quite shed its image as a consolation prize, what it lacked in form and style it made up for in substance.

Like Nixon, Lyndon Johnson was a more vigorous vice president than had previously been the norm, but, as a member of John F. Kennedy's administration, he never became part of the president's inner circle. Personality conflicts between LBJ and the Kennedys were a secret to no one, and mutual respect was not always in evidence either. Still, LBJ's political skill and domestic-policy experience were an evident asset, and the administration relied on his help in areas that were eventually addressed more closely through LBJ's Great Society. Reflecting a trend that has characterized presidential politics during the past few decades, LBJ's true value for JFK lay not in his talents as vice president but in his electoral influence. During the television age, as the further popularization of politics supported the rise of a public presidency, presidential candidates sought to minimize electoral vulnerabilities through running mates who compensated for their perceived weaknesses. JFK was a Catholic from the Northeast with a patrician background, which did not endear him to many voters in the South, so in the 1960 campaign he picked Johnson as his vice president to help in delivering the South to secure the presidency.

President Eisenhower and Vice President Richard Nixon, August 21, 1954 *(Dwight D. Eisenhower Library and Museum)*

During the next 40 years, the process of picking the appropriate running mate became a political art perfected through polling, lengthy deliberations, and careful vetting of prospective candidates. Presidential nominees and their advisers have focused on vice-presidential choices who provide balance and optimize electability, focusing on what a potential running mate brings to the ticket. As such, presidential tickets often yield strange pairings whose logic is dictated not by mutual compatibility and respect but by cost-benefit analysis and cold calculation. That is why John McCain chose Sarah Palin in 2008 and George H. W. Bush selected Dan Quayle in 1988. These political odd couples, though common, are not universal, as the Clinton-Gore ticket in 1992 demonstrated, but the need to have running mates who complement nominees' strengths and mask their weaknesses has been the overriding factor in decision making. Bill Clinton and Al Gore may have been personally better suited for each other than many other presidential candidates and their running mates, but Al Gore would not have been considered by the Clinton team had he not brought something substantial, such as his federal government experience and his family name, to the ticket.

The most immediate consequence of the increased scrutiny of vice-presidential candidates had been a corresponding increase in public awareness, so vice presidents are no longer the obscure figures they were less than 60 years ago. By no means as visible or recognizable as America's presidents, many of its vice presidents have nonetheless become household names, augmenting the stature of an office once considered superfluous. As may be obvious, not all modern vice presidents have fared equally well, nor have they all benefited from the vice presidency's greater exposure. Vice-presidential gaffes have become fodder for a press eager to catch public officials off guard, and they have made the administrations of which they have been a part guilty by association. Spiro Agnew's resignation in 1973 due to his criminal activities did not help an already embattled Richard Nixon, nor did it do much for a vice presidency that had only recently emerged from the shadows. Walter Mondale was an honest man, but his plodding style and uninspiring approach to politics did nothing but confirm the public's lack of affection for the Carter administration. His successor, George H. W. Bush, despite serving with one of the most popular presidents in history, did little to improve the image of the institution, while Dan Quayle, who was vice president in the Bush administration, actually damaged it.

In contrast, Al Gore was unquestionably the most effective vice president since the creation of the American republic, eclipsing many presidents in terms of his accomplishments. Intimately involved in policy making, and taking a special interest in environmental issues, bureaucratic reform, and information technology, Gore was a trusted adviser to President Clinton and an integral member of the administration. He elevated the profile of the office and repaired the damage inflicted on it by his predecessors. When Gore decided to seek the presidency himself in 2000, nobody questioned his qualifications after eight years as the most powerful vice president to date in American history. Unfortunately for Gore, he lost an extremely close race to George W. Bush, who had named Dick Cheney as his running mate. During his two terms, Cheney became even more powerful than Gore had been, leading some of his detractors to refer to him mockingly as the real president. A seasoned veteran of two previous administrations with a take-no-prisoners mentality, Cheney was the president's point man on national security issues. Viewed as the leading advocate of war in the Middle East, Cheney possessed unprecedented authority over strategic planning and military operations, and he held substantial responsibility over diplomatic issues.

According to his critics, Cheney's expansive use of vice-presidential powers may have done the institution as much harm as good, since it exposed an unconstitutional accumulation of authority within an institution that was intended to have little of it. Of course, Cheney's supporters claim such arguments to be hypocritical and disingenuous, based not on substantive reasoning but on a personal dislike of the former vice president. In fact, both sides are right. The vice presidency has surely become something the framers

Vice President Dick Cheney speaks to a crowd of service members at Balad Air Base, Iraq, on March 18, 2008. This photograph was taken by Senior Airman Julianne Showalter. *(Wikipedia)*

would not have sanctioned, but, at the same time, no one seems dissatisfied with the outcome or willing to complain about it unless a political opponent is in charge. The attention the office has attracted over the past several years may cause future occupants to err on the side of caution, if for no other reason than the unwillingness of the president under whom they serve to tolerate potential liabilities. Indeed, Barack Obama's vice president has chosen a less confrontational path by reducing the profile of the office during his first year on the job. Perhaps prophetically, as an experienced legislator with impressive foreign policy credentials, Vice President Joseph Biden has, consciously or unconsciously, steered the institution back toward the standard set by Richard Nixon in the 1950s. Nixon was far from docile or subservient, yet he acknowledged the vice presidency's inherent limitations, and he attempted to make the most of its capabilities within them by never attempting to outshine his chief executive. Whether this is the direction in which the vice presidency is now headed is too early to tell, but it may offer this historically neglected but recently overstretched institution greater legitimacy.

THE CABINET AND THE PRESIDENTIAL STAFF

George Washington arrived in New York, the nation's temporary capital, during spring 1789 to head an administration smaller than most city governments today. In fact, the entire executive branch comprised the sparse remnants of the Continental army, President Washington, Vice President John Adams, and a handful of public officials inherited from the Confederation government. As Congress assumed its constitutional duties and began creating an institutional infrastructure, the presidency did not grow by much. By the mid-1790s, the legislature had added the secretaries of war, state, and the treasury, a postmaster general, an attorney general but no Justice Department, a minimal navy and its secretary, and a few tax officers. That was all. It did not provide for a presidential staff, nor even a personal secretary for Washington, a man who had become accustomed to numerous servants, aides, and slaves on his Mount Vernon estate. Deprived of the resources available to modern presidents, Washington composed his own speeches, wrote his own letters and memoranda, and ran his own errands. The early presidency was neither glamorous nor elaborate, lacking the luxuries and complexities that presidents today take for granted.

Overwhelmed by clerical tasks, America's third president, Thomas Jefferson, broke new ground by hiring several aides. However, because Congress would not provide presidents with a salaried assistant until the late 1850s, Jefferson paid them out of his own pocket. His successors would have to wait until the 20th century for more substantial gains, which, after modest increases during the Progressive Era, finally came with FDR's election. By then, Congress had augmented the cabinet, establishing several new departments between 1849 and 1913. In 1939, it also created the *Executive Office of the President* to address the needs of the modern White House, and the number of experts, assistants, and advisers increased exponentially during the ensuing years. Ultimately, the president's circle of aides became large enough to populate a small town, while the legions of nonpolitical workers servicing the White House, its grounds, and its employees dwarfed the resources available to many cities.

History and Presidential Advisers

Unlike vice presidents, executive aides of one sort or another have been a continuous presence among regimes since the beginning of politics. Rulers have traditionally relied on an inner circle of confidants, friends, or family members for advice, support, and guidance. Although these advisers were not part of a cabinet or institutional framework of some kind until quite recently, their contributions have been indispensable. In England during the late Middle Ages, as the responsibilities of kingship became increasingly complex and monarchs required input regarding the various interests of the realm, the foundations of the royal court began to emerge. Informal executive councils appeared alongside royal officials whose roles varied according to the monarchy's evolving needs. By the early 16th century, the most significant of these had become the Privy Council, which, over the ensuing 200 years, functioned as the monarchy's principal advisory and administrative body.

Aside from their councils, English kings benefited from a steadily expanding staff of personal aides, servants, and admirers who formed the core of a royal court that was almost as elaborate as today's White House. The royal court was an impressive creation, remembered as much for its impact on English politics as for its opulence and sheer size. Lacking the organizational logic of today's bureaucracies, it was often sprawling and wasteful, but effective monarchs were able to use it to their fullest advantage. In the early part of the 18th century, institutional innovations brought greater efficiency and tighter control, but political patronage frequently undermined professionalism and competence. The Privy Council gave way to the modern cabinet, as government by ministers replaced the decentralized and somewhat amorphous practices of the past. The prime minister and his cabinet were not just the king's political advisers, but also the chief policy makers and top administrators in the kingdom.

The framers of the Constitution heeded the British example, deciding to steer clear of a strong cabinet and an extensive presidential bureaucracy. The implications of the British model were disturbing, not least because an active cabinet could easily overpower the presidency and destabilize the republic. The new government would be limited in scope and authority, and the British executive model could not be reconciled with those intentions. In addition, given the presidency's modest requirements, a large executive staff would have been unnecessary, not to mention offensive to a public that equated extravagance with corruption. So the framers settled on a weak cabinet comprising no more than the most essential executive departments and fulfilling an advisory, not administrative, role. Rejecting the idea of cabinet members as ministers, which is what they have actually become over the past century, the framers wanted to restrict the authority of executive departments, so they never even mentioned the cabinet in the Constitution. Except for an indirect reference to heads of executive departments in Article II, the document is silent on the matter. The framers' silence is as telling a signal of their intent as any amount of explanation would have been.

As for a presidential staff, the Constitution ignores the topic altogether. Anything more than a bare-bones executive infrastructure would have been incompatible with a comparatively small and unobtrusive presidency. Moreover, due to their aversion to a burgeoning British bureaucracy that supposedly promoted the corruption of imperial rule prior to American independence, the framers wanted to put nothing in place that resembled a royal court in any fashion. By the mid-18th century, the royal court had become a symbol of luxury, laziness, and moral decay, so the framers of the Constitution took care to avoid authorizing the establishment of a similar institution within the new American government. That presidents were denied even a minimal staff illustrates the framers' intent to make the American presidency as nonimperial, or maybe anti-imperial, as possible. Of course, this goal was achievable because presidential duties and responsibilities were limited during the early republic and, as such, not overly resource intensive. Still, it was a lasting goal that confined the growth of the presidency for quite some time.

The Cabinet

The president's cabinet was the object of prolonged controversy during the 1790s, with Congress attempting to tie the president's hands at every turn. Debate raged about the amount of independence department secretaries should have and the control presidents would have over them. While some members of Congress believed that giving secretaries discretionary authority over respective policy areas was prudent, most feared that an assertive cabinet would either rival the president for power and status or increase the authority of the president himself beyond acceptable limits. As a result, the creation of even the most essential departments was fraught with contention and turmoil, discouraging efforts to expand the cabinet for years. Congress eventually provided the president with three cabinet secretaries, who were the heads of the Departments of State, War, and the Treasury, which hardly broke new ground since they were inherited from the Confederation government. The legislature added an attorney general to prosecute all cases involving the U.S. government, but it did not create a Justice Department until 1870.

As intended by the framers, the early cabinet was primarily an advisory body with few administrative responsibilities. Without a doubt, during the 1790s, the most prominent of the three departments was the Treasury, mostly so because of its first secretary, Alexander Hamilton. Almost immediately, Hamilton tested the department's limited authority by spearheading the administration's effort to create centralized financial markets that would encourage industrial growth. George Washington's financial and economic policies were Hamilton's brainchild, which aroused anxiety over the Treasury secretary's political influence within the administration. Ironically, as one of the authors of the *Federalist Papers*, Hamilton was as familiar as anyone with the framers' intent because he had been one of those framers himself, yet his tenure at Treasury contradicted almost every prevailing assumption about the president's cabinet. Hamilton's motivations for his apparent about-face remain the subject of debate, but the change of heart demonstrates the difficulty of preserving a correspondence between intentions and practices in the real world.

Over the course of the 19th century, as the nation's territorial expansion drove foreign policy, the secretary of war played an increasingly important role, though the effectiveness of individual secretaries was frequently

National Security Advisor Zbigniew Brzezinski, Secretary of the Treasury Michael Blumenthal, President Carter, and Secretary of State Cyrus Vance aboard Air Force One, traveling to London for the G7 Economic Summit 1977 *(Jimmy Carter Library)*

compromised by their lack of strategic vision and leadership ability. Indeed, during the Civil War, Abraham Lincoln was so dissatisfied with the War Department's management of the conflict that he became the chief strategist in the administration. Nevertheless, the significance of the Department of War had been firmly established by then, and its role would expand during the subsequent decades. Like the War Department, the State Department proved itself to be an indispensable part of presidential administrations. The United States was beset by various unresolved border disputes that had lingered since the Revolutionary War period, and the resolution of those disputes was a top priority for the young nation. As the presidency's diplomatic arm, the Department of State took the lead in those efforts and, in so doing, promoted the country's international legitimacy.

The State Department was so valued and respected that the office became the stepping-stone to the presidency of the early republic. In fact, five of the first eight presidents had been secretaries of state, with only Washington, Adams, and Andrew Jackson excluded. Thomas Jefferson, James Madison, James Monroe, John Quincy Adams, and Martin Van Buren had come from the Department of State, which confirmed its enviable stature within the executive branch. Together with the secretaries of war and the treasury, secretaries of state would enjoy an elevated status within presidential administrations, and, as Congress began creating additional departments, the initial three formed part of an emerging inner cabinet. Not all offices represented in the extended cabinet were equally important, while, as the cabinet grew, not all of its members needed to be involved in most aspects of presidential policy making. The inner cabinet better reflected national priorities and the realities of presidential politics in modern America, so its prevalence rose steadily. After Congress created the Justice Department, America's attorney generals joined this inner circle of advisers and policy makers, as did secretaries of defense following the conversion of the War Department into the Department of Defense.

Since World War II, some of the nation's greatest public servants have been members of the so-called inner cabinet, occasionally eclipsing their presidents in terms of status and prestige. Likewise, some of America's most controversial figures have also been part of this group of presidential confidants. Famous or infamous, they have become household names, inspiring as much debate and political discussion, to say nothing of scholarship, as anyone else—in politics or otherwise. George Marshall, John Foster Dulles, Robert Kennedy, Henry Kissinger, Janet Reno, Colin Powell, Donald Rumsfeld, and Hillary Clinton have been just a few of those who have generated significant attention from the American people, the press, and those who study the presidency. Whether they have helped the presidency or hindered it, members of the president's inner cabinet have been top-level advisers. An impressive political pedigree may be no guarantee of competent or effective leadership, but these individuals were chosen, at least in part, because of their pedigrees, which underscores the significance of the departments they have represented.

In 1849, Congress created the Interior Department to manage public lands and the nation's natural resources. The rapid growth of federal territories during the 19th century strained government resources, which put pressure on legislators to provide the presidency with an adequate means of meeting rising responsibilities. Unlike the president's inner cabinet, the Interior Department was largely administrative and did not exist for advisory purposes. This should not imply that the inner cabinet did not have administrative duties, for those increased dramatically during the 20th century, but its advisory privileges set it apart from the extended cabinet. Whereas the four key executive departments were established both to advise American presidents and to address administrative requirements, the others arose purely out of an institutional demand for resources and bureaucratic specialization. As changing economic and social conditions stretched the capabilities of the executive branch, Congress built a bureaucratic infrastructure for the industrial age around new cabinet departments and regulatory agencies. Although a few of the secretaries of these departments have been extraordinarily close to their presidents, that has not been typical, nor was it ever anyone's intent.

By the beginning of the 20th century, ongoing social and economic change spurred the addition of the Departments of Agriculture, Commerce, and Labor to the cabinet, enhancing the presidency's ability to promote targeted education, research, and regulation. These three departments were established in direct response to mass industrialization, as Congress resolved to help workers, farmers, students, and businesses affected by the transformations that were then ongoing. The rise of the welfare state produced momentum for further additions, such as the Departments of Health and Human Services, Housing and Urban Development, and Education, while regulatory pressures resulted in the Departments of Energy and Transportation. In 1989, efforts to institutionalize aid for America's war veterans culminated in the Department of Veterans Affairs, and the 15th and final cabinet department, Homeland Security, appeared following the terrorist attacks on September 11, 2001.

The Presidential Staff
The framers were convinced the presidency would maintain its modest proportions because nothing in the Constitution pointed to the contrary. Despite anxieties over other aspects of the new government, they felt reassured about the presidency. Convinced that the presidency would never resemble the British Crown, they dismissed fears of an unmanageable executive behemoth akin to the royal court as groundless. After all, their intentions regarding the extent and scope of the American presidency were widely acknowledged and respected, so why should anyone have thought that those fears were actually warranted. The eventual emergence of just such a behemoth is one more of those ironies that have marked the evolution of the presidency. Repelled by the British royal court, the framers worked diligently to establish a presidency that would be its opposite, but, by the late 20th century the presidency looked more like its twin.

Indeed, the presidency today is, in many ways, the modern equivalent of the 18th-century British court. Obviously, it lacks a hereditary monarch, royal family, and private attendants, but it shares many of the older institution's traits. The modern presidency may be professionally organized, while the royal court was poorly structured, if not shapeless, but the composition and purpose of both institutions are strikingly similar. Like the royal court, the modern presidency includes scores of aides and advisers, throngs of followers and admirers whose careers depend on their relationship with the boss, a number of executive councils that address different areas of foreign and domestic policy, and a small but powerful circle of confidants who have the chief executive's ear and control access to him. Furthermore, like the royal palaces of old, the White House is a strategic stronghold. Protected like no other structure in the United States and built to sustain the first family and its staff, the White House is a city onto itself. With its own security force, service and maintenance personnel, provisions, and support facilities, its purpose is to keep the president inside and practically everyone else outside.

With the establishment of the Executive Office of the President (EOP), the White House became more than just the place in which America's chief executives lived and worked. The appearance of the EOP spurred the presidency's development into a bureaucratic giant. The cold war and escalating threats from within and without, on the other hand, fueled the transformation of the executive residence into a fortress. Both factors have been responsible for the evolution of the White House toward something its early occupants would not have recognized or admired. Nevertheless, the creation of the EOP was necessary because the administrative requirements of the modern presidency had become too complex for business as usual. The EOP facilitates policy making through various councils whose specialized expertise promotes informed decision making at the top levels. The EOP also serves as a vital link between presidents and the American people, processing vital information concerning public opinion, national needs and demands, and political priorities.

The most critical part of the EOP is the White House staff, a central administrative network that houses some of the most influential officials in Washington. At almost 500 employees, the staff runs the White House and coordinates policy making within the presidency. With a staff ranging from clerical help to the presidents' top lieutenants, it is the bureaucratic nerve center of the executive branch. All roads to the president converge at the White House, and no one gets through without the knowledge or permission of the chief executive's closest aides. The gatekeeper at the White House, and arguably the linchpin of an effective presidency, is the *chief of staff*, who is the highest ranking member of the EOP. A position used, if not created, by Dwight Eisenhower and modeled on its military namesake, it did not become a regular part of the presidency until some 20 years later. Most presidential scholars acknowledge H. R. Haldeman, who was appointed by Richard Nixon, as the first actual chief of staff. Given Haldeman's involvement in the Watergate scandal and his subsequent conviction for federal crimes, that the position survived is a testament to the importance of the office. That survival not only confirms the centrality and value of the chief of staff, but also demonstrates the need for professional management of a presidential staff whose resources and organizational requirements dwarf those of most corporate executives.

Although the chief of staff has frequently been called the second most powerful person in Washington, a select group of presidential assistants is just as powerful. Others, such as cabinet secretaries, may have more constitutional authority, but, aside from the president, no one has more real power than a small circle of people within the White House. These are the individuals whom presidents trust most, and theirs are the opinions that matter. Perhaps not as visible or as prominent as cabinet secretaries, vice presidents, or agency heads, the president's confidants among the White House staff are indispensable. With deceptively ordinary titles such as adviser, counsel, assistant, or aide, their importance and influence may not be evident to outsiders, but their value is clear to all insiders. They shape policy, provide political analysis, set the president's agenda, manage his communication and interaction with practically everyone, and promote his objectives with Congress and other Washington institutions. Without them, the modern presidency would come to a halt.

Despite their relative anonymity, the television age has catapulted a handful of these presidential power brokers to stardom, bestowing on them a celebrity status that is rare even for politicians. Names such as David Gergen, Pat Buchanan, George Stephanopoulos, and Karl Rove have become almost as recognizable as those of the presidents they served. The public exposure of the president's closest advisers has not been a welcome development, attracting unneeded attention by the press and a spotlight over one of the most sensitive parts of the presidency. Whereas presidents have become increasingly visible, they have worked hard to keep the political games, manipulations, and horse trading that characterize policy making away from the public eye. Common sense dictates that greater scrutiny of the most intimate and private relationships in the White House can undermine the effectiveness of the president and his leverage over others in Washington. In this regard, as with the vice presidency, the Obama administration may be breaking new ground by minimizing the profile of its principal aides and downplaying their popular appeal, so even stars like David Axelrod seem unusually subdued, especially in comparison with Clinton and Bush advisers Stephanopoulos and Rove, respectively. However, Obama's more cautious approach may be either the beginning of a trend or an aberration.

AMERICA'S FIRST LADIES

In this and previous chapters, much has been made of historical precedent, political tradition, and their influence over the emergence of the presidency. Some aspects of the presidency can be traced to ancient times, while others have a much shorter heritage, but none has been a universal component of executive politics. The first family is an exception. Every monarch, emperor, dictator, prime minister, president, and even pope has had an extended family, while almost all have had immediate families of their own. If politics has only one universal truth, it is that chief executives must contend with their families in some way and that those families will affect the way they govern. Not all of those families have been similar, however, and not all of their relationships with the chief executive have been stable or supportive—far from it. In fact, those relationships have varied as much as the cultures, circumstances, and geographies that have separated them, and they have made the existence of other universal truths about ruling families highly unlikely.

History and the First Lady

These days, presidents and their counterparts around the globe go out of their way to shield their families from public attention and protect them from the stark realities of politics. This has been a relatively recent trend, because ruling families have traditionally been used as political assets to consolidate power and increase leverage over political rivals and enemies. Consequently, all able-bodied family members played pivotal roles in their patriarchs' political schemes, enabling them to realize key objectives and maintain political advantage, power, and influence. Wives had the unenviable task of producing male heirs to the throne, while daughters were married to kings, princes, or nobles across Europe to secure strategic alliances and political friendships. Sons were groomed to be sovereigns from the time they were born, and extended family members were placed in key posts and given elevated titles to promote dynastic interests.

In most parts of the world today, the situation is vastly different. Families are no longer political instruments to be used for personal gain but are instead part of a private sphere with which the political world has minimal contact. Though not always out of bounds, they are generally considered off limits by the political establishment, and their privacy, if not consistently respected, is at least acknowledged. America's first families are by and large no exception in this regard, shying away from the spotlight and preferring to remain as anonymous and ordinary as possible. Occasionally, however, they choose to be more public or their missteps attract attention from the media and the American people. Billy Carter, brother of Jimmy Carter, was an example of the latter, as were Jenna and Barbara Bush, daughters of George W. Bush. On the other hand, America's first ladies have been the most conspicuous examples of the former, gradually stepping out of the shadows of their powerful husbands and creating their own public personas and even pursuing their own political agendas.

Given the prevailing attitudes toward women during most of the nation's history, the political assertiveness of its first ladies has been a comparatively recent phenomenon. Nevertheless, some of America's earliest first ladies were no wallflowers. Abigail Adams, wife of the second president, though observant of contemporary social graces, was opinionated and outspoken, offering advice and counsel to John throughout his political career. Likewise, James Madison considered his wife, Dolley, an invaluable aide while president, relinquishing control over the presidential residence to her and relying on her to coordinate the evacuation of the White House during the War of 1812. Still, it would be disingenuous and misleading to suggest that these early first ladies, even the most notable of them, had any real power or stature aside from their ceremonial role as the wives of America's chief executives. The historical bias against women as anything but docile, even feeble-minded, companions would not fade substantially until well into the 20th century, and the nation's first ladies would remain part of the backdrop of presidential history until then.

The first presidential spouse to break the mold was Edith Wilson, who, for all intents and purposes, ran the presidency following Woodrow Wilson's stroke in 1919. Obviously, most of the activities on her husband's behalf were hidden from the media and the public, but they were essential. Edith Wilson may have been distinctly different from previous first ladies, but she was pushed into service by unusual circumstances, as was Franklin Roosevelt's wife, Eleanor. FDR contracted polio in 1921 and depended on Eleanor for his political survival thereafter. In fact, had it not been for his wife's extraordinary efforts to maintain his public image and electoral viability, FDR never would have become governor of New York or president of the United States. Eleanor campaigned vigorously for her husband, managed his schedule, acted as his closest adviser, and did as much as anyone to sustain the myth of a vigorous and healthy president. During FDR's presidency, she spoke out against sexism and discrimination, worked hard for the realization of life-long progressive political goals, and transformed the purely ceremonial role of first lady into a substantive presence within the White House.

From both a political and a social perspective, Eleanor Roosevelt's accomplishments were formidable. As first lady, her power rivaled that of FDR's key aides and cabinet secretaries, demonstrating an influence over the president that was rare for anyone, while, as a woman, her activism served as an inspiration to other women, a traditionally silent and neglected majority. Eleanor Roosevelt clearly represented an untapped potential for the nation's chief executives during a time when many in the United States the kind of assertiveness and candor from a woman that she demonstrated. The Nineteenth Amendment gave women the vote in 1920, but women would have to wait a long time to be taken seriously by men, especially in a paternalistic political environment that affirmed masculinity as an ideal. And, in fact, considerable resistance came from women themselves, many of whom had grown accustomed to their subordinate, if not subservient, roles and were content to sustain the status quo. Consequently, many women were even less prepared then their spouses to embrace mavericks such as Eleanor Roosevelt, who were viewed as nothing more than an aberration. This is one of the principal reasons why John Kennedy's wife, Jacqueline, was so eagerly welcomed by Americans, though her youth, grace, and approachably patrician personality proved equally attractive.

The Modern First Lady

Jackie Kennedy was a prominent first lady exactly because she seemed the perfect wife, mother, and hostess. She redecorated the presidential residence, offered advice on fashion and child-raising, managed White House social functions, and largely ignored politics. Jackie Kennedy appeared to be the wife every husband wanted, the mother all children wished they had, and the hostess all women wanted to be. At least, that was the image the media created and the Kennedys promoted. As arguably the most popular first lady to date, Jackie occasionally overshadowed her magnetic husband, leading JFK to remark that he was simply the man who accompanies Jackie Kennedy, but she was not politically progressive or socially daring. Unlike Eleanor Roos-

Jacqueline Kennedy

The role of the first lady, as wife of the president, is a private one with public duties. No constitutional mandate or description of the job exists, yet many first ladies have served their husbands as policy advisers and political assistants. The public role of the first lady has mostly been a social one, yet several first ladies provide distinct examples of the power and influence that can come with the position. Each woman has been allowed to determine her own role within her husband's administration. Jacqueline Kennedy was one of the most revered first ladies of the 20th century.

First Lady Jacqueline Kennedy *(Library of Congress)*

Jacqueline Lee Bouvier (1929–94) met John F. Kennedy in 1951 while he was a member of the U.S. House of Representatives and she was the "inquiring photographer" for the *Washington Times-Herald*. They married in 1953, Kennedy's first year in the U.S. Senate. The couple had four children: a girl that died at birth in 1956, Caroline Bouvier Kennedy (1956-), John Fitzgerald Kennedy, Jr. (1960–99), and Patrick Bouvier Ken-

evelt, Jackie Kennedy was most comfortable working within prevailing stereotypes and using them to her advantage. Hardly an iconoclast, she did not step outside those stereotypes or leverage Eleanor Roosevelt's achievements in any way. As a result, some scholars have claimed that, despite her prominence in the White House and among the American people, Jackie Kennedy actually served as a regressive model for women.

Whether her critics are right or not, Jackie Kennedy set a standard difficult to follow. The next four first ladies, Lady Bird Johnson, Pat Nixon, Betty Ford, and Rosalyn Carter paled by comparison and did little to compensate for their husbands' lack of charisma. Not helped at all by the high standards of femininity and social charm established during Jackie's time at the White House, her successors were handicapped at the gate. Of the four, Betty Ford had the greatest appeal, attracting widespread sympathy and support during her battle with breast cancer. Her defense of the *Roe v. Wade* decision in 1973, which overturned state bans on abortion, and of the Equal Rights

nedy, who died two days after birth in August 1963. Upon her husband's election to the presidency in 1960, Mrs. Kennedy became one of the youngest and most admired first ladies in history, due in part to her fashionable and trend-setting appearance and her commitment to the arts. She was an invaluable political asset to her husband on the campaign trail and during state dinners and trips abroad. She spoke French, Spanish, and Italian, and she was greeted by adoring crowds on numerous international visits, including a trip to France, where she reportedly charmed the French president Charles de Gaulle. The excitement generated by her visit prompted her husband later to quip that he was the man who had accompanied Jacqueline Kennedy to Paris.

Early in the Kennedy administration, Mrs. Kennedy devoted herself to the restoration of the White House. She helped to set up the White House Historical Association as well as the White House Fine Arts Committee. She also procured legislation designating the White House as a museum, and she oversaw the first-ever publication of a White House guidebook. In 1962, she gave a televised tour of the newly restored White House to the nation. Mrs. Kennedy will be remembered most for her courage in the days following her husband's assassination on November 22, 1963. Her public composure and dignity during the funeral, which she had planned based on Abraham Lincoln's funeral following his assassination in 1865, earned her the respect of a grieving nation. In 1968, following the assassination of Robert Kennedy, Mrs. Kennedy married the Greek shipping magnate Aristotle Onassis. After Onassis's death in 1975, she worked as a book editor in New York until her death in 1994.

Amendment for women disturbed her husband's Republican supporters, as did her frank comments on television about teenage sexual habits. Rosalyn Carter, on the other hand, though intelligent and informed, did not help herself or her husband by speaking publicly or being politically active. The American people generally dismissed her as yet another obtrusive member of the Carter family, which had drawn much public criticism during Jimmy Carter's years at the White House.

Rosalyn Carter's successor could not have been more different from the woman she followed into the White House. In many ways, Nancy Reagan, the widely popular but controversial wife of the 40th president, was a Republican version of Eleanor Roosevelt. Controlling, outspoken, and someone with her own political agenda, Nancy Reagan took an active interest in a wide range of matters, but she simultaneously promoted the image of an obedient wife. Working hard to preserve a public persona that maintained a stress on family values cherished by Republicans, Nancy Reagan did not flaunt her power and influence before the cameras, substantial as those were behind the scenes. President Reagan trusted her judgment supremely and even consulted her regarding staffing decisions in the White House and major policy objectives. During her time as first lady, she was the architect of the highly publicized "Just Say No to Drugs" campaign, which attracted scorn and even ridicule from the Democratic opponents and some talk-show hosts. Despite the many substantive contributions, both positive and negative, to the role of first lady, Nancy Reagan will probably be remembered best for protecting and insulating her husband from his critics, both personal and political. Contrary to what has been the case with many presidential marriages, the Reagans appeared truly devoted to each other, and Nancy Reagan's first priority was always her husband's well-being.

As much as the Reagans were devoted to each other, the Clintons, who came to Washington four years after the end of Ronald Reagan's second term, were dedicated to their political careers. A marriage marred by Bill Clinton's marital infidelities before and during his presidency, this was no great love affair, but, strangely, it was a partnership that worked. At least as ambitious as her husband, if not more so, Hillary Clinton was the prototypical baby boomer. Strong-willed, outspoken, and shrewd, she had a take-no-prisoners attitude that did not sit well with the Washington political establishment, which expected its first ladies to observe customary protocols. During her time as America's first lady, Hillary Clinton impressed and offended in equal parts, inspiring a younger generation of women professionals to outperform men at their own game, while alienating traditionalists across the board with her brash and irreverent comments. Unlike the first ladies who preceded her, she set a precedent in acting more as a co-president than as a presidential spouse.

From a political standpoint, Hillary Clinton was the most knowledgeable first lady in history, but her command of the facts was not always an asset. During her much publicized involvement with health-care reform, her intellect and rhetorical skill came across as arrogance and political gamesmanship, which hurt her image and the health-care initiative she championed so tirelessly. Nevertheless, despite the softening of her public profile during her husband's second term, Hillary Clinton remained true to form. Fighting her husband's impeachment and confronting his critics, she was a formidable advocate of what often seemed like a lost cause. Her accusations about right-wing conspiracies notwithstanding, she had sufficient political capital to parlay her experience as first lady into a successful run for the U.S. Senate. After several years as the junior senator from New York, she competed for the Democratic presidential nomination in 2008, losing by the slightest of margins to the eventual president, Barack Obama. She now serves as his secretary of state, making her the most accomplished former first lady ever.

The Clintons campaigned as the quintessential outsiders but became the ultimate insiders. The first lady came to Washington as one of the country's most prominent iconoclasts, and she left the White House as a member of the political establishment she had originally challenged. Senator Clinton became one of Capitol Hill's pillars of centrism, a cautious legislator not willing to take chances or make waves. Gone was the inflammatory rhetoric, as were the progressive ideas and idealistic fervor. They had been replaced by a calm and purposeful demeanor that apparently enhanced her public appeal and reinforced traditional political values. Had the Hillary Clinton who ran for president in 2008 been co-opted by the very forces she had tried so hard to defeat? Her fans claim she had merely matured after eight years as America's first lady into a more seasoned and effective politician, one more capable of pleasing her supporters and critics alike. Never willing to give her the benefit of the doubt, her opponents argue that she is nothing more than a chameleon, adapting her personality and professional approach to the prevailing political winds in Washington.

Where the truth lies is difficult, if not impossible, to determine. Nevertheless, Hillary Clinton's transformation, whether genuine or disingenuous, confirms an unfortunate political truth about women in Washington. To be successful, effective, and electable, a woman cannot become too much of a political liability for the men around her. As far as America's first ladies are concerned, that means the country will not tolerate anyone stronger or more assertive than Nancy Reagan, who, though an active and outspoken spouse, did not overshadow or rival her husband. Certainly, the nation's current first lady, Michelle Obama, is aware of reigning stereotypes and public expectations, and she has been a much more unobtrusive and congenial presence in the White House than was Hillary Clinton. Although Michelle Obama reminds people of Jackie Kennedy, the resemblance is more apparent than real. Michelle Obama's professional achievements have been no less impressive than her husband's, so she would hardly be content as America's homemaker in chief. Still, she has tempered professional ambition with the kind of grace and reserve that suits the public and satisfies those who want their first ladies to err on the side of familial responsibility and social obligation. In this way, Michelle Obama may actually serve as the most viable model for future presidential spouses and also accommodate the American public's seeming need for a first lady who is equal parts Eleanor Roosevelt and Jackie Kennedy.

CONCLUSION

An old French saying advises that "the more things change, the more they remain the same," and nothing better captures the evolution of the executive bureaucracy in the United States during the past 225 years. In 1776, America's founding fathers formally renounced the British Crown and many of its political traditions. Although the American government owed much to its English heritage and the framers of the Constitution proudly embraced a number of British customs, certain institutions were roundly rejected. Monarchy was one of them. Among other things, monarchy had become a symbol of luxury, corruption, and waste, all of which were believed to cause political instability and societal decay. Above all, these characteristics had become associated with the royal court, which was a fount of extravagance and bureaucratic sprawl, according to the framers. Therefore, the American presidency would be the opposite of the royal court, a model of modesty, prudence, and republican wisdom. Limited political authority and institutional moderation were the overriding objectives of the framers' design for the executive branch, and humility would be its ideal.

Unfortunately, the framers' intentions did not endure. By the 20th century, changing circumstances and a new kind of presidential leadership were transforming a once humble and unobtrusive institution into a bureaucratic giant. Industrialization and internationalization pushed the executive branch into the forefront of American governance, encouraging an accumulation of power and resources that outstripped those of its legislative and judicial counterparts. The latter half of the 20th century witnessed the emergence of an imperial presidency replete with many of the trappings of a royal court. Complete with servants, personal attendants, aides, and throngs of advisers, not to mention a cabinet, additional executive councils, and a politicized first family, the presidency today would make America's former British monarchs envious. Furthermore, the presidential residence would put most royal palaces to shame, its security infrastructure would arouse the envy of the Romans, and the arsenal at its disposal would astonish Napoléon. The executive bureaucracy could populate a small city, the president's personal staff could run a Fortune 500 company, and the maintenance and service crew at the White House could outfit a flotilla.

Obviously, this is not what the framers of the Constitution intended. They worked diligently to reshape the prevailing political environment into one that would never tolerate a creation such as the modern presidency. Through the republic they established, the framers revolutionized politics and ensured that change, if it came, would not be regressive. Despite their wish to anchor American political practices to tradition, precedent, and history, they clearly moved forward—beyond the British executive model. Yet, after everything they did and all of the developments of the last 225 years, executive authority appears to have returned to the very place the framers were convinced they had abandoned forever. Of course, the American presidency is not actually a royal institution, but its defining features look surprisingly royal. From the president's expansive powers to an extensive bureaucracy, to say nothing of personal staff and private resources, the modern presidency bears an uncanny resemblance to the royal court of old. Its constitutionality, or lack thereof, is evident, but its feasibility and future are a function of public consent. If the American people are willing to live with an imperial presidency, it will survive, its constitutional status notwithstanding.

CHAPTER 7

The Presidential Policy-Making Process

The word *policy* must be one of the most frequently used, or abused, words in the English language. Strictly speaking, it makes sense only in a political context, but it appears everywhere. Businessmen talk of marketing policy, financial policy, and organizational policy, to name just a few, while athletes focus on defensive policy, offensive policy, and training policy. Churches tout their religious policy, schools promote an educational policy, and doctors uphold medical policy. According to the news and entertainment media, even gangs are not exempt, as they have often been credited with having a criminal policy. The use of the word has become so widespread that the narrator of a recent nature program commented on the social policy of apes. Where will it stop? As amusing as some of these examples may be, such indiscriminate application of a term whose intended focus was rather narrow has made it almost totally irrelevant. Consequently, those who write about policy within its natural political setting must first recover, or reconstruct, its original meaning. This is no easy task.

Unfortunately, political scholars themselves are not immune from misuse of a word that is not as general as they have made it seem. They often inundate readers with references to every kind of policy imaginable and portray the concept itself as something that accommodates all types of political activity. So policies have been equated with rules, guidelines, standards, norms, options, choices, decisions, priorities, criteria, and other related concepts, while the specificity and precision of the original meaning have become lost.

Contrary to much of the available evidence, policy represents a particular type of political activity that is confined to the highest levels of federal, state, and local government. Not all public officials are policy makers, though many of them are involved in various aspects of *policy making*, and not all political acts come from related policies. Instead, policy and the process through which it is created refer just to those acts and officials that define the animating agendas of politics.

The policy-making process creates a link between those agendas and the foundational principles of government by providing a constitutional basis and political rationale for institutional action. Specifically, it applies such principles to targeted political objectives whose realization is critical for effective governance. Complex, intricate, and often confusing, policy making is made up of a number of institutions and scores of individuals, none who is more important than the president of the United States. Although the president was originally overshadowed by Congress, he has become the U.S. policy maker in chief. Congress, interest groups, the media, and the American people all play central roles and occasionally even preempt the president, but only he has the potential to dominate policy making consistently. Of course, this will not happen with a president who lacks the required leadership ability or is generally ineffective. However, no institution other than the presidency is capable of controlling the policy-making process in the same way. Through its public exposure, bureaucratic and political expertise, prospective influence over legislators, and access to other relevant players, the modern presidency is uniquely equipped to set governing agendas.

POLICY, POLICY MAKERS, AND POLICY MAKING

Nothing ever goes the way it was intended. The last several chapters should provide ample evidence of this. The policy-making process is no exception. Scholars, commentators, and politicians often agree on its basic framework, but prevailing realities depart from expectations. Academic models assume stable conditions and universal characteristics, yet political environments are anything but stable and universal. Therefore, the theories and practices of policy making are inherently mismatched, if not divergent, and the gaps that separate them can be significant. Still, theories of policy making are important because they define key concepts, institutions, and procedures and also demonstrate how the process should work. Those theories serve as standards, or guidelines, and they provide the criteria by which the effectiveness and legitimacy of policy making are judged. Because familiarity with how the process should work is critical for an understanding of policy making as a whole, the following section of this chapter will focus on theoretical aspects. The next two sections will examine how it actually works.

What Is Policy?

The introduction to this chapter asserts that policy is not what people commonly presume, but the question remains: "What is policy?" Quite simply, it is the link between constitutional principles and the political means employed in their pursuit. Stated differently, policy connects constitutional politics with ordinary politics and, in so doing, transforms ideals into realities. Unfortunately, this deceptively unassuming answer masks an inherent complexity that defies simple explanation. No amount of rhetorical elegance can convey the intricate combination of ideas and relationships that constitute policy without further elaboration, and, though a basic discussion such as this one cannot do justice to the topic, it can more than adequately summarize its fundamental features. Despite its drawbacks, the above definition serves as a useful starting point, for it identifies the central political dynamic policy making is intended to address, and it highlights the crucial correspondence between constitutional principles and policies that is often ignored, or forgotten.

Policy making animates the most significant relationship in the American political system and, thus, sustains its defining dynamic. The relationship between what the political scientist Bruce Ackerman called "constitutional" and "ordinary" politics lies at the core of American governance, and the resulting dynamic has determined American political development since the founding of the republic. According to Ackerman, by basing a political system on a fundamental law that generates government, the framers of the Constitution created two levels of political activity. The primary, or higher, level is the constitutional level, and it involves the definition of foundational principles, while the secondary, or lower, level is the ordinary level and comprises all legitimate practices that arise from the primary. Obviously, constitutional politics has produced the Constitution, its amendments, and relevant Supreme Court rulings, which, as the theoretical underpinnings of American government, have established both the limits and ideals of ordinary politics. Naturally, since Americans rarely engage in constitutional politics, ordinary politics has been more prolific, reflected in the thousands of statutes, regulations, and actions enacted, but its legitimacy has always derived from the Constitution.

Since the Constitution is not self-executing, the secondary, or ordinary, level of political activity exists only to implement corresponding constitutional principles. Ordinary political practices make sense of the country's binding constitutional theories, which inspire its institutions and public officials. However, the implementation of constitutional principles is neither obvious nor automatic, so the establishment of a connection between constitutional and ordinary politics, though necessary and required, is not guaranteed. This is where policy comes in. It enables officials and institutions to translate lofty constitutional principles into everyday actions that are relevant, warranted, and legitimate. By linking constitutional with ordinary politics, policy making serves as a pathway for the conversion of constitutional authority into political action and the targeted use of power and resources. As such, policy making can be viewed as the glue that holds the political system together, or, alternatively, the indispensable ingredient in American politics.

Policy making produces the nation's political objectives, which are the ends of ordinary politics, and turns them into real programs and initiatives. Policies themselves are nothing more than those very objectives, but, once again, this is not as simple as it appears. In strictly political terms, an objective is a good, which is the end of a process or activity. As the purpose of such a process or activity, a good is desirable and inherently valuable, but, above all, it is legitimate. Therefore, a policy is an objective that represents the implementation of a particular constitutional principle or a specific aspect of that principle. Legitimacy is secured through a clear connection to the Constitution but is lost in the absence of such a connection. A more or less coherent set of policies, or political objectives, representing the intersection of constitutional principle and ideology makes up an agenda, which is a presidential game plan for policy making. Political agendas may be partisan by nature, but they are legitimate only so long as they maintain their constitutional basis.

An agenda is not just a random group of policies, or one with nothing more than a common theme. Rather, an agenda is a comprehensive effort to implement a unified and purposeful constitutional vision through focused political action. A reflection of an administration's political intentions, an agenda is a road map that plots political objectives according to that vision and directs the implementation of relevant constitutional principles. Individual policies within presidential agendas lead to related programs and initiatives whose realization represents the final step of the policy-making process. Aside from the success or failure of these programs and initiatives, the viability of the policies themselves largely determines the effectiveness of presidential agendas. Popularity and the accommodation of partisan priorities also influence effectiveness, as does the ability to articulate political objectives in a persuasive and engaging manner. (Of course, presidents are not the only ones with political agendas, which are common to all political institutions, but they are beyond the scope of this chapter.)

The Policy-Making Process

At the outset, a distinction must be made between policy and the policy-making process. The former is a part of the latter, so the two are not synonymous, but they are inherently joined. The policy-making process has four stages, the first of which is the identification, or definition, of policy. The second is the formulation of strategy, and the third and fourth concentrate on operations and tactics, respectively. Thus, the first two parts of the policy-making process are devoted to planning, while the last two deal with implementation. Policy naturally comes before the others, since it establishes the objectives that policy making is intended to achieve. Without it, the process would be senseless, devoid of the necessary structure and logic that lend it purpose. The subsequent stages are just as important, enabling the realization of political goals and the ultimate translation of constitutional ideals into concrete results. As the product of all four parts working in unison, the policy-making process is the political engine of the American republic, sustaining its political activities and adapting its constitutional principles to contemporary circumstances.

Although each phase of the policy-making process is critical in its own way and, therefore, indispensable, the identification of policy is arguably the most significant. Unless this is done properly, everything that follows can go awry, no matter how skillfully executed. First, a viable policy must be constitutionally sound, so connection to an actual constitutional principle or provision is essential. Otherwise, a political objective lacks legitimacy and will attract debilitating constitutional and statutory scrutiny. Even if the measures produced by such a policy survive scrutiny, their effectiveness will be undermined by the lack of legitimacy. Second, and this may appear obvious, policies must be achievable. Elected officials may be famous for promising their constituents the moon, but they also know that empty promises do not win votes. More important, unrealistic or otherwise unachievable political objectives are harmful, compounding inefficiencies and creating waste that can paralyze the political process. Third, policies must promote valid political objectives whose value is not determined solely by partisan priorities. Agenda setting may be intrinsically partisan, but policies whose partisan interest outweighs national interest are patently invalid.

Other characteristics are desirable but not necessary, and their presence cannot be guaranteed. For example, since valid policies promote the national interest, they should have public support. However, some legitimate political objectives are not overly popular yet are clearly warranted by circumstances. During the 1950s and 1960s, many civil rights policies lacked the backing of the American people, but they were legitimate nonetheless. Still, popularity is important, as a steady decrease in political capital and public approval will quickly undermine an administration's political agenda. Policies should also be simple and clear, which makes them more marketable and, consequently, easier to sell to the American public. Aside from popularity and simplicity, another factor contributing to the viability of political objectives is something legal scholars call ripeness. Ripeness is directly related to achievability, and it refers to a society's ability to confront an issue that has not yet crystallized. In other words, some issues, regardless of their legitimacy, lack critical mass and are not adequately "ripe" as targets of political reform, in terms of either public awareness or political will.

After the definition of policy comes the formulation of strategy. Like policy, *strategy* is a word that has been so widely used and abused that its meaning has been obscured. Its origins stem from its military use, and it is still most closely associated with warfare and national security. In fact, the term can be traced to the ancient Athenian *strategos*, which means general or commander. It has spread today to fields such as business management, economics, sports, religion, and almost every other aspect of modern culture. The military and political definitions are functionally identical, not least because, as the German military expert Carl von Clausewitz stated in the 19th century, war is just an extension of politics. To military personnel and politicians, strategy refers to an overall plan for the realization of corresponding policy and includes a justification of proposed methods and expected resources. A viable strategy not only demonstrates how a political objective will be achieved, but also provides a rationale for the subsequent implementation of subordinate programs. It truly is an overarching plan, offering, among other things, a clear defense of the achievability of a related policy.

The strategic phase of policy making is followed by the operational, which initiates the implementation of political objectives through legislative, and occasionally executive, action. Operations include the various tasks and material demands defined during strategic planning, so they address the physical, or concrete, needs of the policy-making process. Obviously, this is a crucial step because, without it, everything else is just talk and conjecture. It turns policy and strategy into reality by allocating required resources and authority for actual programs, whose existence is merely hypothetical until then. Focusing on performance, execution, and service as opposed to mere concepts and ideas, operational activities enhance governmental capabilities and build infrastructural support through congressional statutes, executive orders, or regulatory decrees, with the first of the three being by far the most common. Finally, once designated programs are created, they are activated and administered during the tactical phase of policy making, which involves the mobilization of allocated resources toward the realization of policy objectives. This includes military campaigns; the provision of health, welfare, and educational services; federal law enforcement; improvements in transportation and communication networks; scientific research and exploration; and many, many more kinds of tactical activities whose aim is the implementation of the nation's policies and related political strategies.

Policy Makers
To the untrained eye, policy making may appear to be dominated by the president and several close advisers. At least, that is how the news media often

portray it. Indeed, the customary discussion and analysis, especially on television, presents something like a Shakespearean drama in which presidents singlehandedly devise foreign and domestic policy and manipulate their colleagues to maximize political advantage. Unfortunately, though commentators and the public at large have become accustomed to praising America's chief executives for apparent successes and blaming them for political failures, such a one-sided view of the policy-making process does little to advance the public's comprehension of it. Like it or not, policy making is complicated, and it involves scores, if not hundreds, of individuals and several institutions. At its best, it is a collaborative process that leverages the combined expertise of its participants toward effective results. At its worst, it is a chaotic sprawl captured by petty jealousies and political hyper-competitiveness, promoting nothing more than partisanship and personal ambition. Reality usually lies somewhere between these two extremes.

Theoretically, of course, policy making is approximated by the former, not the latter. Envisioned as a collaborative process based on the consideration of viable alternatives, its intentions are best conveyed through the so-called *rational-actor model* of executive decision making. Pioneered by the political scientist Graham Allison after studying the activities of the Kennedy administration during the Cuban missile crisis of 1962, the rational-actor model describes how key decisions should be made by political leaders, especially in democratic environments. Allison originally focused on the ability of political actors to act rationally in crisis situations, but his conclusions have since been applied to all types of decision-making scenarios. From presidential politics to corporate management, the rational-actor model has served as an instructive tool for understanding organizational behavior at the highest levels. Although, like any other model of political behavior, it is far from perfect or completely predictive, it more than adequately illustrates how policy making should work.

Since the rational-actor model focuses on decision making, its insights regarding planning are greater than those concerning implementation. Not unexpectedly, it is most helpful in explaining policy and strategy and less so operations and tactics. Still, the framework can be extended to the operational stage with some benefit, especially with respect to the determination of standards for effectiveness, efficiency, and feasibility. Overall, this model of decision making hinges on the concept of rationality, not the ordinary kind of rationality referenced in everyday speech but the concept that economists, for example, use to describe market dynamics. When economists state that participants in a free market act rationally, they are not implying that market transactions are based on reason rather than emotion. Rather, they are assuming that decisions to buy and sell are based on free choice and the consideration of valid alternatives. Moreover, rational choices promote decision makers' interests and represent optimal outcomes, or outcomes predicted to be optimal. Crudely speaking, transactional choices maximize potential profits and minimize expected risks through the best available options.

Likewise, in politics, rationality presupposes deliberation and the existence of viable options. It also assumes that decisions will reflect the most favorable balance of costs and benefits regarding the public's welfare. As such, legitimate decisions are not unilateral nor do they ignore alternatives, and they cannot endorse outcomes that promote partisan objectives or do not optimize national interests. Obviously, because presidents have ultimate political authority, the process is not wholly democratic, and final decisions are theirs; they accept responsibility for this role and are accountable to the public as a result. Nevertheless, policy-making decisions cannot simply begin and end with the president. If the rational-actor model is any guide, legitimate policy making depends on the president's ability and willingness to consult others and to consider their contributions seriously. According to the model, the key decision maker, which is the president, delegates the preparation of appropriate alternatives to a group, or groups, of experts and advisers with whom he or she deliberates predicted outcomes, costs, and benefits. Those involved in the discussions make recommendations, from which the president makes decisions.

Once again, the linchpin in all this is rationality, which enhances both the legitimacy and the effectiveness of the policy-making process. Decisions without reflection, representative participation, or awareness of valid options are inherently flawed, as are those that arise from coercion, manipulation, or dishonesty. A mock collaboration intended to bias the process toward predetermined outcomes is irrational and, therefore, lacks merit. The identification of policy and the formulation of strategy must be a function of true collaboration and an earnest consideration of alternatives, and the final decision must optimize the public interest and support the constitutional principles at stake. Above all, the process, though headed by a president who has the ultimate power and authority to make decisions, must be sufficiently democratic to permit free competition among ideas and, thus, enable the survival of the most viable options. The president may have the constitutional right to make decisions without consultation, but the need for rationality contradicts such an approach.

PRESIDENTIAL POLICY MAKING IN THE REAL WORLD

In the United States today, the president is arguably the most important policy maker in Washington, dominating the planning stages, if not the operational one also, and directly engaging both the public and the press to win approval of his or her policies. With few exceptions, such as the Republican-led Contract with America in 1995, presidential agendas are more prominent than their congressional counterparts and, due to the fractured nature of legislative politics, more cohesive and consistent. At present, presidential policies, if properly and skillfully handled, have a substantially higher probability of success than do those that originate in Congress, and they often set, or at least heavily influence, the nation's political priorities. Contrary to what had been the case for more than a century after the country's founding, Congress no longer controls the policy-making process, but it also lacks the leadership capacity and public backing to establish long-term political agendas. In the absence of effective presidential leadership, policy making is typically rudderless, leading to political gridlock or paralysis, which demonstrates how crucial presidents have become to a process that originally marginalized their contributions.

Policy Making and Irrationality

Despite their significance, presidents' contributions to policy making do not necessarily arise from the kinds of circumstances the rational-actor model predicts. Far from being uniformly rational, presidential policy making can deviate from the norm considerably. It is not always collaborative, nor is it predominantly deliberative. Presidents frequently steer toward predetermined political objectives and their decision making can be more idiosyncratic than logical, all of which precludes free choice and competition. Connection to overriding constitutional principles, though necessary in theory, is often tenuous at best, and national interest habitually takes a back seat to selfish interest. The president's personal ambitions, as well as those of advisers, party, influential legislators, and powerful interest groups, more than occasionally occupy center stage, while the news media exploit political differences among policy makers to feed consumer demand for sensational stories. The result, though far from disastrous, is also far from the ideal represented by the rational-actor model.

Graham Allison's research showed that, under extraordinary circumstances, executive decision making is anything but rational. In crisis situations, decision making is usually dominated by the president or a few key advisers, and they customarily produce predetermined outcomes. An apparently collaborative effort is used to steer policy makers toward the president's favored options, while alternative choices are seldom considered seriously. During the Cuban missile crisis, for example, John Kennedy crafted a response to Soviet deployment of nuclear weapons in Cuba through the so-called Executive Committee, which he and his brother Attorney General Robert Kennedy, actually utilized to advance their own strategic and tactical priorities. The consensus among Kennedy's top advisers pointed in a direction the president refused to follow until the president persuaded most of his colleagues to change their minds. The American response to the Soviet action was ultimately successful and probably averted a nuclear war, but it was hardly rational.

President John F. Kennedy meeting with his ExComm group during the Cuban missile crisis, October 29, 1962 *(John F. Kennedy Library)*

Similarly, George W. Bush's Middle East policy after terrorist incursions against the United States in 2001 was anything but rational. The available evidence indicates that President Bush came to Washington with the desire to reshape geopolitical dynamics in the Middle East and, if possible, to complete the destruction of the Iraqi regime begun by his father 10 years earlier. After the terrorist acts in fall 2001, President Bush, Vice President Dick Cheney, and Secretary of Defense Donald Rumsfeld advocated a strategy that called for the democratization of rogue states through the invasion of Iraq and the pursuit of terrorist networks throughout the region. The administration short-circuited serious deliberations and scuttled the consideration of alternatives so it could press for the adoption of its foreign policy goals, which were eventually accepted by a Congress reluctant to make difficult decisions and more than willing to pass them on to the president. In addition, the public, smarting from the first attacks on U.S. soil since 1941 and eager for revenge, posed few obstacles to the realization of Bush's objectives.

According to the rational-actor model, the above examples illustrate illegitimate decision making. Nevertheless, they were constitutionally valid and definitely within the law and binding political precedents. More than anything, these two incidents provide proof that decision making processes do not always work the way they should. They may also be evidence that the rational-actor model does not hold for crises, but, as it turns out, it does not hold Universally in any context. It certainly cannot explain the creation of health-care policy in the Clinton administration during 1993, which undermined rationality from the start. The process was definitely deliberative, but only within a like-minded group of policy experts, yet it was also exclusive, minimizing the opportunity for free exchange and the presentation of alternatives. President Bill Clinton delegated considerable responsibility to others, but, in the end, too much authority lay with Hillary Clinton, who seemed unwilling to compromise on key points. The Clintons' health-care policy became one of their first political casualties and stigmatized the administration's related domestic policies for some time.

Even effective, beneficial policies are not immune from irrationality. No one would dispute that FDR's New Deal and LBJ's Great Society were the products of comprehensive effort and diligence by all involved, especially the many lawmakers and experts who made critical contributions. However, despite their success and popularity, to say nothing of their long-term viability, both were conceived and pushed through Congress by presidents with a single-minded purpose that did not brook compromise or extensive deliberation. Particularly in LBJ's case, he and his closest aides presented the extended cabinet and lawmakers with a done deal that many thought was forced upon them. This should not imply that congressional and executive policy makers outside of the president's inner circle did not favor the proposed reforms, nor does it mean that those reforms were ill-advised, but the design and passage of key Great Society measures was not a function of the kind of collaborative give-and-take the rational-actor model demands. Indeed, LBJ engaged in substantial horse trading with legislators to secure acceptance of his program, but consideration of major alternatives was never part of the process.

Presidents and Policy Making

In the end, these examples and others like them say a lot about what policy making is not, but they also reveal something about what it is. The process is not so much irrational as it is less rational than scholars would like. Presidents and their key aides often dominate the identification of policy because they wish to fulfill campaign promises and, more important, ensure the acceptance of those political objectives most dear to them. Rationality may require the identification and deliberation of actual policy alternatives, especially since this leads to more prudent and balanced decision making, but reality does not afford presidents this luxury. The American public expects its political leaders to be resolute, decisive, and forthright by offering a recognizable political agenda that sets immediate priorities. Because presidents have distinct and definite policy goals, many of which invariably reflect choices they made prior to assuming office, they are dedicated to the realization of their goals and not someone else's. Thus, to assume that any president would be willing to set his or her political agenda by committee is foolish. For better or worse, presidential agendas largely reflect the personal preferences and choices of America's chief executives, and, while those agendas are also influenced and shaped by other policy makers and pressure groups, they do not usually emerge through democratic input.

Graham Allison's observations notwithstanding, presidential policy making is probably most collaborative and democratic, hence rational, during crises or extraordinary circumstances. This is so because presidents adequately prepare for the unexpected. Unable to predict the future, they inevitably face situations that surprise and confuse them and their advisers. At such times, due to the comparative lack of preparation and readiness, not to mention information, presidents customarily require greater assistance and cooperation from other policy makers, whose primary responsibility becomes the development of viable and informed alternatives for presidential action. Such was the case immediately after World War II, as President Harry Truman struggled to define effective international policies to counter the growing Soviet threat. The doctrine of *containment*, the principal U.S. foreign policy during the cold war, at least until the Reagan administration, was the outcome of a concentrated collaborative effort by the Truman administration. Although the final product was Truman's, it represented the active and ongoing participation of numerous experts, advisers, military officers, legislators, and friends working in concert with the president to find an appropriate response to recent Soviet expansion.

Partisanship also plays a strong role in policy making, affecting presidents in a way academic models do not allow but reality always permits. Like it or not, presidents, as all public officials, are political animals with ideological leanings and partisan loyalties whose careers are facilitated, if not made, by the very same parties many commentators are so willing to criticize. The golden age of political parties passed a few decades ago, but the current era of candidate-centered politics is just as dependent on their existence. Without the political backing, financial resources, and broad social networks of the two big parties, candidates for office have little chance of victory, while officeholders face almost insurmountable obstacles to success. This is perhaps the principal reason why independents and third-party candidates perform so poorly and why the American public rarely takes them seriously. Becoming president requires more than good ideas, and presidential candidates cannot prevail without the dedicated support of a major party, so, by the time they get elected, presidents will invariably accumulate a number of partisan debts that must be paid during their tenures in office.

Consequently, some policy priorities will be dictated by partisan interests. In exchange for assistance throughout their careers but especially during election campaigns, presidents often defer to their parties on pivotal issues. With few exceptions, regardless of a president's personal stand on those issues, partisan interests will prevail, or the president will eventually lose key constituencies and vital resources. President George H. W. Bush discovered as much when he approved tax increases over party opposition in 1991. However, some policies are not as important to party identity as others, and, in those areas, presidents generally have the greatest latitude. Still, core policies are so closely associated with either Democrats or Republicans that party leaders will not jeopardize them. These policies include those that deal withthe economy, abortion, the death penalty, gun control, taxes, entitlements, gay rights, and illegal immigration, followed closely by the environment, affirmative action, religion, and medical research. Only a highly talented president with a wide base of public support can challenge his or her party on such policies, and even then, cannot do so too frequently without depleting political capital. President Bill Clinton was able to do so with his welfare reform initiative in 1996 and the 1993 compromise over homosexuals in the military, both of which left party stalwarts disgruntled.

Aside from partisan pressures, another prevalent influence over presidential policy making is popularity. Although academic models of decision making expect presidents to do what is right and not necessarily what is popular, the distinction is often lost on policy makers in the real world. To presidents and their advisers, and practically everyone else in Washington, popularity makes right, which means that, barring exceptional circumstances, unpopular policies that are otherwise legitimate are neither feasible nor effective. Because presidents owe those who voted for them as much as they owe their parties and they continuously strive to maximize public approval, certain policies are essentially the products of public opinion. Bill Clinton was often criticized for running the country by opinion polls, but the truth of the matter is that every president is deeply worried about public approval and the popularity of his agenda. Some have pointed to George W. Bush, his successor, as a counterexample, yet President Bush's defiance of public opinion regarding foreign policy was less a function of his disregard for popularity than his surprisingly dogged adherence to religious and ideological principles over political reality.

Policy Makers in Washington

For all the benefits of academic theories, one of the greatest drawbacks is their static nature. No matter how complex or intricate, theories are not dynamic, as they aim for regularity and standardization. They define people and institutions as set in stone, without making allowance for change and variation. Obviously, theories would not be very useful as explanatory tools if they comprised as many exceptions as rules, yet, at the same time, they fail to take into account the unpredictable and the unusual, especially for processes such as policy making whose cast of characters and institutions is always different. Presidential policy making does indeed inevitably involve the president and his or her chief advisers, but little else is constant from policy to policy. The list of participants varies according to circumstance, need, and political priority, and their activities as well as resulting interactions are just as diverse. This does not mean that the process defies all generalization in that regard, but it underscores the difficulty of defining a normal pattern of relationships for the policy-making process.

In one way or another, presidential policy making always begins and ends with the president, even if the chief executive's ideas are not those that initiate discussions. Granted, some administrations have fostered the impression, intentionally or inadvertently, that presidential oversight of policy making is minimal, but that is not the case. For instance, Ronald Reagan delegated most of the work to others and seemed to be interested in only the broadest and most general matters, apparently content with the role of a grandfatherly preacher imparting moral lessons to his domestic and foreign audiences. That was the perception anyhow, and his administration did little to dispel it. He may not have been a tireless negotiator such as LBJ or a policy aficionado such as Bill Clinton, but Reagan exercised largely effective leadership over policy making during his tenure and was intent on putting his stamp on critical policies, particularly those concerning national security and economic regulation. On the other hand, Jimmy Carter, who was Reagan's immediate predecessor, could do nothing to dismiss the public image of a chief executive incapable of controlling the runaway train that was presidential policy making. Unfortunately, this image stemmed from the president's lack of leadership and poor managerial skills, which nothing could reverse.

Aside from the president, a small cadre of trusted aides runs the policy-making process, acting as both advisers and gatekeepers, managing access to key personnel, acting as liaisons between the White House and other participants, and delegating the various tasks. Depending on the type of policy, these aides invariably involve various groups within the Executive Office of the President, such as the Council of Economic Advisors, National Security Council, Office of Management and Budget, and others. The executive councils are often the real workhorses, doing the heavy lifting during policy making by compiling data, performing analyses, preparing strategy, providing expertise, and fulfilling any number of related jobs assigned to them by the president or presidential staff. They are joined by relevant cabinet members and staff, who occasionally work at cross-purposes with the White House due to issues of territoriality, especially among departments, but their expertise and assessments can be crucial to the success of presidential agendas. In addition, presidents sometimes solicit advice from outside experts, such as academics or industry specialists, whose roles in the policy-making process can vary widely, but whose input can be quite valuable on controversial or complicated issues.

At some point, at least by the operational stage but customarily much earlier, legislators become involved in the process. Without them, the implementation of presidential policy is mere fantasy, so presidents must secure the cooperation of Congress as early as possible. In many, if not most, cases, presidents or their aides consult selected congressional leaders, which can include the Speaker of the House, majority or minority leaders of either chamber, heads or ranking members of pertinent committees, and other prominent representatives or senators. Congressional support for presidential policies is indispensable, because lawmakers have the ability to stall, derail, or alter intended legislation and undermine presidential agendas altogether. Conventional wisdom among pundits holds that presidential agendas have a higher probability of success if the presidency and Congress are controlled by the same party, thereby facilitating collaboration and compromise, but the historical evidence has not been as clear. Both Bill Clinton and Barack Obama faced strong opposition over their health-care policies despite Democratic majorities in both houses, and George W. Bush certainly did not get his way on everything during his time in office with Republican majorities.

Policy Makers outside Washington
Beyond the executive and legislative branches, the roles of other participants are more difficult to define, not necessarily because they are do not provide regular input but because their numbers can be large and their activities questionable. The most significant of these are the various interest groups and campaign contributors who have a disproportionate effect on national politics. Not a single policy that survives initial discussions among the president and presidential aides becomes implemented without early and continuous intervention by lobbyists. Interest groups represent practically every cause and idea and seem to include anyone with a political agenda. Active on issues involving both foreign and domestic policy, they enable certain constituencies to exert political pressure that far outweighs their number. Their ranks include AARP (formerly the American Associations of Retired Persons), the American Israel Public Affairs Committee, the National Association of Manufacturers, the National Rifle Association, NARAL Pro-Choice America, the National Right to Life Committee, the AFL-CIO, and thousands of other organizations that serve the political objectives not only of American constituents, but also of foreign interests.

Interest groups are not the only ones with disproportionate influence over politics and access to the policy-making process. Other participants who wield such clout include the wealthy individuals who fill party coffers and finance presidential campaigns. Through direct contributions, indirect assistance, and social networking, they provide candidates and parties with money, which is the indispensable ingredient for political success. As Jesse Unruh, the longtime California politician who became one of the most significant personalities in Democratic politics, once remarked, "Money is the mother's milk of politics." So, because presidents and their political parties need their cash cows, those with money have unique leverage over policy makers. No politicians, particularly not presidents, can afford to alienate those who keep the cash coming, and financial contributors will always have access to them and other policy makers. The simple truth is that donors give money for selfish reasons, and they expect political favors that promote their personal interests.

In the United States, the political system cannot survive without money, so those with wealth seem especially important. During Ronald Reagan's two terms in the White House, a group of business moguls, mostly from Reagan's home state, advised the president on economic and financial matters, often affecting his domestic policy decisions more than his closest official advisers or his department secretaries. Holmes Tuttle, the prominent California automobile dealer, and Joseph Coors, the beer magnate, were two of the dozen or so wealthy party contributors who formed Reagan's so-called kitchen cabinet and who enjoyed unprecedented access to the White House and the policy-making process. Of course, Reagan was not an anomaly in this regard, as most modern chief executives nurtured their relationships with the rich and famous. President Clinton was chided by his opponents for his close ties to powerful individuals and was even accused, perhaps tongue-in-cheek, of selling admission to the Lincoln bedroom, which is part of a guest suite in the White House, but his actions constituted nothing unusual. The Clintons attracted criticism from cultural conservatives for their friendships with Hollywood's elite, especially because of the movie industry's status as a bastion of leftist politics. The first couple's perceived extravagances did nothing to dispel outlandish rumors of a conspiracy between the president and Hollywood radicals. Yet, Bill Clinton's political relationships with film icons constituted standard practice.

As long as money continues to play such a critical role in politics, wealthy individuals will have access to the White House. Despite the American people's supposed uneasiness over the influence of money in politics and the occasional outcry by reform-minded legislators, money is here to stay. An open, competitive, and market-driven system dominated by two major parties cannot break its close ties to private finance, and the Supreme Court agrees. The public presidency depends on private financing for its existence and influence, and the American public, its less half-hearted complaints notwithstanding, seems to have accepted this fact. Very few people appeared concerned by JFK's ties to entertainers, movie stars, labor leaders, or newspaper publishers, and not many were overly worried about George H. W. Bush's links with the Saudi royal family, not to mention his relationships to other foreign interests. George W. Bush's favorable treatment of oil executives, government contractors, and steel magnates did not bother any of his supporters, while the bailouts of investment bankers, automakers, and mortgage lenders, though condemned by many, passed without sufficient backlash to derail them. Even Barack Obama, who campaigned against the entrenched moneyed and special interests in Washington, ultimately won because of them. Raising record amounts of money to secure his election and incurring numerous political debts in the process, President Obama has been no more successful than his predecessors at distancing himself or the White House from America's wealthy and powerful.

With respect to major policy makers outside government, last but not least come the news media. They are not official players, but their ability to change or influence policy is as profound as it is inevitable. The American political environment is shaped, if not defined, through the media, who have an unparalleled access to Washington and its key personalities. Political victories and defeats, wars, scandals, and routine events unfold on America's televisions and computers. These days, everything within the White House

President Bush and King Fahd, at the Royal Pavilion in Saudi Arabia, discuss the situation in Iraq, November 21, 1990. *(George Bush Presidential Library)*

is fair game, so very little is private, secret, or unavailable. Unfortunately, at least for the presidents and their staffs, nonstop cable and Internet coverage attracts relentless scrutiny that the policy-making process cannot always survive. Final products as well as the most preliminary of ideas are dissected, examined, and reexamined by scores of analysts and pundits who concentrate on a handful of the most accessible, if not sensational, details and offer opinions as freely as smiles. This much media attention invites controversy, which, despite increasing viewership and ratings, does little to help deliberation and compromise and often forces policy makers to make premature or ill-advised changes. Of course, greater exposure also results in greater transparency, to which the American people are certainly entitled, and media coverage often leads to policy improvements, but the media no longer simply report the news. As active, albeit indirect, participants in the policy-making process, they have become part of the news.

TWO KINDS OF POLICY MAKING

Today's philosophers reject the existence of universal truths. However, some things at least appear to be universal. One of America's most famous and colorful authors, Mark Twain, numbered death and taxes among them, but he could have added foreign and domestic policy to the list. Regardless of time, geography, or ideology, regimes past and present have pursued these two basic types of policy. Whether the Soviet Union or the United Kingdom, the Roman Empire or imperial China, Mesopotamia or Mauritania, not a single government has escaped this truth. The United States is obviously no different in this respect. For American politicians, like their counterparts across the globe, foreign policy and domestic policy are the only games in town, so all policy making is of one type or the other. This is only natural, as nations have both internal and external priorities, which are addressed through their leaders' political agendas. In the United States, these agendas are realized through separate yet overlapping domestic and foreign policy establishments that intersect at the White House and are unified through executive leadership and an underlying national interest.

Domestic Policy

Of the two types of policy, domestic seems the more essential, if not the more important. Although this characterization is open to dispute, the centrality of domestic policy should not be. Internal politics is the lifeblood of any country, and, though defense and national security are vital concerns, Americans today could not survive without an active domestic agenda. Even during the early republic, when the range of federal activity was quite limited, domestic policy was responsible for the provision of services and resources crucial to life in the United States. Over the last several decades, the federal government has become involved in many aspects of American life. Americans' reliance on the federal government is so deep that they expect continuous attention from their public officials and depend on federal assistance, regulation, and protection every day.

This reliance transcends issues of subsistence and basic survival and includes expectations regarding the government's responsibility to enhance quality of life and personal success. These demands clearly do not reflect traditional ideas about the government's role in society, but Americans have accepted them as normal and necessary, and federal policy makers are keenly aware of it. Consequently, the president and presidential staff must devote sufficient attention to a broad array of policy areas in their efforts to meet public demand and fulfill the government's domestic duties. Of the many different kinds of domestic policy, perhaps none is more important to the American people, particularly as voters, than economic policy. Ironically, the public has always given presidents far too much credit for contemporary economic conditions, blaming them for recessions and praising them for recoveries. Presidents and their advisers have far less ability to affect the economy than the public believes, and they cannot control either the market or the business cycle. Still, most people are convinced that their chief executives are at least indirectly responsible for the nation's economic woes and successes, which is a perception enthusiastically promoted by the news media, so presidents must take economic policy very seriously.

Economic policy itself consists of *monetary policy* and *fiscal policy*. Of the two, monetary policy is by far the more obscure, understood mainly by specialists and subject to minimal interference from the president. He or she appoints the chairman of the Board of Governors of the Federal Reserve System, the vice chairman, and the remaining governors, who serve on the 12-member Federal Open Market Committee (FOMC), which controls interest rates and the nation's money supply. Federal Reserve governors serve 14-year staggered terms, while the chairman is selected from among the governors for a four-year renewable term, so the president's influence over monetary policy extends no further than powers of persuasion and appointment authority under relevant congressional statutes. Although the decisions of prominent Federal Reserve chairmen, such as Alan Greenspan, are occasionally associated with presidential economic agendas, presidents have limited influence over monetary policy. This does not mean that the FOMC operates without regard for economic policies of presidents, as the Treasury Department often consults with FOMC members, but presidents do not formulate monetary policy nor do they manage it.

On the other hand, presidential involvement in fiscal policy is much more profound, and it can frequently determine the fate of an entire presidency. Although the implementation of fiscal policy belongs to Congress, since it has the constitutional authority to initiate revenue and appropriations measures, the nation usually takes its cue from its presidents in this regard. Fiscal policy covers taxing and spending and can be as potentially polarizing as some high-profile social issues such as abortion and gay marriage. Despite the inflammatory partisan rhetoric on both sides, differences over fiscal policy between Democrats and Republicans are hardly as stark as they appear. In truth, neither party favors high taxes, yet, because each party caters to its core constituencies, debate arises about who should reap the benefits or bear the burdens of an unequal tax system. Likewise, the customary stereotypes concerning spending and fiscal discipline are misleading, not least because both parties are more than willing to provide monetary support for key constituencies. Whereas Democrats have often advocated increased spending on social services, Republicans have pushed for various industrial subsidies that aid their supporters.

With respect to spending, both Democrats and Republicans have been less than responsible. In an effort to maintain public support, both parties have customarily made unrealistic promises to their constituents, which has not promoted fiscal discipline. Spending has been spiraling out of control for several decades, producing annual deficits that eclipse the national incomes of many countries. America's total debt almost equals its GDP (gross domestic product) and will soon surpass it, but budget deficits will continue for some time. As a result, the United States, once the world's leading creditor, is now its biggest debtor. Therefore, effective fiscal management is a priority for all American presidents, because, if history has shown anything, it has demonstrated that financial vulnerability eventually leads to political instability. America's chief executives are undoubtedly aware of this, and fiscal discipline has been a policy priority for most of them, but, due to their courtship of high approval ratings, they have been unwilling to inflict the short-term pain a long-term cure would cause Americans. In the end, their unwillingness, or inability, to act does not diminish the significance of fiscal policy, nor does it change the likelihood that fiscal policy will some day make or break presidents. That day may be coming sooner than most people think.

From a more immediate perspective, fiscal policy is so significant because every type of domestic policy affects it in some way. Since federal programs require money and resources, they also affect the bottom line. In some way, whether through new taxes or diversion of existing revenues, presidents have to pay for their initiatives, and their fiscal policies must account for other domestic policies. From that perspective, the most consequential of these other policies is welfare policy, which includes not only the portions narrowly known as welfare but also the related and substantially more expensive entitlements such as Social Security, Medicare and Medicaid, disability and unemployment insurance, and additional social services. Entitlements consume the largest portion of American tax revenues, and their skyrocketing

President Barack Obama, Vice President Joe Biden, and senior staff react in the Roosevelt Room of the White House as the House passes the health-care reform bill. *(Wikipedia)*

costs are a formidable obstacle to effective financial management, but presidents have been reluctant to do anything more than tinker with programs that mean so much to so many voters. As the American population continues to age and the demand for social services keeps growing, the financial burdens on the federal government will increase, which will only attract even more attention to presidential welfare policy and the need to find a feasible solution to this burgeoning problem.

Aside from welfare policy, health-care policy has become a prominent concern for Americans and their presidents. Health-care policy is related to welfare policy, and they share many of the same issues, but policy dealing with health care is arguably more complex because it straddles the public and private sectors. Although the federal government's regulatory authority over the health-care industry has grown exponentially over the last 50 years, America's capitalist economy has traditionally resisted too much government interference in market activities. The nation's health-care industry is heavily regulated but is still largely controlled through private enterprise, which has created a strange and uneasy partnership between public and private institutions. Overall, the United States boasts one of the most elite health-care systems in the world, but, at the same time, it neglects or ignores a disturbing number of people. Whether this is a result of too much government intervention or not enough is a question that fuels angry debates in this country, but the fact remains that close to 50 million Americans are uninsured. Consequently, as evidenced by the Obama administration's efforts during its first year in the White House, health-care policy will continue to occupy center stage in American politics for an indefinite period.

Domestic policy includes various other kinds of policy. Some among the more relevant examples include social policy, environmental and conservation policy, crime policy, industrial and labor policy, transportation and communication policy, and education policy. Of these, social policy has been the most controversial, encompassing the so-called culture wars of the last four decades and promoting causes that one of the two major parties invariably opposes. Oddly enough, though politicians and their constituents alike, to say nothing of the parties themselves, inflate the importance of issues such as abortion, homosexuality, prayer in public places, evolution, and medical research, presidents have not been eager to confront them. Some presidents have issued executive orders regarding the expenditure of federal funds for abortion services or embryonic research, but they have mostly confined their involvement to the use of the bully pulpit to influence others. Presidents realize that these are personal issues whose pursuit could deplete their political capital, so they prefer to concentrate on those battles that are winnable without incurring the high political casualties these others could entail. In addition, due to the federalist structure of American politics, state and local governments have often been the engines of social policy, and many presidents have been willing to defer to them in all but the most high-profile cases.

Foreign Policy

Without a doubt, domestic policy appears more relevant to the everyday existence of ordinary Americans. Presidential candidates prioritize domestic over international issues during their campaigns. Due to the lack of foreign policy experience of many candidates, most naturally steer toward the domestic policy topics with which they are most familiar. However, as presidents, many become preoccupied with foreign policy to the exclusion, or detriment, of the domestic policies on the basis of which they won election. Thus, it is incorrect to say that foreign policy is less significant than domestic policy. Moreover, if foreign policy truly is a secondary concern, what explains the fact that it has been the source of some of the greatest social unrest in this country's history? New York draft riots in 1863 produced clashes between civilians and federal troops; antiwar agitation from 1916 to 1918 led to violent confrontations with police and federal authorities; social upheaval over the Vietnam War tore the nation apart during the 1960s and early 1970s; and President Bush's decision to invade Iraq unleashed protests across the nation. Clearly, foreign policy touches a nerve that resonates with Americans. It may not be the constant irritant some domestic policies are to their opponents, but foreign policy, especially issues dealing with war and national defense, can invoke the very questions of national existence that determine survival as a republic.

As you know from the earlier chapters, the inability to coordinate foreign policy was one of the main deficiencies of the Confederation government and, thus, a principal reason for the creation of the presidency by the framers of the Constitution. Given the narrow authority of the early presidency, particularly in domestic affairs, foreign policy stood out as one of the key responsibilities of the nation's first several presidents. In addition, though the new nation did not have a large standing army, its defense was a top priority for the Founding Fathers, and security issues were of paramount importance to everyone. Obviously, no American wanted the recently created republic to perish due to an inability to defend itself, so its presidents were immediately aware of the need to craft effective foreign policies that would preserve and adequately protect the United States. If some Americans question the significance of foreign policy today, no one did so when the nation was founded, as the recent experience of war had convincingly demonstrated the need for a successful foreign policy.

Foreign policy includes two complementary but distinct concerns, diplomacy and national security, whose goals and priorities, though supposedly unified, are not always easily reconciled. Theoretically, one is an extension of the other, so that, where diplomacy ends, national security begins, the two working together seamlessly toward identical political objectives. Whether through failure or success, diplomacy should in some way set the stage for the execution of national security policies that follow. The negotiation, deliberation, and debate that characterize diplomacy should go hand in hand with the strategic and tactical activities that national security demands. However, despite the inclusion of diplomatic and national security interests under a common foreign policy, presidents do not always successfully align those interests, and their diplomatic and national security establishments do not always read from the same script. Diplomacy and national security may be the two areas addressed by foreign policy, but their execution is not uniformly coordinated.

One reason for the institutional, if not inherent, inconsistency between diplomatic and national security policy is that they seem to have different aims. While they should both target the same political objectives and, therefore, support identical policies, one rejects war while the other depends on it. By definition, diplomacy focuses on peaceful promotion of strategic goals and prevention of war, whereas national security concentrates on military advancement of strategic objectives and preparation for war. Take the cold war policy of containment mentioned earlier in this chapter, for example.

While both the diplomatic and the defense teams were committed to the policy itself, they often worked at cross-purposes. During the 1970s, as diplomats promoted détente, or a cooling of tensions between the United States and the Soviet Union, the military still pursued its strategy of mutually assured destruction (MAD). Though hardly something defense leaders wanted or anticipated, MAD called for the total deployment of the nation's nuclear arsenal against the Soviets. Despite the fact that MAD was, first and foremost, a deterrent, its implementation was not merely hypothetical.

Another reason for inconsistencies between diplomatic and national security objectives arises from institutional territoriality. The Departments of State and Defense may answer to the same president, but they have developed different cultures and different priorities, which has often led to friction between the two. Partly, this is due to the disconnect between national security and diplomacy discussed above, so the diplomats have at times viewed those at Defense as warmongers, while the national security team has occasionally dismissed its colleagues in the State Department as naive peaceniks. However, their differences are mainly a product of divergent evolutionary paths that have produced two distinct institutions. In the context of international politics, this fact has manifested itself in some unusual and perhaps unexpected ways, because the diplomatic and defense establishments have developed divergent priorities and allegiances. For instance, defense personnel have been staunchly pro-Israeli, even anti-Arab, with respect to Middle East policy, but their diplomatic counterparts have been much more willing to view Arab causes, especially the plight of the Palestinians, sympathetically. Maybe the most glaring recent example of the tension between the two departments is President George W. Bush's antiterrorism policy. The Defense Department's strategy of preemptive strikes against sponsors of terrorism encountered strong opposition from the State Department and caused pronounced problems during Bush's first term.

As important as agreement between the president's major foreign policy teams may be to the overall effectiveness of an international agenda, their strategic differences cannot account for the increasing cost of national security. Both the State and Defense Departments have been enthusiastic supporters of the defense buildup during the past several decades, and neither has done much to instill fiscal prudence among their ranks. The creation of vast strategic and tactical arsenals during the cold war was considered necessary by all involved, and, despite ongoing negotiations with the Soviets regarding arms reductions, defense spending kept rising. The end of the cold war never brought the peace dividend for which many had hoped, and defense expenditures did not decrease. The uncertainty of a post-Soviet world seemed to demand better, smarter, and more expensive weapons, and the events of September 11, 2001, merely affirmed U.S. commitment to state-

President George W. Bush is applauded after his address at the Pentagon memorial service on October 11, 2001, in honor of those who perished in the terrorist attack on September 11. *(Department of Defense)*

of-the-art defense capabilities. Like entitlement spending on the domestic side of the ledger, a steadily growing defense budget feeds the U.S. ballooning debt, and, though defense costs may not be as large as those incurred by the welfare bureaucracy, they are nonetheless significant.

Other Types of Policy

All that has been said in the preceding two sections confirms the existence of only two kinds of policies. It appears that foreign policy and domestic policy really are the only games in town. In other words, the basket that is presidential policy making, though containing an assortment of various shapes, sizes, and colors, has only two kinds of fruit, apples and oranges. Some may resemble tangerines, lemons, or pears, but they are either citrus or pomes (apple family). However, if you dig deeper, you will find fruits that are not wholly one or the other. Hybrids of some sort, they share traits of both and display characteristics that straddle the division between the two. While America's oldest fruit baskets may have included only apples and oranges, times have become more complicated and the needs of the modern-day republic have grown in number and complexity, which has fostered the emergence of hybrids that can more appropriately address the demands of a mature society.

Neither foreign nor domestic policy appropriately applies to internal defense, or what has become known as homeland security. As evidenced by the recently created Department of Homeland Security, this area encompasses facets of both foreign and domestic policy. It draws on resources from federal law enforcement, foreign espionage and intelligence, domestic intelligence and counterterrorism, the military, federal transportation authorities, state and local organizations, and other domestic and national security sources. Maintenance of the country's internal defense capabilities is a task that covers so many different areas of both foreign and domestic policy that it cannot be pigeon-holed into just one of the two. Likewise, the federal antidrug effort is a hybrid that combines external and internal strategies to achieve the nation's objectives, fusing domestic law enforcement with interdiction abroad. Executive antidrug policies would not be successful without this mixture of foreign and domestic resources. Another prominent example is the federal attempt to confront illegal immigration. While this matter definitely has a foreign policy component, as do all immigration issues, it also comprises several internal initiatives that aim at the apprehension of illegal immigrants.

Like national defense and federal law enforcement, particular economic issues, such as international trade and commerce, are hybrids too. They do not fall squarely under the purview of foreign or domestic policy since they are both. As an oft-repeated observation confirms, the world is getting smaller, which means it is becoming increasingly interconnected, especially through economic globalization. International trade and commercial networks are of paramount importance to the preservation of extended markets and the sale of American goods and services in other countries. The negotiation of trade agreements and the establishment of official ties with foreign nations are largely matters of economic diplomacy, but identification of the overarching economic policies that guide them is primarily the job of the president's domestic policy team. Foreign economic policy constitutes an inherent extension of domestic objectives, so the pursuit of international economic goals falls to the domestic and foreign policy establishments together. In today's global business environments, separating domestic from foreign, or national from international, ventures is impossible, so the promotion of American economic interests does not rest with only one side.

Finally, the discussion comes to an entirely different species altogether, one that can best be described as global policy, or, to use a fancier term, transnational policy. As hinted above, the United States has become part of a smaller world defined through extensive political and economic relationships that influence national development as much as domestic circumstances themselves. Some of these relationships are formal, perpetuated through international agreements and treaties, but many more are informal,

NATO

The North Atlantic Treaty Organization (NATO) was a quintessential product of the cold war, and its original purpose was aptly summarized by a British official who claimed that NATO exists to keep the United States in Europe, the Soviet Union out, and Germany down. Such a characterization may be an anachronism in a post-Soviet world no longer driven by East-West rivalries, but NATO was indeed established as a bulwark against Soviet expansionism in Europe and a guarantee against German military resurgence. Since the last round of enlargements in 2009, NATO is made up of 28 states in Europe and North America. Its headquarters is located in Brussels, Belgium, and its membership has grown considerably over the past two decades. Contrary to what had been the case for most of its history, NATO now includes members from eastern and central Europe and is, thus, no longer an exclusive club for the United States, Canada, and their western European allies.

Principal political authority lies with the North Atlantic Council, which is a deliberative decision-making body that acts through consensus rather than by voting, thereby ensuring unity of purpose and strategic coordination for NATO initiatives. NATO is led by the secretary-general, who, as head of the North Atlantic Council, represents NATO in dealings with states and other international organizations. The alliance's political structure is complemented by a unified military command structure, which is controlled by U.S. military personnel but supported by a staff made up of personnel from all member countries. Despite NATO's obvious political role, it is, first and foremost, a military alliance. NATO exists to protect its members from

nurtured through the regular and ongoing interactions among nations, their institutions, and their peoples. Over the years, resulting interdependence has led to ever-closer collaboration among world governments and the emergence of something akin to global policy. In concert with other heads of state, American presidents have become a unique sort of policy maker, a transnational policy maker. Transnational policy makers are no doubt aware of their nations' interests, but they craft policies that secure global interests.

Transnational means beyond nations and nationhood, for it transcends both the national and the international by engaging the global. In the context of world politics, it includes not only the challenges that face humanity as a whole, such as climate change, overpopulation, water scarcity, pandemic, and world hunger, but also the solutions to those problems. This may appear

attack by common enemies and to ensure the physical integrity of the territories of its members.

NATO was created in 1949 to promote two geopolitical objectives above all. First, the reconstruction of Europe, both physically and politically, had to be secured in a way that would promote the establishment and maintenance of long-term stability and prosperity in western European states. Second, and just as significant, European leaders needed to create an international, or at least regional, structure that would prevent the outbreak of future wars in Europe. The United States and its western European allies may not have agreed on all aspects of postwar international policy, but they were unified in their fears of Soviet aggression and the growth of Soviet influence in Europe, and they realized that American military might was absolutely indispensable to deter or repel potential Soviet initiatives in the West. The founding members included Great Britain, France, the Benelux countries, the United States, Canada, Denmark, Norway, Portugal, Italy, and Iceland, which was permitted to join the alliance without a standing army. By the early 1950s, the communist threat in Greece and Turkey had subsided, so these geopolitically critical states also became members. In addition, following the political stabilization of West Germany, it was invited to join in 1955. The only other country to join NATO prior to the post-Soviet increase in membership starting in the 1990s was Spain in 1982. On the whole, NATO's membership during its first 50 years reflected its origins as an anti-Soviet military alliance designed to prosecute the cold war and protect Europe from potentially expansionist and aggressive designs of the antidemocratic forces of the Soviet bloc.

to be nothing more than foreign policy on a different plane, but such a characterization misses the point. Whereas the purpose of foreign policy is the promotion of American strategic priorities through political and economic advantage, and, if necessary, military force, the aim of transnational policy is the subordination of those priorities to something broader. Foreign policy places the American president in the driver's seat, but, as a global policy maker, he is just one of a crew of navigators. He is part of something distinctly unique, something for which the framers of the Constitution could not have planned, something that lies outside the normal responsibilities of the U.S. head of state. As an American president, he still has inordinate influence over his colleagues, which is a consequence of America's international status and power, yet, at the same time, he participates in a process than does not officially recognize that status or power.

CONCLUSION

If this chapter has accomplished anything, it has validated the assertions in its introduction. Throughout, references to this and that kind of policy have been so numerous that, by now, their number may seem larger than the population of a small country. You have encountered foreign as well as domestic policy, fiscal policy and monetary policy, diplomatic policy, national security policy, welfare policy, health-care policy, education policy, social policy, Middle East policy, cold war policy, post-Soviet policy, abortion policy, religious policy, and countless other types of policy. The word *policy*, you learned, has a very specific meaning for those who study politics, but its application has been so widespread in this chapter that it may obscure the intended clarity of the explanation. However, this too has served a purpose. As the above description of hybrid policies illustrates, the lines that divide different policies are frequently unclear. Indeed, the use of such labels as foreign and domestic, or diplomatic and military, or even national and international, is more a matter of convenience than it is a matter of establishing actual boundaries that separate these policy types. Such labels allow informed discussion of the many areas that constitute presidential agendas, but they represent fluid rather than static categories that can overlap as much as they can remain distinct.

The chapter also focused on the relationship between policy making as theory and policy making as political practice, offering the rational-actor model of executive decision making as the ideal toward which the process aspires. Along the way, the shortcomings of the academic model became abundantly clear, or, viewed from another perspective, the inability of reality to match the ideal became just as clear. The stumbling block proved to be rationality, because actual policy making, often a helter-skelter sprawl of activity intended to affirm presidential priorities, leans toward irrationality. Still, the process appears rational enough to produce effective results most of the time, and presidential decisions themselves are ultimately subject to public consent through the ballot box, so democratic principles are upheld. Moreover, since presidents are the ones accountable to the public, and because they are the nation's elected chief executives, the dominance of their predetermined policy goals is only natural, if not warranted. In the end, the process may not coincide with the academic model in all respects, but it works and it also reflects public expectations.

A greater failure than irrationality is something substantially more serious, and it is an entirely different problem altogether. The very legitimacy of the policy-making process is at stake, and the American public and its representatives are either unaware or apathetic. Somewhere along the way, probably seven to eight decades ago, the connection between policy and constitutional principle was severed, and the gap between the constitution and policy making has grown steadily ever since. These days, the identification of policy has very little if anything to do with corresponding constitutional provisions, as it represents the promotion of naked political priorities. These priorities are driven by partisan, personal, and ideological agendas whose constitutional foundation is irrelevant. Policy makers no longer ask questions about constitutional requirements but concern themselves with purely political demands. Over the last several decades, this increasingly illegitimate process has survived, and only a few skeptics have dared to ask how. This is obviously one of those issues, mentioned earlier in this chapter, that is not sufficiently "ripe" for public consideration, but at some point it will be. When that time comes, both the people and their representatives will have to face difficult questions.

Articles of Confederation An agreement unifying the former British colonies in North America. Ratified in 1781, it was replaced by the Constitution in 1787.

bureaucracy A merit-based network of institutions, offices, and personnel that manages the resource requirements of modern governments through regulatory and administrative services

cabinet The president's chief advisory body made up of the heads of the 15 executive departments

candidate-centered politics An electoral system in which political parties play subsidiary roles as fund-raising organizations for presidential candidates, providing the infrastructure and support to run successful campaigns

checks and balances The set of interbranch relationships intended to prevent the accumulation of too much power by a single branch of government

chief of staff The head of the Executive Office of the President, the chief of staff is in charge of the White House bureaucracy and serves as the key link between the president and other public officials.

cold war The political rivalry between the United States and the Soviet Union lasting from 1945 to 1991, which included proxy wars, covert action, and support of satellite regimes across the globe

containment The principal cold war foreign policy before the 1980s, which opposed Soviet expansion and attempted to limit communist influence to areas where it already existed

domestic policy A presidential administration's internal political objectives reflecting the economic, social, and cultural needs of the American people

Electoral College The body designated by the Constitution to elect the president. Prior to 1824, with no popular vote, electors chose presidents on their own, but today their role is purely ceremonial.

enumerated powers Those powers specifically identified in the Constitution as belonging to the president

executive authority The president's right to use power as delegated by the American people and mandated by the Constitution

Executive Office of the President The bureaucratic core of the executive branch, which includes the White House staff, various advisory councils, the cabinet, and the president's closest aides and assistants

executive power The president's ability to coerce, influence, or persuade others through physical force, political status, or moral authority

fiscal policy The part of domestic policy that deals with taxes and expenditures

foreign policy Presidential diplomatic and national security objectives as they relate to national interest and strategic advantage

Great Society President Lyndon Johnson's social and cultural program that significantly expanded the welfare state through measures for the uninsured, elderly, poor, and otherwise needy and through legislation that authorized assistance to students, minorities, artists, musicians, teachers, and women

implied powers The powers not specifically identified in the Constitution but nevertheless implied as inherent by explicit provisions

independent agency A regulatory or administrative institution usually within the executive branch with broad authority to set, enforce, and interpret relevant regulations or provide specific services

Manifest Destiny   The belief, popularized in the 1840s, that the United States is destined through divine providence to control all the lands between the Atlantic and Pacific Oceans

monetary policy   Largely controlled by the Federal Open Market Committee, which is part of the Federal Reserve System, the management of interest rates and the nation's money supply

national security state   The bureaucratic machinery erected during the cold war to secure American strategic interests, including the Department of Defense, the National Security Council, the armed forces, the intelligence community, and various support personnel

New Deal   The group of domestic initiatives implemented by the administration of Franklin Roosevelt as a response to the Great Depression of the 1930s. It established the foundations of America's welfare state and greatly expanded the reach of federal regulatory authority.

policy   A desirable political objective that has both constitutional and political value and whose implementation is the focus of day-to-day governance

policy making   The process of converting the political objectives that compose presidential agendas into actual programs and initiatives

popular sovereignty   The Enlightenment idea that ultimate rule rests with the people at large and that government should be based on popular consent

Progressive Era   Approximately the first two decades of the 20th century, during which political reformers, or progressives, began to address the social and economic consequences of industrial capitalism. It is regarded by many as a precursor to the New Deal.

public presidency   The modern presidency as it has developed during the television age, based on the executive practice of "going public," or directly engaging the American people, and bypassing Congress, through the president's role as communicator in chief

rational-actor model   An academic theory that claims executive decision making should be rational, or based on collaboration and the open consideration of viable alternatives

separation of powers   The American constitutional practice of dividing governmental authority into separate executive, legislative, and judicial spheres

sovereignty   The ultimate, or final, right to rule and exercise political power

spoils system   A system of political patronage prevalent throughout the 19th century through which political parties distributed appointments to federal jobs to loyalists, supporters, and contributors

welfare state   The social services bureaucracy created by the New Deal and Great Society that administers Social Security, Medicare, Medicaid, welfare, unemployment and disability insurance, subsidies and financial assistance for the poor, and a host of other programs for the economically or socially dislocated

SELECTED BIBLIOGRAPHY

Burke, John. *The Institutional Presidency*. Baltimore: Johns Hopkins University Press, 1992.

Canes-Wrone, Brandice. *Who Leads Whom? Presidents, Policy, and the Public*. Chicago: University of Chicago Press, 2006.

Cohen, Jeffrey E. *Presidential Responsiveness and Public Policy-making: The Public and the Policies That Presidents Choose*. Ann Arbor: University of Michigan Press, 1997.

Cronin, Thomas E., and Michael A. Genovese. *The Paradoxes of the American Presidency*. 3d ed. New York: Oxford University Press, 2010.

Edwards, George C. III. *On Deaf Ears: The Limits of the Bully Pulpit*. New Haven, Conn.: Yale University Press, 2003.

Edwards, George C. III, and Stephen J. Wayne. *Presidential Leadership: Politics and Policy Making*. 8th ed. Boston: Wadsworth, 2010.

Genovese, Michael A. *The Power of the American Presidency 1789–2000*. New York: Oxford University Press, 2001.

Genovese, Michael A., and Lori Cox Han, eds. *The Presidency and the Challenge of Democracy*. New York: Palgrave Macmillan, 2006.

Greenstein, Fred I. *The Presidential Difference: Leadership Style from FDR to Barack Obama*. Princeton, N.J.: Princeton University Press, 2009.

Han, Lori Cox. *Governing from Center Stage: White House Communication Strategies during the Television Age of Politics*. Cresskill, N.J.: Hampton Press, 2001.

Heith, Diane J. *Polling to Govern: Public Opinion and Presidential Leadership*. Palo Alto, Calif.: Stanford University Press, 2003.

Jones, Charles O. *Separate but Equal Branches: Congress and the Presidency*. 2d ed. New York: Chatham House, 1999.

Kernell, Samuel. *Going Public: New Strategies of Presidential Leadership*. 4th ed. Washington, D.C.: CQ Press, 2007.

Kessel, John H. *Presidents, the Presidency, and the Political Environment*. Washington, D.C.: CQ Press, 2001.

Lammers, William W., and Michael A. Genovese. *The Presidency and Domestic Policy: Comparing Leadership Styles, FDR to Clinton*. Washington, D.C.: CQ Press, 2000.

Maltese, John Anthony. *Spin Control: The White House Office of Communications and the Management of Presidential News*. 2d ed. Chapel Hill: University of North Carolina Press, 1994.

Milkis, Sidney M., and Michael Nelson. *The American Presidency: Origins and Development*. 5th ed. Washington, D.C.: CQ Press, 2007.

Neustadt, Richard. *Presidential Power*. New York: Wiley, 1960.

Patterson, Bradley H., Jr. *The White House Staff: Inside the West Wing and Beyond*. Washington, D.C.: Brookings, 2000.

Pfiffner, James P. *The Modern Presidency*. 6th ed. Boston: Wadsworth, 2010.

Pika, Joseph A., and John Anthony Maltese. *The Politics of the Presidency*. 7th ed. Washington, D.C.: CQ Press, 2010.

Rose, Richard. *The Postmodern President*. 2d ed. Chatham, N.J.: Chatham House, 1991.

Rossiter, Clinton. *The American Presidency*. New York: Harcourt, Brace and World, 1956.

Rudalevige, Andrew. *Managing the President's Program: Presidential Leadership and Legislative Policy Formulation*. Princeton, N.J.: Princeton University Press, 2002.

Schlesinger, Arthur M., Jr. *The Imperial Presidency*. Boston: Houghton Mifflin, 1973.

Skowronek, Stephen. *The Politics Presidents Make: Leadership from John Adams to George Bush*. Cambridge, Mass.: Belknap/Harvard Press, 1993.

Stuckey, Mary E. *The President as Interpreter-in-Chief*. Chatham, N.J.: Chatham House, 1991.

Tulis, Jeffrey K. *The Rhetorical Presidency*. Princeton, N.J.: Princeton University Press, 1987.

Warshaw, Shirley Anne. *The Keys to Power: Managing the Presidency*. New York: Longman, 2000.

Wayne, Stephen J. *The Road to the White House, 2008*. Boston: Thomson, 2008.

Weko, Thomas J. *The Politicizing Presidency: The White House Personnel Office, 1948–1994*. Lawrence: University of Kansas Press, 1995.

INDEX

Note: *Italic* page numbers indicate illustrations. **Boldface** page numbers denote major treatment of a topic. Page numbers followed by *t* denote tables, charts, or graphs.